Microsoft®
Office
Excel 2003
fast&easy™

Microsoft® Office Excel 2003

fast&easy™

Diane Koers

Premier

Press™

The Premier Press logo and related trade dress are trademarks of Premier Press and may not be used without written permission.

SVP, Retail Strategic Market Group: Andy Shafran
Publisher: Stacy L. Hiquet
Senior Marketing Manager: Sarah O'Donnell
Marketing Manager: Heather Hurley
Manager of Editorial Services: Heather Talbot
Associate Marketing Manager: Kristin Eisenzopf
Project Editor: Jenny Davidson
Technical Reviewer: Greg Perry
Retail Market Coordinator: Sarah Dubois
Interior Layout: Danielle Foster
Cover Designer: Mike Tanamachi
Indexer: Sharon Shock
Proofreader: Dan Foster

Microsoft, Office, Excel, Word, and Access are either registered trademarks or trademarks of Microsoft Corporation in the United States and/or other countries.

All other trademarks are the property of their respective owners.

Important: Premier Press cannot provide software support. Please contact the appropriate software manufacturer's technical support line or Web site for assistance.

Premier Press and the author have attempted throughout this book to distinguish proprietary trademarks from descriptive terms by following the capitalization style used by the manufacturer.

Information contained in this book has been obtained by Premier Press from sources believed to be reliable. However, because of the possibility of human or mechanical error by our sources, Premier Press, or others, the Publisher does not guarantee the accuracy, adequacy, or completeness of any information and is not responsible for any errors or omissions or the results obtained from use of such information. Readers should be particularly aware of the fact that the Internet is an ever-changing entity. Some facts may have changed since this book went to press.

ISBN: 1-59200-079-7
Library of Congress Catalog Card Number: 2003105360
Printed in the United States of America
04 05 06 07 08 BH 10 9 8 7 6 5 4 3 2

Premier Press, a division of Course Technology
25 Thomson Place
Boston, MA 02210

To everyone at Bosma Industries for the Blind
Serving the needs of others

Acknowledgments

I am deeply grateful to the many people at Premier Press who worked on this book. Thank you for all the time you gave and for your assistance. While I can't name everyone involved, I'd like to especially thank Stacy Hiquet for the opportunity to write this book and her confidence in me; to Greg Perry for his wonderful technical advice; to Dan Foster and Danielle Foster for their outstanding contributions; and a very special thank you to Jenny Davidson for all her patience and guidance in pulling the project together and making it correct. It takes a lot of both to work with me!

Lastly, a big hug and kiss to my husband, Vern, for his never-ending support. For thirty-five years we've been a team, and it shows!

About the Author

DIANE KOERS owns and operates All Business Service, a software training and consulting business formed in 1988 that services the central Indiana area. Her area of expertise has long been in the word-processing, spreadsheet, and graphics area of computing as well as providing training and support for Peachtree Accounting Software. Diane's authoring experience includes over two dozen books on topics such as PC Security, Microsoft Windows, Office, Works, WordPerfect, Paint Shop Pro, Lotus SmartSuite, Quicken, Money, and Peachtree Accounting, many of which have been translated into other languages such as Dutch, Bulgarian, Spanish, and Greek. She has also developed and written numerous training manuals for her clients.

Active in her church and civic activities, Diane enjoys spending her free time traveling and playing with her grandsons and her two Yorkshire Terriers.

Contents at a Glance

Contents

PART II
WORKING WITH FORMULAS AND
LARGER WORKSHEETS 103

Introduction

Welcome to the world of Microsoft Excel.

This new *Fast & Easy* book from Premier Press will help you use the many and varied features of one of the Microsoft Office products—Microsoft Excel, the most popular and powerful worksheet program in the world.

What is a worksheet program? A worksheet is a program with a huge grid designed to display data in rows and columns where you can create calculations to perform mathematical, logical, and other types of operations on the data you enter. You can sort the data, enhance it, and manipulate it a plethora of ways including creating powerful charts and graphs from it. Whether you need a list of names and addresses, or a document to calculate next year's sales revenue based on prior years' performance, Excel is the application you want to use.

You will find the information that you need to quickly and easily get the jobs done in the *Microsoft Office Excel 2003 Fast & Easy* guide. This book uses a step-by-step approach with illustrations of what you will see on your screen, linked with instructions for the next mouse movements or keyboard operations to complete your task. Computer terms and phrases are clearly explained in non-technical language, and expert tips and shortcuts help you produce professional-quality documents.

Microsoft Office Excel 2003 Fast & Easy provides the tools you need to successfully tackle the potentially overwhelming challenge of learning to use Microsoft Excel. Whether you are a novice user or an experienced professional, you will be able to quickly tap into the program's user-friendly integrated design and feature-rich environment.

Through this book you learn *how* to create worksheets; however, *what* you create is totally up to you—your imagination is the only limit! This book cannot teach you everything you can do with Microsoft Excel, nor does it give you all the different ways to accomplish a task. What I *have* tried to do is give you the fastest and easiest way to get started with this fun and exciting program.

How This Book Is Organized

This book is divided into five parts, an appendix, and a glossary of terms. Each part focuses on a different area of Excel and at the end of each part, you'll find ten review questions to help you test your understanding of the covered materials.

In Part I, I show you how to create a basic worksheet. While it's not the most exciting section of the book, it's certainly the most practical. Look out after that—things start to be lots of fun! In Part II, you learn about creating formulas to make Excel do all the calculating work for you, while in Part III you discover how to make it all look appealing and interesting to your audience. Part IV shows you how to use some of Excel's powerful analysis tools and tools that improve your worksheet quality. In Part V you learn how easily Excel integrates with other people and other Office applications. Finally, the helpful appendix will show you how to save your valuable time with keyboard shortcuts.

Who Should Read This Book?

This book can be used as a learning tool or as a step-by-step task reference. The easy-to-follow, highly visual nature of this book makes it the perfect learning tool for a beginning computer user as well as those seasoned computer users who are new to Microsoft Excel. No prerequisites are required from you, the reader, except that you know how to turn your computer on and how to use your mouse.

In addition, anyone using a software application always needs an occasional reminder about the steps required to perform a particular task. By using the *Microsoft Office Excel 2003 Fast & Easy* guide, any level of user can look up steps for a task quickly without having to plow through pages of descriptions.

Added Advice to Make You a Pro

You'll notice that this book uses steps and keeps explanations to a minimum to help you learn faster. Included in the book are a few elements that provide some additional comments to help you master the program, without encumbering your progress through the steps:

TIP

Tips often offer shortcuts when performing an action, or a hint about a feature that might make your work in Excel quicker and easier.

NOTE

Notes give you a bit of background or additional information about a feature, or advice about how to use the feature in your day-to-day activities.

Read and enjoy this *Fast & Easy* book. It certainly is the *fastest and easiest* way to learn Microsoft Office Excel 2003.

—Diane Koers

PART I

Building a Basic Worksheet

1

Exploring the Excel Screen

Previously, you may have used a paper, pencil, and calculator to track information, whether to figure a simple calculation or track a list of items in alphabetical order. Excel handles those tasks and many more, including very complex calculations. At first glance, however, the Excel opening screen can feel very intimidating with all of its buttons, options, rows, and columns. Once you understand the purpose for all those options, you will feel much more comfortable with the Excel screen.

In this chapter, you'll learn how to:

- Open the Excel program
- Explore and move around the Excel screen
- Understand cell addresses
- Work with the task pane
- Use Excel menus
- Use Excel Help

Starting Excel

There are a number of different methods to access the Excel application. One method is from the Start button.

1. Click on the **Start button**. The Start menu will appear.

2. Click on **All Programs**. A menu of available programs will appear.

3. Click on **Microsoft Excel**. The Microsoft Excel program will open with a blank worksheet screen.

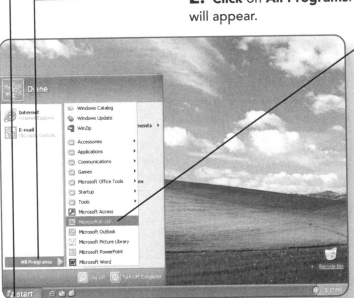

TIP

If you have a Microsoft Excel icon on your Windows desktop, you can double-click it to quickly access Excel.

Exploring the Worksheet Screen

Many items that you see when you open a new worksheet (also known as a spreadsheet) are standard to most Microsoft Office programs. However, the following list illustrates a few elements that are specific to a spreadsheet program. These include:

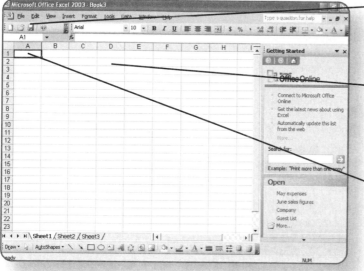

- **Toolbars**. A selection of commonly used Excel features. A single click on a toolbar item activates the feature.

- **Worksheet area**. A rectangular grid, consisting of rows and columns. Columns are labels with letters across the top, and rows are indicated by numbers.

- **Cell**. The intersection of a row and a column. Also known as a cell address. When referring to a cell address, Excel references the column letter first then the row number. For example, Excel refers to a cell address as B6 not 6B. A selected cell has a heavy border around it.

NOTE

Each worksheet has 256 columns and 65,536 rows, for a total of 16,777,216 cells in each worksheet.

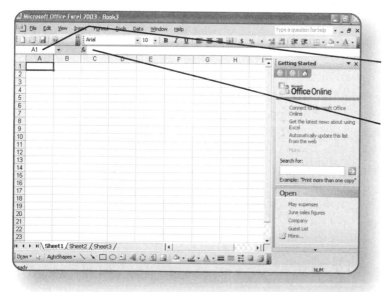

- **Edit line**. The edit line consists of two parts:

- **Selection Indicator**. Shows the address or name of the currently selected cell.

- **Contents Box**. Displays the contents of the currently selected cell.

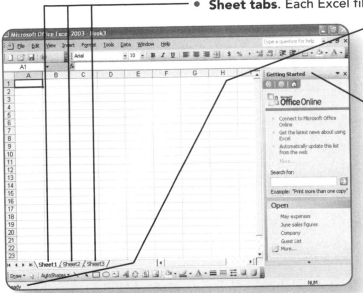

- **Sheet tabs**. Each Excel file can contain 256 worksheets.

- **Status Bar**. Displays information about the current selection and what Excel is doing.

- **Task pane**. Small windows that assist you when working with Excel. Task panes store collections of important Excel features and present them in ways that are easy to find and use.

Working with the Task Pane

Excel contains several different task panes, each of which appears when you use various Excel tasks. One task pane assists you in creating new worksheets, whereas another task pane helps you add clip art to your worksheet.

Changing Task Panes

By default, Excel displays the Getting Started task pane. The Getting Started task pane lists common features associated with opening an existing worksheet or creating a new worksheet. As you select different Excel features, the task pane may change.

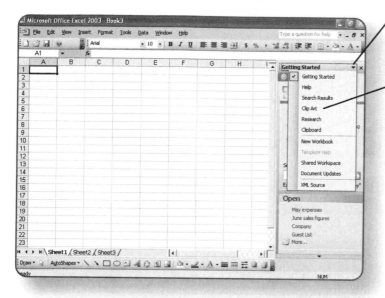

1. **Click** on the **task pane drop-down menu**. A list of other task panes will appear.

2. **Click** on a **task pane name**. The selected task pane will appear.

Closing and Redisplaying the Task Pane

While the task pane can be very helpful, it also uses up valuable screen space. You can close the task pane at any time and redisplay it whenever you want it back.

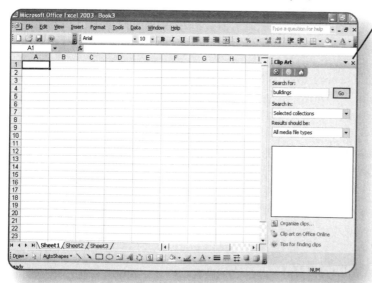

1. **Click** the **task pane close button**. The task pane will close.

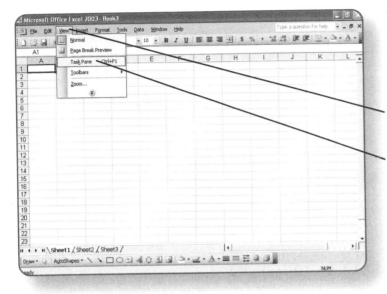

The task pane will reappear automatically when you select an Excel feature that uses the task pane. You can, however, redisplay the task pane at any time.

2. Click on **View**. The View menu will appear.

3. Click on **Task Pane**. The task pane will reopen.

NOTE

For the purposes of this book, most screens will appear without the task pane, unless a feature that uses the task pane is being shown.

Working with Menus

All Windows-based applications use menus to list items appropriate to your program. Excel is no different. As you click a menu choice, you see the options available under that menu. Some menus have submenus which list additional choices from which you can select. A menu option lighter in color than the other options is said to be grayed out and means that particular choice is unavailable at the moment. Menu options become grayed out when they are not applicable to your current selection.

Personalized Menus

Excel includes personalized menus. When the menu is first accessed, only the most common features are displayed. Notice the down-pointing double arrow at the bottom of the menu. This arrow indicates that additional menu features are available. If you pause the mouse over the top item on the menu bar or move it down to the double arrow, the menu will expand to include all available features for that menu.

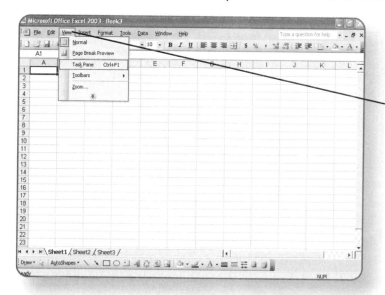

As you use the personalized menus, the features you use most often will appear at the top of the menu.

1. Click on **View**. The View menu will appear with five options.

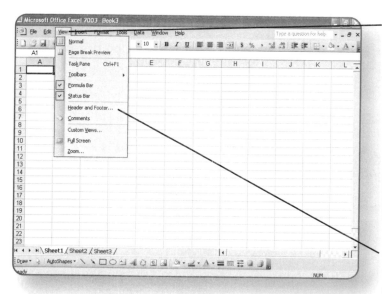

2. Pause the **mouse pointer** over the View menu. The View menu will expand to include 11 items.

TIP

Click on the menu name (such as View) to close a menu without making any selection.

Many selections in a menu are followed by three periods, called an *ellipsis*. Selections followed by ellipses indicate that, if you select one of these items, a dialog box will appear with more options.

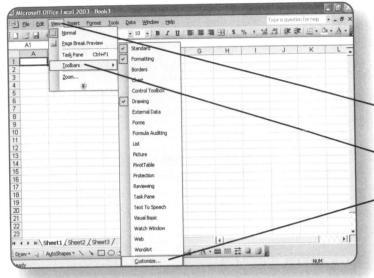

If you find you don't like the personalized menus, you can turn the feature off and all options will automatically appear when you select a menu.

3. **Click** on **View**. The View menu will appear.

4. **Click** on **Toolbars**. The Toolbars submenu will appear.

5. **Click** on **Customize**. The Customize dialog box will open.

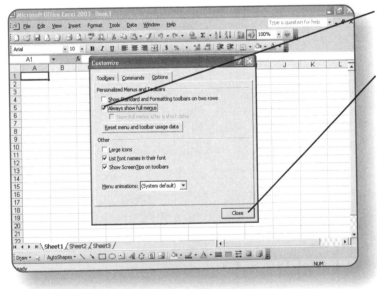

6. **Click** on **Always show full menus**. The option will be selected.

7. **Click** on **Close**. The Customize dialog box will close.

Shortcut Menus

Shortcut menus contain a limited number of commands. The commands you see on a shortcut menu are relevant to what you are doing at the time you open the shortcut menu. Click the right mouse button (called a *right-click*) to open a shortcut menu. Be sure the mouse pointer is in the shape of a white cross before right-clicking to open a shortcut menu.

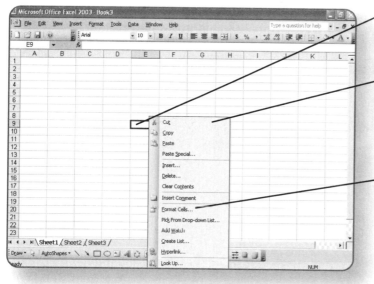

1. **Click** on any **cell** of the worksheet. The cell will be selected.

2. **Press** the **right mouse button**. The mouse pointer will change to an arrow and a shortcut menu will appear on the screen.

3. **Click** on a **menu selection**. The menu action will occur.

TIP

Press the Esc key or click anywhere outside the shortcut menu to close the menu without making a selection.

Using Toolbars

Along the top and bottom of the Excel screen, you see several different toolbars. Toolbars are small icons or buttons that help you access commonly used Excel features without digging through the menus. Excel includes over 20 toolbars to assist you.

When you first use Excel, you see three toolbars displayed by default. The Standard and Formatting toolbars display side-by-side along the top of the Excel screen, and the Drawing toolbar displays along the bottom of the screen.

Standard toolbar

Formatting toolbar

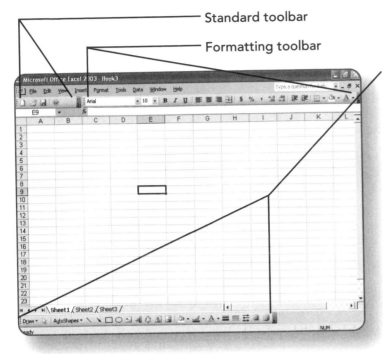

Drawing toolbar

If you look closely, you can see that the toolbar buttons are grouped into related activities. For example, the Alignment buttons (left, center, and right) are together, and options that relate to files, such as saving or opening, are grouped together. You'll learn about using these buttons in later chapters.

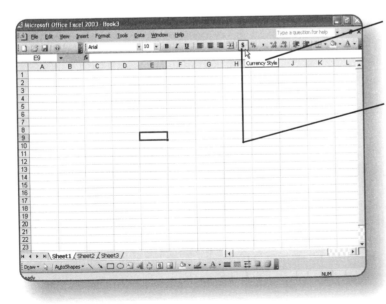

1. **Pause** the **mouse pointer** over any toolbar item. The description of that feature will appear.

2. **Click** on a **toolbar button**. The requested action will occur.

Additional toolbar buttons may be available.

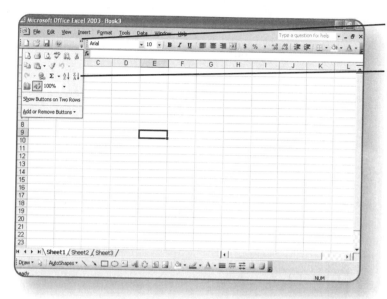

3. **Click** on the **Toolbar options button**.

Additional toolbar buttons appear from which you can select.

Separating Toolbars

Most people find the Standard and Formatting toolbars difficult to use when displayed side-by-side, so you may want to separate them so one is on top of the other, which makes all the tools on these bars much easier to access.

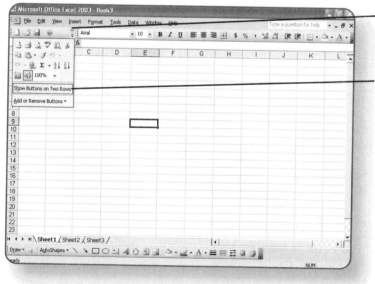

1. **Click** on the **Toolbar options button**. Additional toolbar buttons appear.

2. **Click** on **Show Buttons on Two Rows**. The Standard and Formatting toolbars become separated.

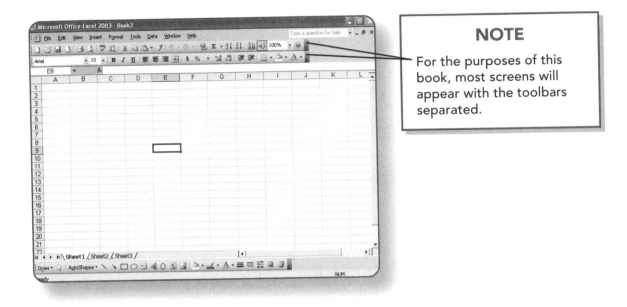

NOTE

For the purposes of this book, most screens will appear with the toolbars separated.

Moving a Toolbar

Most toolbars are docked at the top or bottom of the screen, but if a toolbar is not located in a favorable position for you to access, move it to any position on the screen. Sometimes, you may accidentally move a toolbar into the middle of the screen, blocking your view of your worksheet. It's very easy to move a toolbar into any position.

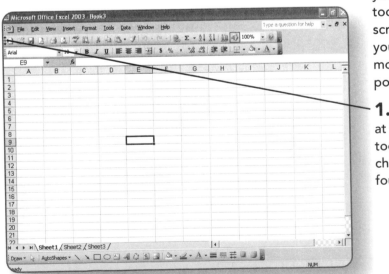

1. **Position** the **mouse pointer** at the far-left side of any toolbar. The mouse pointer changes to a black cross with four arrowheads.

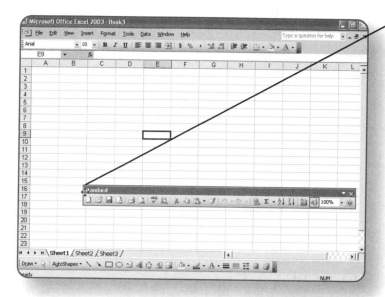

2. **Hold down** the **mouse button and drag** the mouse into the worksheet area. The toolbar may change shape.

NOTE

Although you probably won't want to, you can move the menu bar with the same method.

3. **Release** the **mouse button**. The toolbar will remain in the new position.

TIP

To put a toolbar back to the normal position, press and hold the mouse button over the toolbar title bar and drag it into the desired position, usually at the top of the screen.

Hiding and Displaying Toolbars

You can hide or display any toolbar. This can be very helpful if a particular toolbar is using valuable screen space. For example, if you are not doing any drawing, you may want to hide the drawing toolbar.

1. Click on **View**. The View menu will appear.

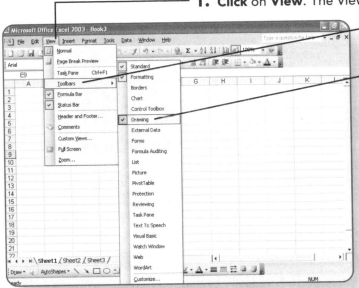

2. Click on **Toolbars**. A list of toolbars will appear.

3. Click on the **toolbar** you want to turn off or on.

Currently displayed toolbars have a check mark next to them. Toolbars without a check mark are not currently displayed.

Moving around the Worksheet Screen

You can use your mouse or keyboard to move around a worksheet. Because of the large size of an Excel worksheet, you need ways to move around quickly.

For illustration purposes, in the following two figures you see a worksheet with a lot of information stored in it. You will learn how to enter information into your worksheets in Chapter 2, "Creating a Simple Worksheet."

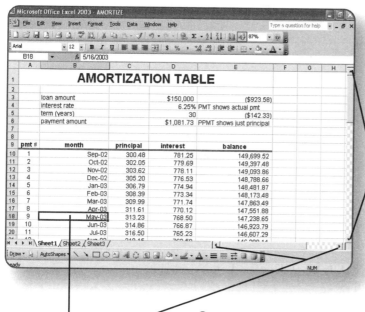

Using the Mouse

Because there are over 16 million possible cells in a single worksheet, you may find that using the mouse is an easy way to move around in the worksheet.

1. **Click** the **vertical scroll arrows** until the row you want is visible.

2. **Click** the **horizontal scroll arrows** until the column you want is visible.

3. **Click** on the desired **cell**. The cell becomes the currently selected cell.

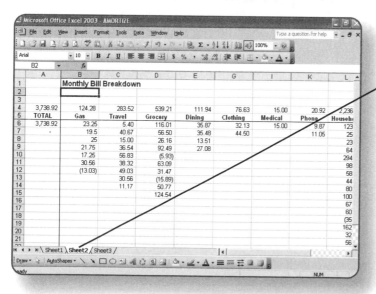

By default, Excel displays three worksheets, labeled Sheet1, Sheet2, and Sheet3.

4. **Click** a **worksheet tab**. The selected worksheet appears on top of the stack.

You'll learn more about working with multiple worksheets in Chapter 8, "Working with Larger Worksheets."

Keystroke	Result
Arrow keys	Moves one cell at a time up, down, left, or right
Page Down	Moves one screen down
Page Up	Moves one screen up
Home	Moves to column A of the current row
Ctrl+Home	Moves to cell A1
Ctrl+Arrow key	Moves to the beginning or end of a row or column
Ctrl+Page Down	Moves to the next worksheet
Ctrl+Page Up	Moves to the previous worksheet
F5	Displays the Go To dialog box which enables you to specify a cell address

Using the Keyboard

As you have just discovered, you can use your mouse to move around an Excel worksheet; however, you may find using the keyboard faster and easier. The table shown here describes keyboard methods for moving around a worksheet.

Accessing the Go To Command

If you have a rather large worksheet, you can use the Go To command to jump to a specific cell or area of the worksheet.

1. Click on **Edit**. The Edit menu will appear.

2. Click on **Go To**. The Go To dialog box will appear.

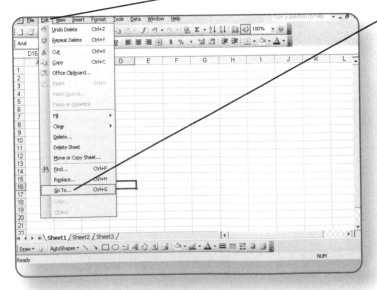

NOTE

If you are using personalized menus, you may not immediately see the Go To command. Pause the mouse over the Edit menu to display the additional options.

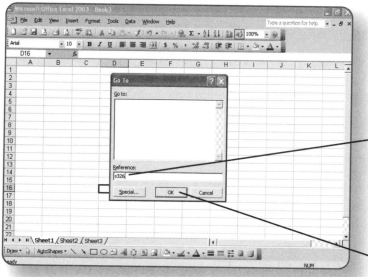

Optionally, press the F5 key to quickly display the Go To dialog box.

3. In the Reference box, **type** the **cell address** you want to locate. Remember to enter the column letter first, then the row number. In this example, we are looking for column S and row 326.

4. Click on **OK**. The specified cell will be selected.

NOTE

Cell addresses are not case sensitive.

Using Excel Help

Many of your questions about Excel can be answered in this book. However, Excel includes an extensive Help system which can include searching the Internet for solutions. The easiest method is to access the very convenient Ask a Question box where you can pose your question or enter a term in plain English.

1. Click in the **Ask a Question box** located in the upper-right corner of the screen. An insertion point will appear in the box.

2. Type your **question or words** that describe what you need help with. You can type a complete sentence or just a few words.

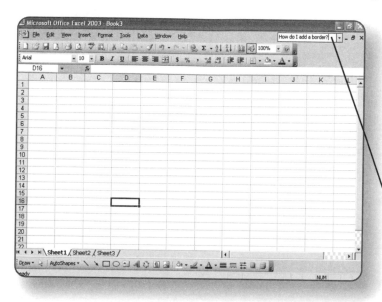

3. Press the **Enter key**. The task pane will display a selection of potential Help topics.

Excel looks for your answer in the Excel Help system; however, if you have Internet access, Excel will attempt to contact Microsoft.com for additional options.

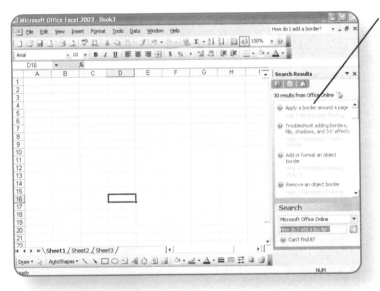

4. Click on the **topic** that best represents the subject with which you need help. A Help window with instructions will appear.

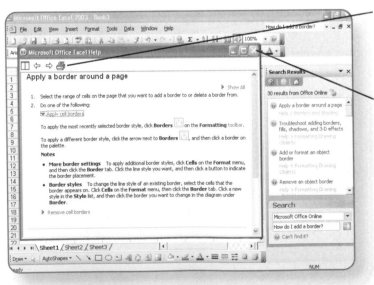

5. Click the **Print button** to print a hard copy of the Help instructions.

6. Click the **Close button** when you are finished with the Help window.

2

Creating a Simple Worksheet

There's an old adage that "you have to crawl before you can walk." That saying applies to Excel worksheets as well. You need to learn the basics before you learn the more complex features of Excel. That's what this chapter is about—the basics.

In this chapter, you'll learn how to:

- Enter labels, values, and dates
- Save, close, and open worksheet files
- E-mail your worksheet
- Create a new worksheet

Entering Data

Worksheet data is made up of three components: labels, values, and formulas. This section discusses entering labels and values, and you'll learn about creating and entering formulas in Chapter 6, "Working with Formulas." When you are ready to enter data into a worksheet cell, you must first click on the cell in which you want the information.

Entering Labels

Labels are traditionally descriptive pieces of information, such as names, months, or other identifying information. Excel automatically recognizes information as a label if it contains alphabetic characters. Don't worry if the entire label does not appear to fit into a cell width. If needed, Excel automatically extends the data past the cell width.

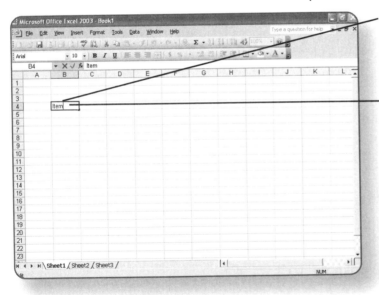

1. **Click** on the **cell** in which you want to place the label. A border will appear around the selected cell.

2. **Type** some **text**. A blinking insertion point will appear.

TIP

If you make a mistake and have not yet pressed the Enter key, press the Backspace key to delete characters and type a correction, or press the Escape key to cancel typing in the selected cell.

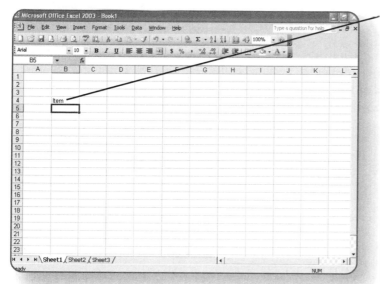

3. Press the **Enter key**. Excel accepts the label and aligns the data along the left edge of the cell. The cell below the one in which you just entered data will then be selected.

TIP

Optionally, instead of pressing the Enter key, press the Tab key and Excel will move to the right of the current cell instead of below it.

4. Repeat steps 1-3 for each label you want to enter. Data will appear in the multiple cells.

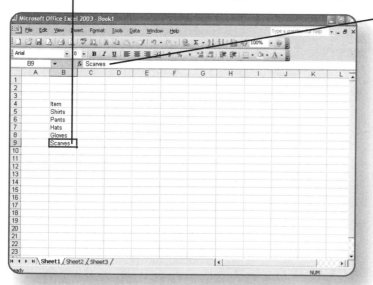

Excel also displays the contents of the current cell in the Formula bar.

NOTE

Optionally, you can press an arrow key instead of the Enter key. This will accept the cell content you were typing and move to the next cell in the direction of the arrow key.

Entering Values

Values are the raw numbers that you track in a worksheet. When you enter a value, you don't need to enter commas or dollar signs. In Chapter 4, "Making the Worksheet Look Good," you'll learn how to let Excel do that for you.

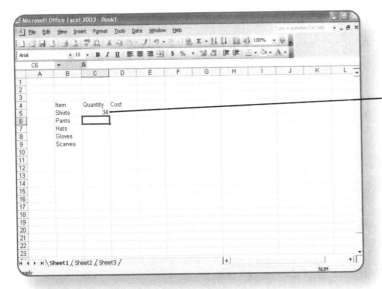

1. **Click** on the **cell** in which you want to place the value. A border will appear around the selected cell.

2. **Type** the numerical **value**. A blinking insertion point will appear.

3. **Press Enter** to accept the value. The number will be entered into the cell and the cell below will then be selected.

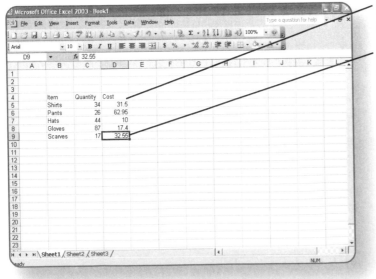

Excel aligns values along the right edge of the cell.

4. **Repeat steps 1-3** for each value you want to enter.

If your value is too large to fit into the cell width, Excel may
display a series of number signs (####) or it may round the
value display. Don't worry about the appearance that displays
in Excel. Remember that you'll discover how to change the
display of your data in Chapter 4. The following table illustrates
some of the ways Excel, by default, displays numeric data:

You enter	Excel may display
1074	1074
0174	174
'0174	0174
39.95	39.95
39.50	39.5
39.501	39.501
4789547.365	4789547.37

Entering Dates

Although dates contain characters and look like a label, Excel
technically considers them values, because Excel can calculate
the time between dates, which you will learn about in Chapter
6, "Working with Formulas." For example, day 1 is January
1st, 1900, day 2 is January 2nd, 1900, and so forth.

When you enter a date, Excel may not display it on the screen
in the same way that you type it. You will discover how to

format dates in different perspectives in Chapter 4. The following table shows how Excel automatically displays dates:

You type	Excel displays
January 23, 2003	23-Jan-2003
January 23	23-Jan
Jan 23	23-Jan
1/23	23-Jan
1-23	23-Jan
1-23-03	1/23/2003
1/23/03	1/23/2003

NOTE

Depending on the Regional and International settings of your computer, your system may display differently, such as displaying only the last two digits of a year.

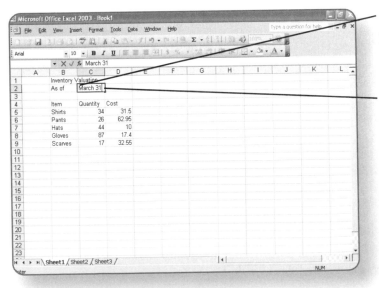

1. **Click** on the **cell** in which you want to enter the date. A border will appear around the selected cell.

2. **Type** the **date**. A blinking insertion point will appear.

3. Press Enter to accept the date. Excel will enter the date into the cell and display it in the default date format.

In the Formula bar, Excel displays the date in numeric *mm/dd/yyyy* format.

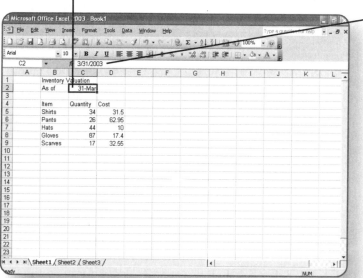

Saving a Worksheet File

Anyone who uses a computer has probably lost data at one time or another. If you don't save your worksheet regularly, it only takes a second to lose hours of work. Fortunately, Excel has a built-in feature to help protect you against this eventuality. However, you still need to save your worksheet so you can refer to it or make changes to it at some future time.

Saving a File the First Time

When you first open Excel, a blank screen appears with the title Worksheet1 in the Excel title bar. The next blank worksheet you create is named Worksheet2, then Worksheet3, and so forth. Those names are temporary names and are not very descriptive, so you need to assign a name that is associated with the worksheet contents.

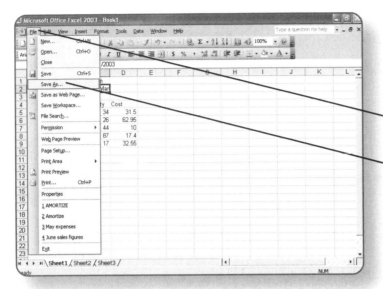

Excel asks for a name the first time you save the worksheet, and after that, the name you assign it will appear in the Excel title bar.

1. **Click** on **File**. The File menu appears.

2. **Click** on **Save As**. The Save As dialog box will open.

NOTE

When you first save an unnamed file, you can use the Save command or the Save As command. Both commands take you to the Save As dialog box.

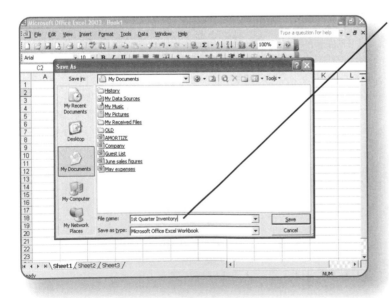

3. **Type** a **name** for your file in the File Name text box. The file name will be displayed.

File names can contain spaces, dashes, and many other special characters, but cannot include the asterisk (*), slash (/), backslash (\), or question mark (?) characters.

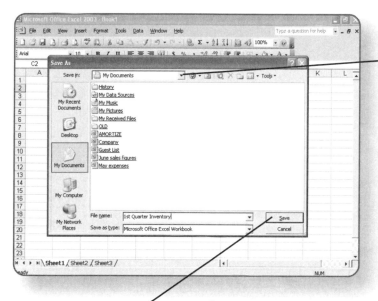

4. Click on **Save**. Your worksheet is saved and the name you specified will appear in the title bar.

Resaving a Worksheet

As you make changes to your worksheet, you should resave it. A good rule is to save your worksheet at least every ten minutes. Excel replaces the worksheet copy already saved on the disk with the newly revised worksheet copy.

1. Click on the **Save button**. The worksheet will be resaved with any changes you made. No dialog box will open because the worksheet is resaved with the same name and in the same folder as previously specified.

TIP

If you want to save the worksheet with a different name or in a different folder, click on File, then choose Save As. The Save As dialog box will prompt you for the new name or folder. The original worksheet will remain, as well as the new one.

Closing a Worksheet

When you are finished working on a worksheet, you should close it. Closing is the equivalent of putting it away for later use. When you close a worksheet, you are only putting the worksheet away—not the program. Excel is still active and ready to work for you.

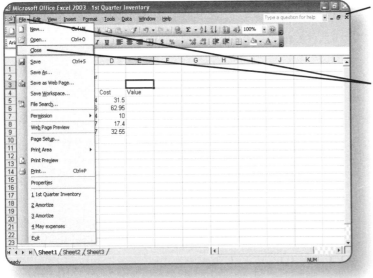

1a. **Click** on the **Close Button**. The worksheet will be closed.

OR

1b. **Click** on **File**. The File menu will appear. **Click** on **Close**. The worksheet will close.

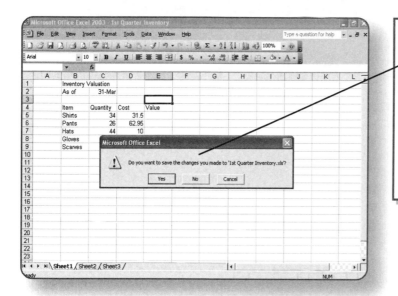

NOTE

If you close a worksheet with changes that have not been saved, Excel will prompt you with a dialog box. Choose Yes to save the changes or No to close the file without saving the changes.

Enabling AutoRecover

Excel has a feature called AutoRecover, which periodically saves a temporary version of your worksheet for you. When you close Excel normally, the temporary versions disappear, but if you don't get the chance to exit Excel (say, due to a computer freeze up), when you reopen Excel, the program opens a recovery version of the worksheets you were working on at the time of the crash. You can then choose to save them or not.

You can specify the time intervals for the AutoRecover to save your work.

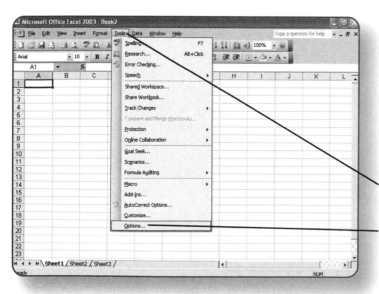

1. Click on **Tools**. The Tools menu will appear.

2. Click on **Options**. The Options dialog box will open.

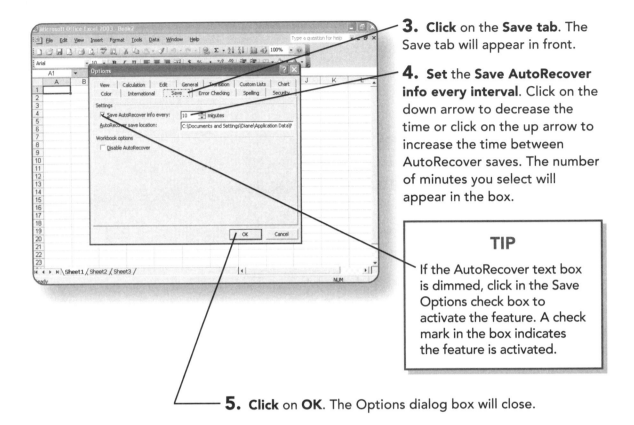

3. **Click** on the **Save tab**. The Save tab will appear in front.

4. **Set** the **Save AutoRecover info every interval**. Click on the down arrow to decrease the time or click on the up arrow to increase the time between AutoRecover saves. The number of minutes you select will appear in the box.

TIP

If the AutoRecover text box is dimmed, click in the Save Options check box to activate the feature. A check mark in the box indicates the feature is activated.

---

5. **Click** on **OK**. The Options dialog box will close.

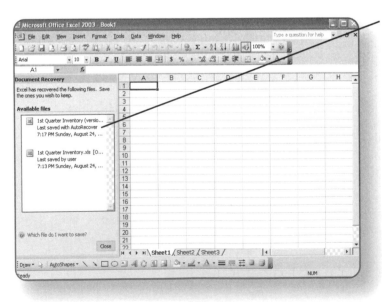

In the event of a system crash, when you reopen Excel, it lists both the original saved version and the recovered version. You can select which version of the worksheet you want to open and save.

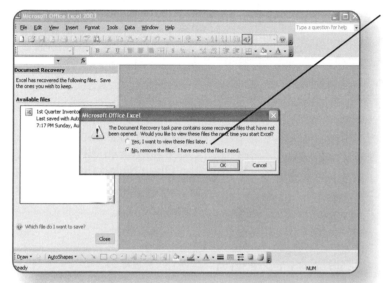

If you opted not to open and save a recovered file, when you exit Excel normally, you can decide to keep the recovered version of the file for later use or let Excel go ahead and delete it normally.

Opening an Existing File

Opening a worksheet is putting a copy of that file into the computer's memory and onto your screen so that you can work on it. If you make any changes, be sure to save the file again. Excel provides several different ways to open a worksheet.

Displaying the Open Dialog Box

Worksheets you have previously saved can be reopened on your screen through the Open dialog box.

1. Click on **File**. The File menu will appear.

2. Click on **Open**. The Open dialog box will appear.

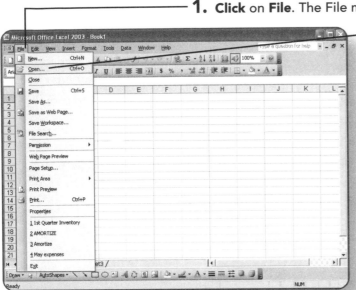

TIP

Optionally, click on the Open button to display the Open dialog box.

3. Click on the **file name** you want to open. The file name will be highlighted.

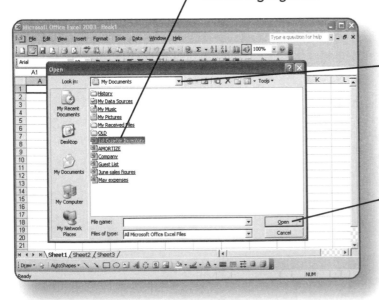

NOTE

If your file is located in a different folder than the one displayed in the Look in list box, click on the drop-down menu to navigate to the proper folder.

4. Click on **Open**. The file will be placed on your screen, ready for you to edit.

Opening a Recently Used Worksheet

Both the File menu and the task pane list several of the worksheets you've recently used, allowing you to quickly locate and open a worksheet.

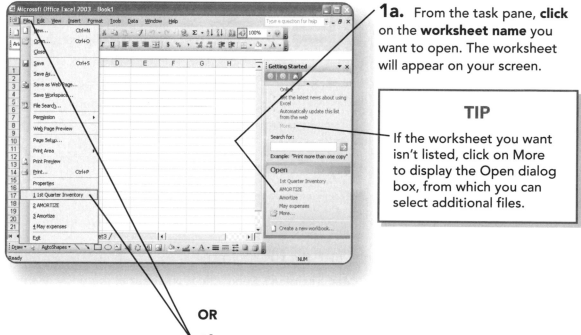

1a. From the task pane, **click** on the **worksheet name** you want to open. The worksheet will appear on your screen.

TIP

If the worksheet you want isn't listed, click on More to display the Open dialog box, from which you can select additional files.

OR

1b. **Click** on **File**. The File menu will open. **Click** the **worksheet name** you want to open. The worksheet will appear on your screen.

E-Mailing a Worksheet

If you have e-mail access, you can send a worksheet directly to another person. Excel either copies the content of the worksheet into a blank e-mail message or sends the worksheet as an attachment to an e-mail message.

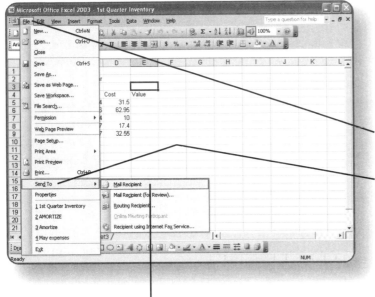

NOTE

You must save your worksheet prior to e-mailing it to someone.

1. **Click** on the **File menu**. The File menu will open.

2. **Click** on **Send To**. The Send To submenu will open.

Excel provides three different ways to e-mail a worksheet:

3. **Click** on the **appropriate option**:

- **Mail Recipient**. Sends the worksheet in the body of the e-mail.

- **Mail Recipient (for Review)**. The recipient will receive a link or an attachment, or both a link and an attachment to the file so they can review the file. When a reviewer opens the file, the reviewing tools are enabled and displayed. The files returned from reviewers automatically prompt you to merge changes. You can then use the reviewing tools to accept or reject the changes. For more information about reviewing tools, see Chapter 18, "Collaborating with Others."

- **Mail Recipient (as Attachment)**. Sends a copy of the worksheet as a file attachment for the recipient to open.

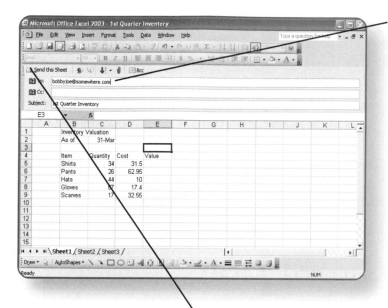

4. Type the **recipient's e-mail address**. The e-mail address will appear in the To box. You can add additional recipients by separating their e-mail addresses with a semicolon.

TIP

Some mail programs also allow you to add additional introductory text.

---

5. Click on **Send** or **Send this sheet**. Excel will send the worksheet to the e-mail recipients.

Starting a New Worksheet

When an Excel session is first started, a blank worksheet appears ready for you to use. However, during the course of using Excel, you may need another blank worksheet. Excel includes several methods to access a new worksheet.

By using the toolbar, creating a new worksheet using the standard Excel settings is only a mouse click away!

1a. **Click** on the **New Blank Worksheet button**. A new screen will appear with the title Worksheet2, Worksheet3, Worksheet4, and so on, depending on how many worksheets you've created during this session.

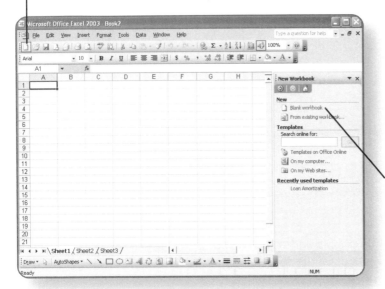

OR

TIP

Click on View, Task Pane if your task pane is not already displayed.

1b. **Click** on **Blank Workbook**. A standard blank worksheet will appear on the screen.

3

Editing a Worksheet

When you create a worksheet, a lot of data entry is usually involved. Excel has features to assist you with some of the repetitive work, but, unfortunately, you'll probably still make mistakes. You may need to edit the entries you made in some cells and you may want to make changes to the construction of your worksheet. Excel includes the ability to reorganize your worksheet without having to reenter any data.

In this chapter, you'll learn how to:

- Edit cell data
- Select cells
- Insert and delete rows, columns, and cells
- Use Undo and Redo
- Use the Clipboard task pane
- Use the Fill feature
- Transpose data

Editing Data

You can edit your data in a variety of ways. You might need to change the contents of a cell or you might want to move the data to a different area of the worksheet.

Replacing the Contents of a Cell

You can make changes to the contents of a cell in two ways. One method is by typing over the existing cell contents.

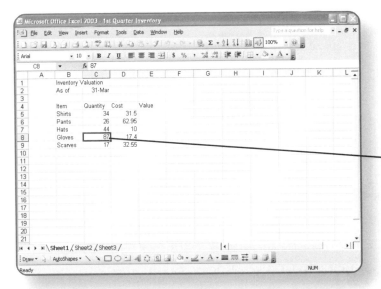

1. **Click** on an occupied **cell**. The cell and its contents will be selected.

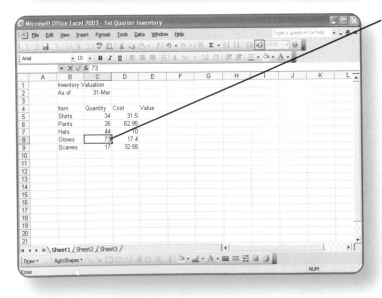

2. **Type** a new **label or value**. The new data will appear in the cell.

3. **Press** the **Enter key**. The new data will be accepted in the selected cell.

Editing the Contents of a Cell

The other method in which you can make changes to the contents of a cell is to use the Edit feature.

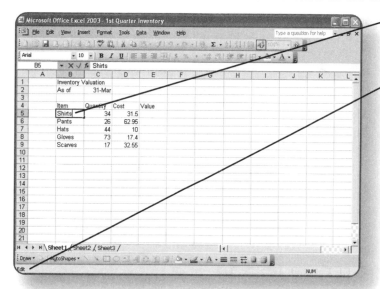

1. **Double-click** on the **cell** you want to edit. The insertion point will blink within the cell.

The status bar indicates that you are in Edit mode.

TIP

You can also press the F2 key to edit the contents of a cell.

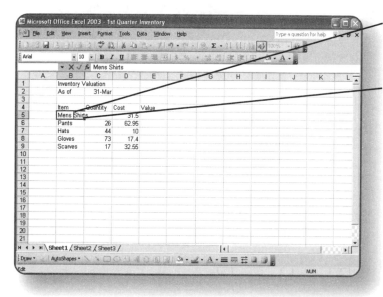

2. **Press** the **left arrow key**. The insertion point will move within the current cell.

3. **Type** the **changes**. The changes will appear in the current cell.

4. **Press** the **Enter key**. The changes will be entered into the current cell.

Clearing Cell Contents

If you enter data into a cell then later decide you do not want the information in the worksheet, you can quickly clear the contents.

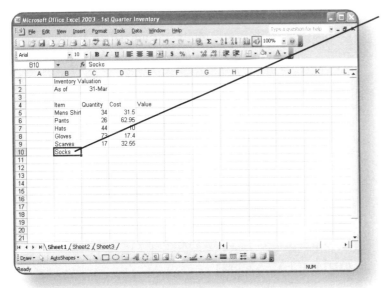

1. Click on the **cell** you want to clear. The cell is selected.

2. Press the **Delete key**. The content of the cell is cleared and the cell becomes empty.

Learning Selection Techniques

To move, copy, delete, or change the formatting of data in a worksheet, you must first select the cells you want to modify. Selected cells appear darker on screen—just the reverse of unselected text, with the exception of the first cell. The first cell does not appear darker; it just has a dark border around it.

TIP

Make sure the mouse pointer is a white cross before attempting to select cells.

The following table describes some of the different selection techniques:

To Select	Do This
A row	Click on the row number on the left side of the screen.
A column	Click on the column letter at the top of the screen.
A cell	Click on the desired cell.
A sequential block of cells	Click on the first cell and drag to highlight the rest of the cells.
A non-sequential block of cells	Click on the first cell, then hold down the Ctrl key and click on any additional cells.

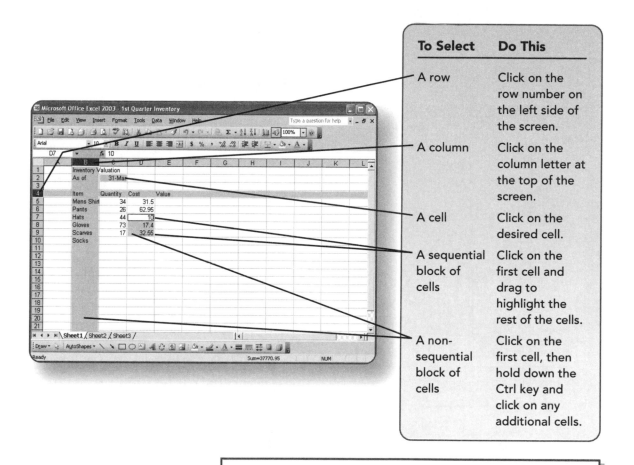

TIP

To deselect a block of cells, click the mouse in any single cell.

Inserting Areas

Occasionally you need to insert a column, row, or a single cell in the middle of existing information. Inserting rows, columns, or cells moves data to make room for new rows or columns.

Inserting Columns

You can insert a column anywhere you need it. Excel moves the existing columns to the right to make room for the new column.

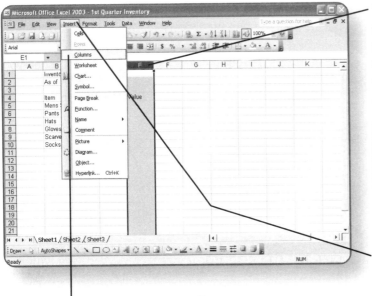

1. Click the heading letter of the **column** *after* which you want to insert the new column. (Excel will insert the new column in front of the selected one.) The entire column is selected.

TIP

To insert multiple columns, select headings across multiple columns.

---

2. Click on **Insert**. The Insert menu will appear.

3. Click on **Columns**. Excel will insert a new column in the selected area.

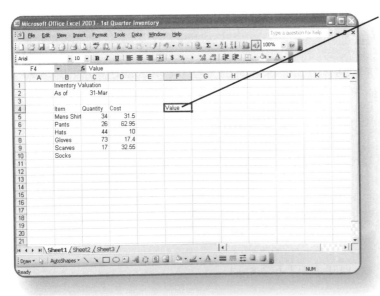

Excel moves information in the previously selected column and all columns to the right of the selected column to the right.

Inserting Rows

You can insert a row anywhere you need it. Excel will move the existing rows down to make room for the new ones.

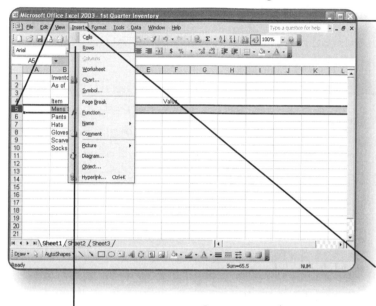

1. **Click** on the row number of the **row** *after* which you want to insert the new row. (Excel will insert the new row above the selected one.) The entire row is selected.

TIP

To insert multiple rows, select cells across multiple rows.

2. **Click** on **Insert**. The Insert menu will appear.

3. **Click** on **Rows**. Excel inserts a new row in the selected area.

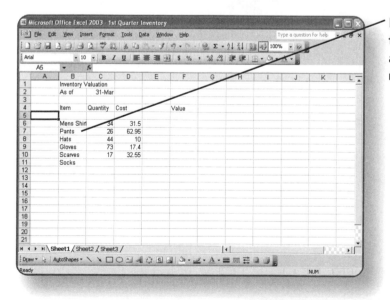

Excel moves information in the previously selected row and all rows below the selected row down.

Inserting Cells

Instead of inserting an entire column or an entire row, you can insert a single cell or even a group of cells. Excel then moves existing data down or to the right, depending on the option you specify.

1. Select the **cells** currently where you want the new cells. The cells will be selected.

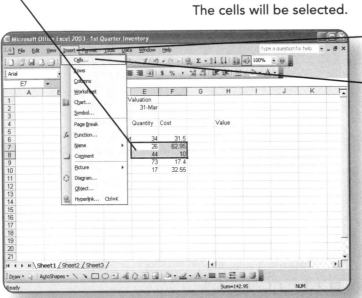

2. Click on **Insert**. The Insert menu will appear.

3. Click on **Cells**. The Insert dialog box will open.

4. Click on **Shift Cells Right or Shift Cells Down**. A dot appears next to the selection.

5. Click on **OK**. The Insert dialog box will close and the new cells will be inserted.

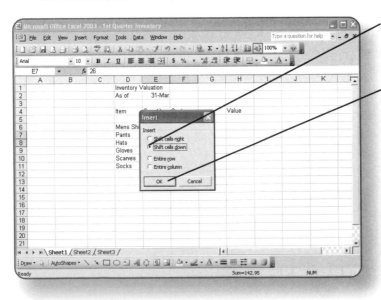

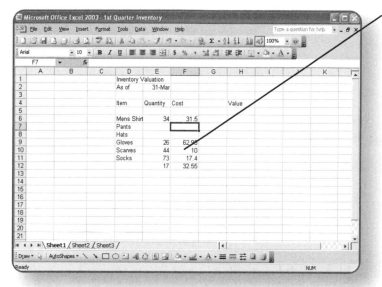

Existing data is moved down or to the right.

Deleting Areas

Use caution when deleting rows or columns. Excel will delete the entire row of 256 columns or the entire column of 65,536 rows. Any data in the selected row or column is deleted as well.

Deleting Columns

When you delete a column, Excel will pull the remaining columns to the left. You can delete a single column at a time, or you can delete multiple columns, whether sequential or non-sequential columns.

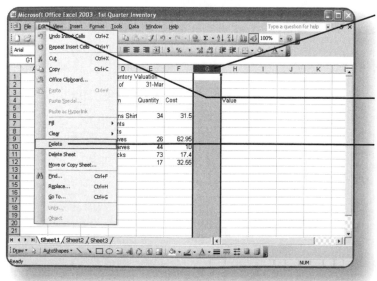

1. **Click** the **column heading letter** of the column you want to delete. The entire column is selected.

2. **Click** on **Edit**. The Edit menu will appear.

3. **Click** on **Delete**. The selected column is deleted.

Deleting Rows

When you delete a row, Excel will pull the remaining rows up. You can delete a single row at a time, or you can delete multiple rows, whether sequential or nonsequential.

1. Click the **row heading number** of the row you want to delete. The entire row is selected.

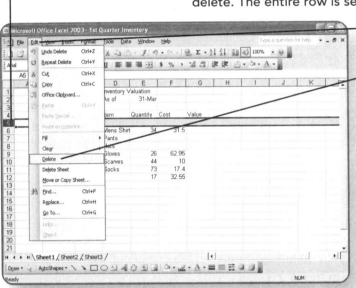

2. Click on **Edit**. The Edit menu will appear.

3. Click on **Delete**. The selected row is deleted.

Deleting Cells

When clearing the contents of a cell, the cell remains in its current location, whereas deleting a cell eliminates not only the contents of the cell but also the actual cell. Other cells move into the deleted cell position.

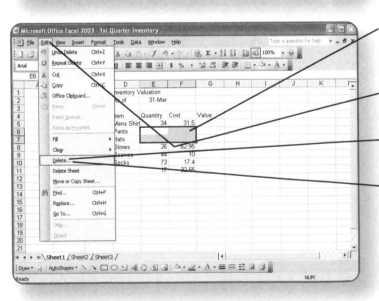

1. Select the **cells** you want to delete. The cells will be selected.

2. Click on **Edit**. The Edit menu will appear.

3. Click on **Delete**. The Delete dialog box will open.

Unlike when a column or row is selected, the Delete menu option has an ellipsis, which indicates a dialog box will open.

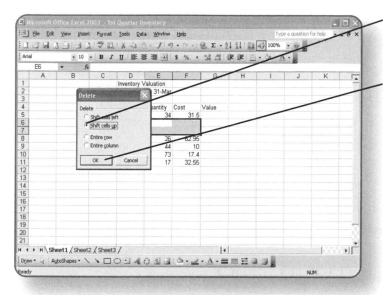

4. Click on **Shift Cells Left or Shift Cells Up**. A dot appears next to the selection.

5. Click on **OK**. The Delete dialog box will close and the selected cells will be deleted.

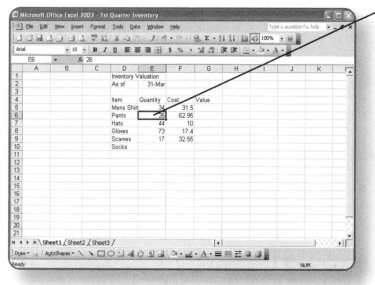

Existing data is moved up or to the left.

Using Undo and Redo

If you make a change, then determine you really didn't want to make that change, Excel provides an Undo feature. You can use Undo to restore text that you deleted, delete text you just typed, or reverse a recently taken action.

An exception to the Undo function is if you save your worksheet—you cannot "unsave" it. Also, if you close the worksheet, you cannot undo changes made in the previous editing session when you reopen the worksheet.

Undoing the Previous Step

You are one mouse click away from reversing your previous action.

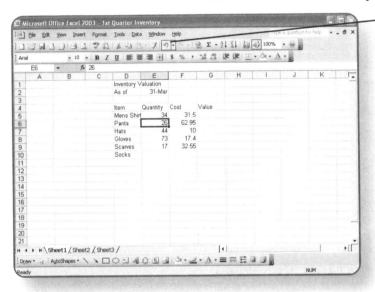

1. Click on the **Undo button**. Excel will reverse the last action you took with the current worksheet.

TIP

Optionally, choose Undo from the Edit menu.

Redoing the Previous Step

If you undo an action and then decide you prefer the worksheet the original way, use the Redo feature.

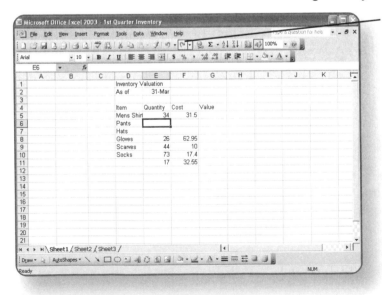

1. Click on the **Redo button**. Excel will reverse the previous undo action.

Undoing a Series of Actions

Excel actually keeps track of several steps you have recently taken. When you Undo a previous step, you also undo any actions taken after that step. For example, imagine you changed the value in a cell then bolded the cell contents. If you undo the typing, Excel also reverses the bolding step.

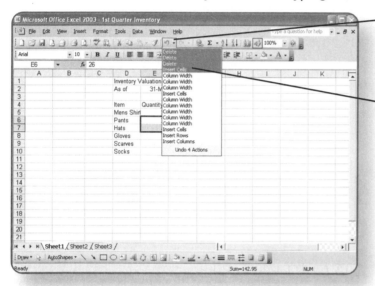

1. Click on the **arrow** next to the Undo button. A list of the most recent actions will be displayed.

2. Click on the **action** you want to undo. Excel will reverse the selected action as well as all actions listed above it.

Moving Data Around

If you're not happy with the placement of data, you don't have to delete it and retype it. Excel makes it easy for you to move it around. In fact, Excel provides several ways to move data.

Cutting and Pasting Data

Excel uses the Windows copy and paste features to assist you with moving data.

1. **Select** the **cells** you want to move. The cells will be highlighted.

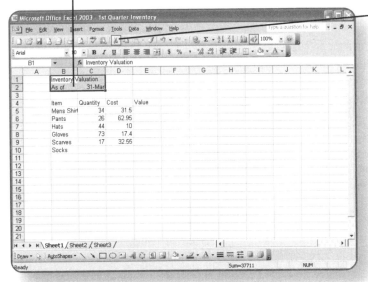

2. **Click** on the **Cut button**. Moving dashes, called a *marquee*, will appear around your selection.

TIP

Optionally, press Ctrl + X or choose Cut from the Edit menu.

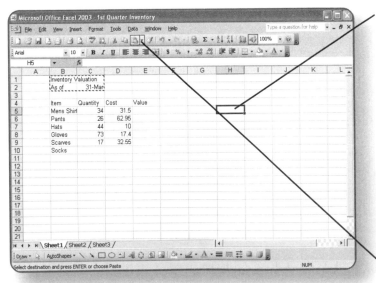

3. **Click** on the **cell** that will be the upper-left corner of the new location of the range. The cell will be selected.

NOTE

There must be enough empty cells in the new location to accommodate the cut data or existing data will be overwritten.

4. **Click** on the **Paste button**.

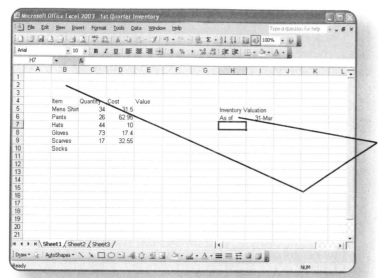

TIP

Optionally, press Ctrl + V or choose Paste from the Edit menu.

The data is pasted into the new location and removed from the previous location.

Using Drag and Drop to Move Cells

Drag and drop is another method used to move data from one location to another. The drag and drop method works best for moving a few cells of data a short distance.

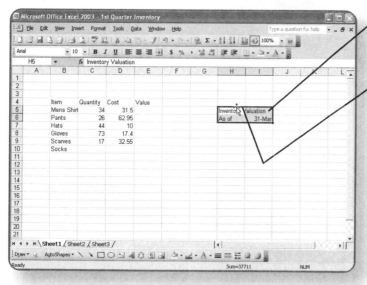

1. Select the **cells** you want to move. The cells will be highlighted.

2. Position the **mouse pointer** on the border edge of the highlighted cells. The mouse pointer will appear as a white arrow pointed to the left with four black arrow heads.

NOTE

Make sure the mouse pointer is a white arrow and not a black cross, which accomplishes a different function.

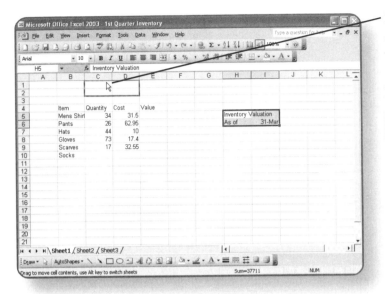

3. Hold the **mouse button** down **and drag** the mouse to the desired location. A gray border appears around the cells you point to.

TIP

To copy text with drag and drop, hold down the Ctrl key before dragging the selected text. Release the mouse button before releasing the Ctrl key.

4. Release the **mouse button**. The cells will move to the new location.

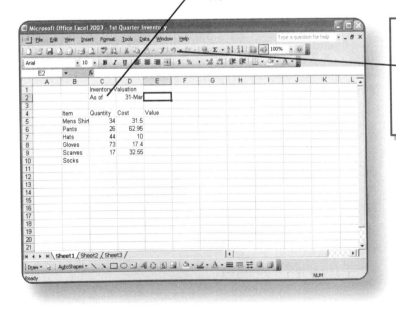

TIP

If you accidentally move cells to the wrong position, click on the Undo button to reverse the move.

Copying Data

If you want to duplicate cell data, again, you don't have to retype it. You can use the Copy command to replicate information.

1. Select the **cells** you want to duplicate. The cells will be highlighted.

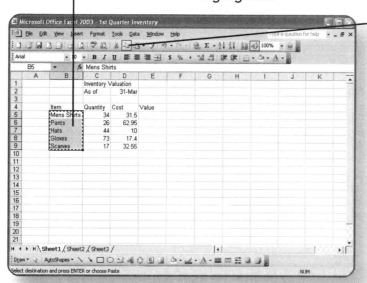

2. Click on the **Copy button.** The marquee, sometimes called "marching ants," will appear around the selected cells.

TIP

Optionally, press Ctrl + C or choose Copy from the Edit menu.

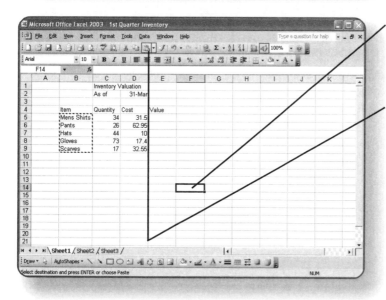

3. Click on the beginning **cell** where you want to paste the duplicated information. The cell will be highlighted.

4. Click on the **Paste** button.

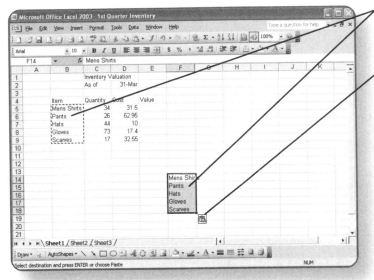

The pasted text will appear in both the original and new location.

In some situations, when you paste information or perform other Excel functions, you may see a small icon, called a Smart Tag, appear to the right of the pasted text. You'll learn about Smart Tags in Chapter 14, "Discovering Tools for Speed and Quality."

TIP

If the marquee does not stop marching, press the Enter key.

Using the Office Clipboard

Excel also uses a special form of the Windows clipboard, called the Office Clipboard. The Office Clipboard allows you to collect text and other items from any Office document or even other programs, then past them into any Excel worksheet. Each item is appended to the clipboard contents and then inserted as individuals or as a group in a new location or worksheet. You copy an item to the Office Clipboard, then paste it into any Office worksheet at any time. The collected items stay on the Office Clipboard until you exit Office.

Depending on the number of times you have copied text, the Clipboard task pane may appear automatically when you paste text.

1. Click on **Edit**. The Edit menu will appear.

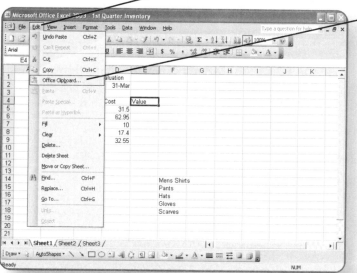

2. Click on **Office Clipboard**. The Clipboard task pane will appear.

The Office Clipboard stores up to 24 items you copied or cut. It doesn't matter whether you used the Edit menu, the cut or copy icons on the toolbar, the shortcut menu, or the shortcut keys.

You can insert any desired item from the clipboard or you can insert all items.

3. Click the **mouse** where you want to insert the Clipboard contents. The blinking insertion point will appear.

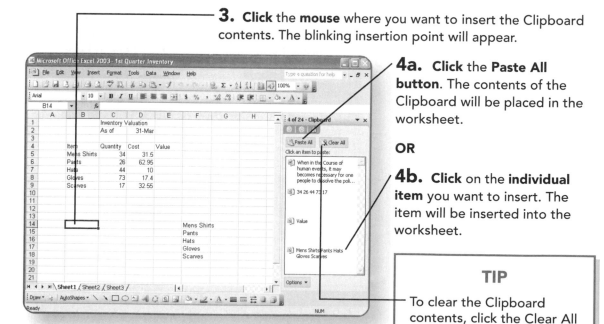

4a. Click the **Paste All button**. The contents of the Clipboard will be placed in the worksheet.

OR

4b. Click on the **individual item** you want to insert. The item will be inserted into the worksheet.

TIP

To clear the Clipboard contents, click the Clear All button.

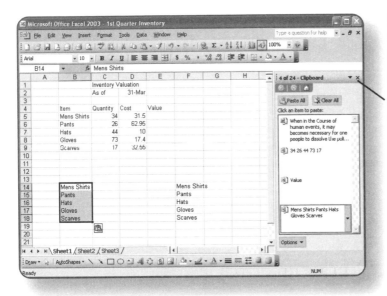

If you are finished with the Clipboard task pane, you may find it helpful to put the task pane away.

5. Click the **Close button**. The Clipboard task pane will disappear.

Using the Fill Feature

Excel includes a great built-in, time-saving feature called *Fill*. If you provide Excel the beginning pattern, such as a Month, Day, or numbers, Excel can fill in the rest of the pattern for you. For example, if you type January, Excel fills in February, March, April, and so on.

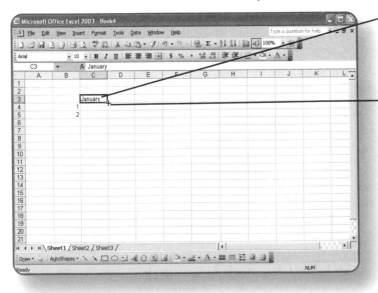

1. Type the beginning **month, day, or number** in the beginning cell. The text will be displayed in the cell.

2. Position the **mouse pointer** on the lower-right corner of the beginning cell. The mouse pointer will become a small black cross.

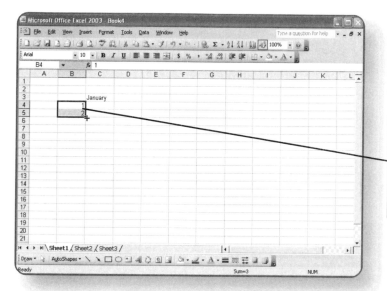

If you want Excel to fill in numbers, you must first give it a pattern. For example, enter the value of **1** in the first cell, and then enter **2** in the second cell.

TIP

For numbers, select both the first and second cells before proceeding to step 3.

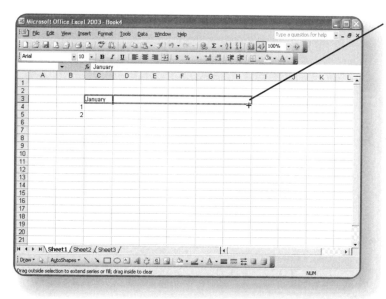

3. **Press and hold** the **mouse button and drag** to select the next cells to be filled in. The cells will have a gray border surrounding them.

4. **Release** the **mouse button**. The pattern will be repeated.

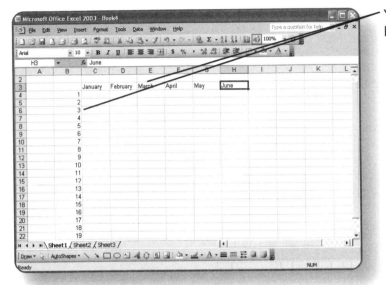

You can fill a series up, down, left, or right in your worksheet.

4

Making the Worksheet Look Good

You can make your worksheets more interesting and easier to read by formatting the worksheet cells. Change the fonts, font sizes, and styles or make the numbers easier to read by adding numeric formatting. Liven up the worksheet with effective use of borders, lines, and colors.

In this chapter, you'll learn how to:

- Use AutoFormat
- Format numbers and dates
- Use fonts and font attributes
- Modify column width and row height
- Adjust cell alignment
- Add cell borders and patterns
- Copy cell formatting

Using AutoFormat

AutoFormat is a quick, easy method to format your worksheet. It allows you to select from a number of professionally designed formats that automatically add colors, fonts, lines, borders, and more to your worksheets. Excel provides 16 different predefined AutoFormat patterns, some color and some black and white.

1. **Click and drag** the **mouse** across the cells you want to format. The cells will be highlighted.

2. **Click** on **Format**. The Format menu will appear.

3. **Click** on **AutoForma**t. The AutoFormat dialog box will open.

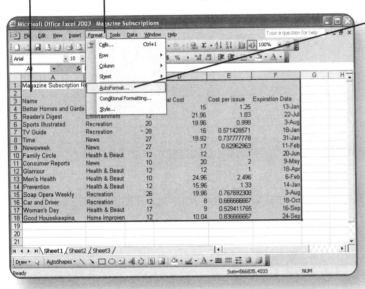

4. Click on a sample **format**. A border appears around the selected format.

Click on the Options button to specify additional preferences.

5. Click on **OK**. The effect will be applied to the selected cells.

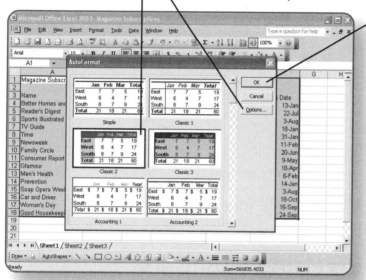

6. Deselect the highlighted **cells** to see the full effect of the AutoFormat. Depending on your selection, AutoFormat may have added color, changed the fonts, applied italics or bolding, and adjusted row heights.

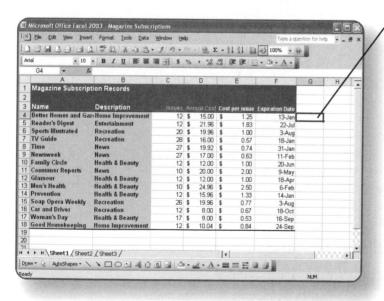

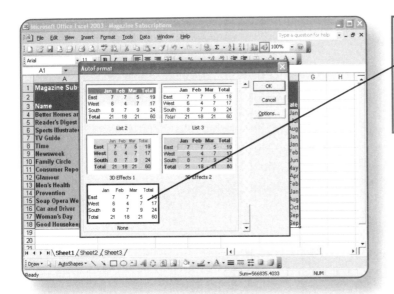

TIP

Apply the AutoFormat option "None" to remove the formatting from any selected cells.

Formatting Numbers

By default, values are displayed as general numbers; however, you can choose to display values as currency, percentages, fractions, dates, and many other formats.

Formatting Numbers with the Toolbar

The Excel formatting toolbar includes three popular number styles: commas, accounting, and percentages. Accounting and comma formats automatically apply two decimal places, whereas the percentage format doesn't apply any decimal points. The accounting style also applies a dollar sign to the number.

Adding Commas

When you apply a comma style to selected values, Excel separates the thousands making the data easier to read.

1. Select the **cells** you want to format. The cells will be highlighted.

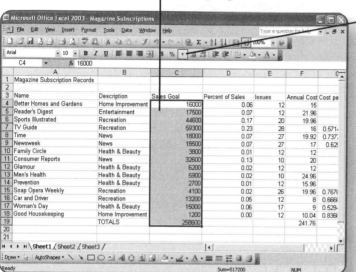

2. Click on the **Comma button**. The cells will be formatted with two decimal places and a comma to separate numbers greater than 999.

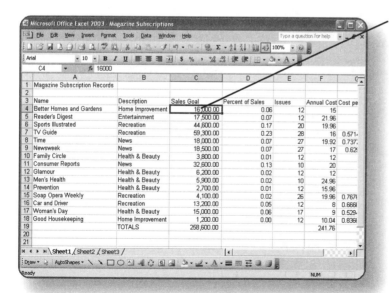

Cells formatted with a comma.

Formatting for Currency

Excel has a little quirk that appears when choosing the Currency button on the toolbar. The Excel tooltip calls this button the currency style; however, it actually applies an accounting style. The difference is in the placement of the dollar sign. In currency style, the dollar sign is right next to the numbers, but in accounting style, the dollar sign is on the left edge of the cell

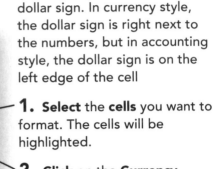

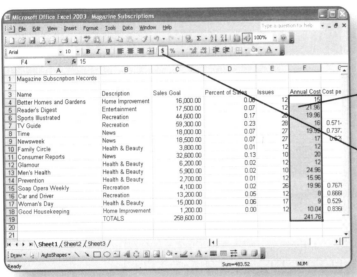

1. Select the **cells** you want to format. The cells will be highlighted.

2. Click on the **Currency button**. The cells will be formatted with a dollar sign and two decimal places.

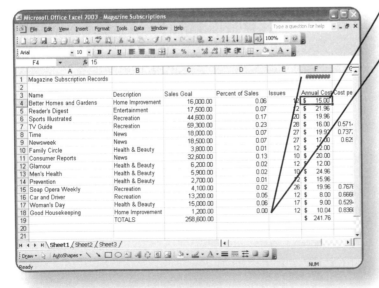

Cells formatted with currency and two decimal places.

If a formatted value cannot fit within the width of a cell, Excel may display a series of ###. You will discover how to widen a column later in this chapter.

Formatting Percentages

Excel provides a button on the toolbar for quick access when changing numbers to display as a percentage. Excel automatically multiplies the cell value by 100 and displays the result with a percent symbol. For example, if the cell has a value of 15, Excel will display 1500%; however, if the cell has a value of 0.15, Excel will display 15%.

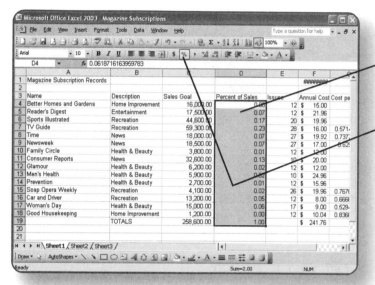

1. Select the **cells** you want to format. The cells will be highlighted.

2. Click on the **Percent button**. The cells will be formatted with a percent sign and no decimal places.

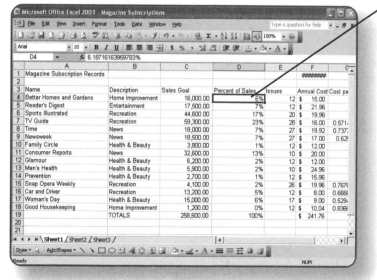

Cells formatted with the percent symbol.

Changing the Decimal Point Values

As mentioned earlier, by default, the comma and currency styles include two decimal places, and percentages don't include decimal points. If you have a number in a formatted cell with more than the two decimal points, Excel will round the number up. So if you enter 75.257 in a cell, then format that cell to comma or currency, Excel will display $75.26. There are toolbar buttons, however, that allow you to increase or decrease the number of decimal places. The maximum number of decimal places is 15 places.

1. **Select** the **cells** you want to format. The cells will be highlighted.

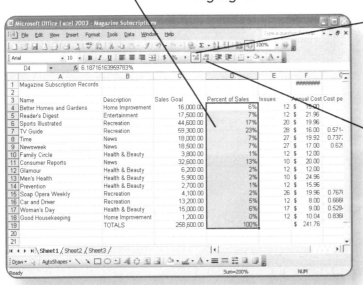

2a. **Click** on the **Increase Decimal button**. Each click increases the number of decimal places.

OR

2b. **Click** on the **Decrease Decimal button**. Each click decreases the number of decimal places.

Formatting Numbers through the Menu

Excel includes a dialog box where you can change all the formatting options in one step.

Formatting Numbers

The Format Cells dialog box allows you to select from several different number formatting styles, including whether to display negative numbers in red, choosing the number of decimal points, and even selecting the desired type of currency symbol. There is also a "Special" category where you can format numbers to match the pattern for telephone numbers or social security numbers.

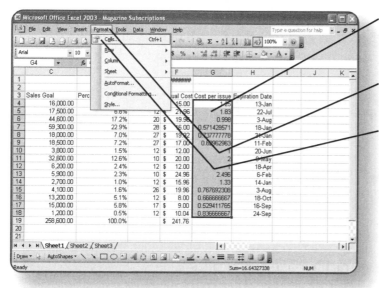

1. **Select** the **cells** you want to format. The cells will be highlighted.

2. **Click** on **Format**. The Format menu will appear.

3. **Click** on **Cells**. The Format Cells dialog box will open.

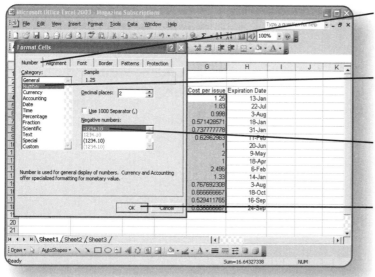

4. If necessary, **click** the **Number tab**. A list of number formats will display.

5. **Click** on a **category**. Available options for the selected category will appear.

6. **Click** on any desired **options**. A sample will appear in the sample box.

7. **Click** on **OK**. The Format Cells dialog box will close and Excel will apply the selected format.

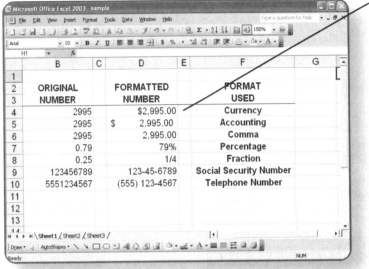

A sample of different number formats.

Formatting Dates

As you learned in Chapter 2, "Creating a Simple Worksheet," Excel may not display a date in the same format as you entered the data. Through the Format Cells dialog box you can select the format you want for cells containing dates.

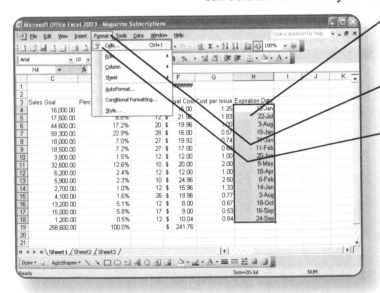

1. **Select** the **cells** you want to format. The cells will be highlighted.

2. **Click** on **Format**. The Format menu will appear.

3. **Click** on **Cells**. The Format Cells dialog box will open.

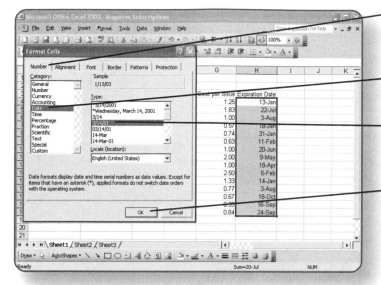

4. If necessary, **click** the **Number tab**. A list of number formats will display.

5. Click on **Date**. A list of available date formats will appear.

6. Click on a **date style**. A sample will appear in the sample box.

7. Click on **OK**. The Format Cells dialog box will close and Excel will apply the date style you selected.

Formatting with Fonts

Excel uses a default font of Arial 10 points, but from the toolbar you can easily change the font typeface, size, style, and color.

Selecting a Typeface

Fonts are typefaces in different styles that give your text character and impact. Your selection of fonts will vary depending on the software installed on your computer.

1. **Select** the **cells** you want to format. The cells will be highlighted.

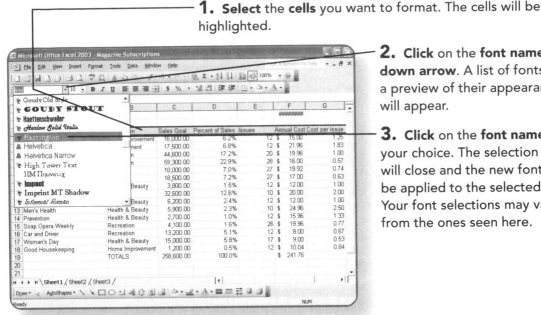

2. **Click** on the **font name down arrow**. A list of fonts and a preview of their appearance will appear.

3. **Click** on the **font name** of your choice. The selection list will close and the new font will be applied to the selected cells. Your font selections may vary from the ones seen here.

Selecting a Font Size

The default font size in an Excel worksheet is 10 points. There are approximately 72 points in an inch, so a 10 point font is slightly less than one-seventh of an inch tall.

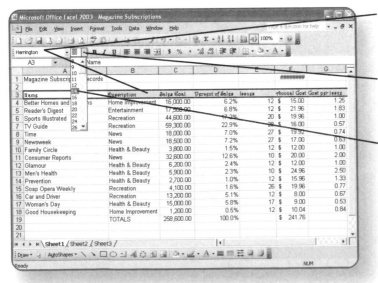

1. **Select** the **cells** you want to format. The cells will be highlighted.

2. **Click** on the **font size down arrow**. A list of available sizes will appear.

3. **Click** on the **font size** of your choice. The selection list will close and the new font size will be applied to the selected cells.

Adding Bold, Underline, or Italics

Excel includes three different font styles you can select from the toolbar. Font styles include **bold**, <u>underline</u>, and *italics*.

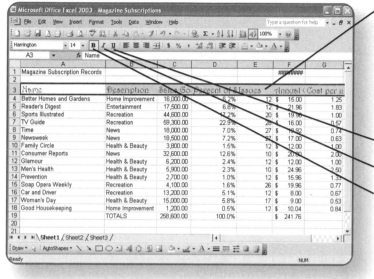

1. Select the **cells** you want to format. The cells will be highlighted.

2. Click on any of the following **options**. The attributes will be applied to the selected cells.

- Underline button

- Italics button

- Bold button

TIP

Shortcut keys include Ctrl + B for Bold, Ctrl + I for Italics, and Ctrl + U for Underline.

The Bold, Italics, and Underline buttons are like toggle switches. Click on them a second time to turn the attribute off.

NOTE

Underlining is not the same as a cell border. Cell borders are discussed later in this chapter.

Working with Font Colors

If you want to add color to your worksheet, try changing the font color.

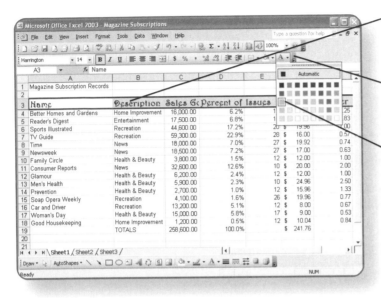

1. **Select** the **cells** you want to format. The cells will be highlighted.

2. **Click** the **font color down arrow**. A color palette will appear.

3. **Click** on a **color**. The color palette will close and the font color will be applied to the selected cells.

Setting Font Options Using the Format Dialog Box

Setting formatting from the toolbar is easy, but Excel also provides a dialog box that offers font choices plus a few extras.

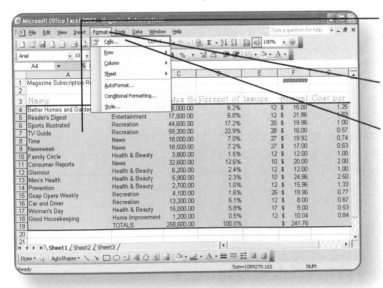

1. **Select** the **cells** you want to format. The cells will be highlighted.

2. **Click** on **Format**. The Format menu will appear.

3. **Click** on **Cells**. The Format Cells dialog box will open.

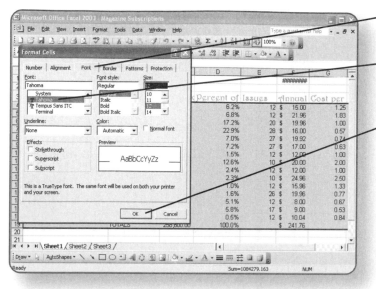

4. Click on the **Font tab**. The Font tab will appear in front.

5. Select any desired **font options** including typeface, size, color, and other options.

6. Click on **OK**. Excel will apply all the font options at once.

Adjusting Column Width

By default, Excel columns are 8.43 points wide. When the content of a cell is too long to fit into its cell, depending on the type of data, Excel may automatically widen the column or display the information in a different format. You can manually resize a column so all data displays correctly.

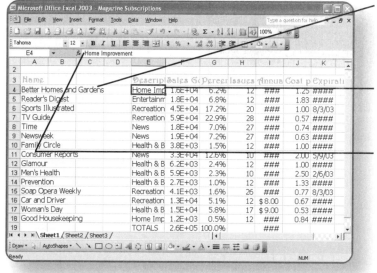

If a label does not fit into the cell, the contents will spill into the next cell to the right, if the next cell is empty.

If the next cell is not empty, Excel displays only the amount of text that will fit into the cell.

The extra text is not cut off, just not displayed.

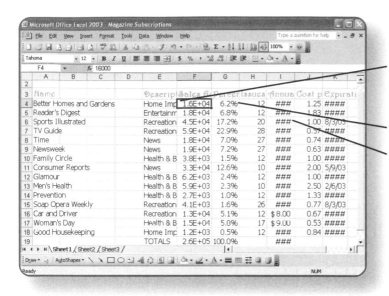

If a value is too wide, Excel may do one of several things:

- Display the number in scientific notation so it displays in fewer characters.

- Automatically widen the cell.

- Display the data as a series of number signs (#).

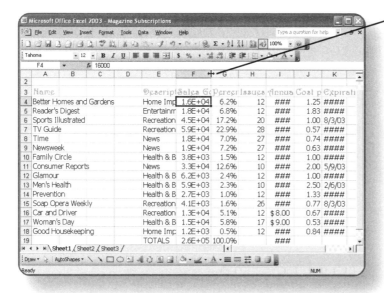

1a. **Double-click** on the **dividing line** to the right of the column heading letters. The column will automatically expand to fit the column contents.

TIP

To resize multiple columns at the same time, select the columns you want to modify.

OR

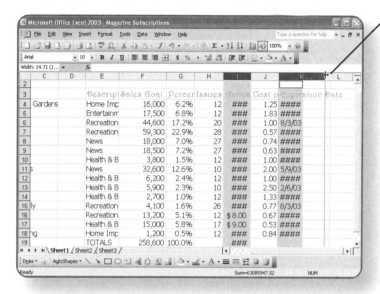

1b. **Position** the **mouse pointer** on the dividing line between the column heading letters until the mouse pointer becomes a double-headed arrow. **Drag** the **line** to the right to widen the column or to the left to make the column narrower. A line will appear showing the new column width. **Release** the **mouse button**. The new column width will apply to the selected column.

TIP

To manually set the column width, click the Format menu, select Column, then Width. Enter the desired column width in points.

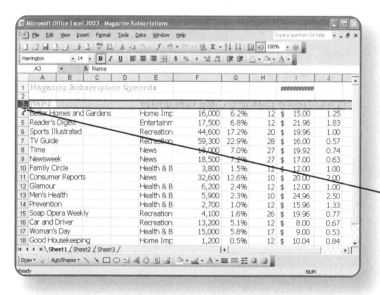

Adjusting Row Height

When you change to a larger font, Excel usually enlarges the row height to accommodate the larger font size. You can also manually resize the row height.

1a. **Double-click** on the **dividing line** below the row that needs to be resized. The row will automatically expand to fit the row contents.

TIP

To resize multiple rows at the same time, select the rows you want to modify.

OR

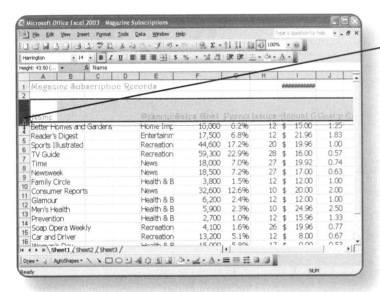

1b. **Position** the **mouse pointer** on the dividing line below the row that needs to be resized until the mouse pointer becomes a double-headed arrow. **Drag** the **line** down to increase the row height or up to decrease the row height. A line will appear showing the new row height. **Release** the **mouse button**. The new row height will apply to the selected column.

TIP

To manually set the row height, click the Format menu, select Row, then Height. Enter the desired row height in points.

Setting Worksheet Alignment

By default, Excel makes labels left-aligned and values right-aligned to their cells. You can change the alignment of either to left, right, centered, or full justified.

You can also wrap text in the cells when the text is too long to fit in one cell and you don't want it to overlap to the next cell.

Adjusting Cell Alignment

You can adjust cells individually or adjust a block of cells.

1. **Select** the **cells** you want to format. The cells will be highlighted.

2. **Click** on **Format**. The Format menu will appear.

3. **Click** on **Cells**. The Format Cells dialog box will open.

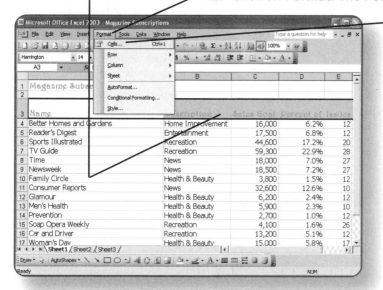

4. If necessary, **click** on the **Alignment tab**. The Alignment tab will come to the top.

5. **Click** the **Horizontal drop-down menu**. A list of options will appear.

6. **Click** an alignment **option**. The option will be selected.

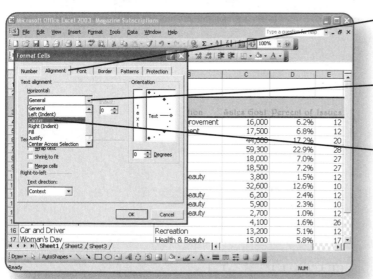

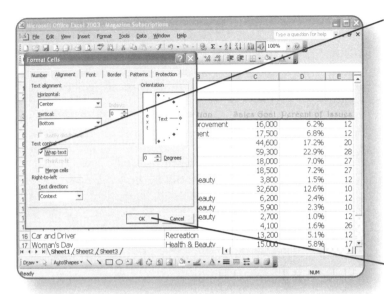

7. Optionally, **click** on a **Text control option** to activate any desired feature. A check mark will appear in the selection box.

TIP

The Wrap text feature treats each cell like a miniature word processor, with text wrapping around in the cell.

8. Click on **OK**. The selections will be applied to the highlighted cells.

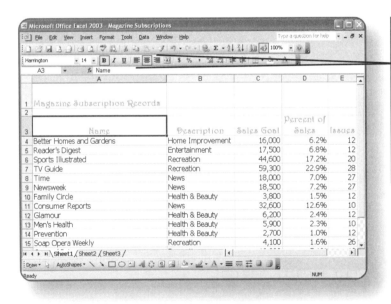

TIP

Optionally, you can quickly align text with the toolbar. Select the text you want to align, then click on one of the three alignment buttons on the toolbar: Left, Center, or Right.

Setting Vertical Alignment

Excel aligns text vertically to the bottom of the row, but you can also center it or align it to the top of the cell. You can also make the entire cell contents display vertically or at an angle.

1. Select the **cells** you want to format. The cells will be highlighted.

2. Click on **Format**. The Format menu will appear.

3. Click on **Cells**. The Format Cells dialog box will open.

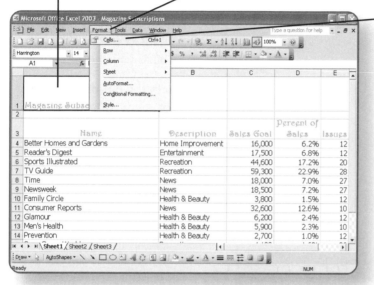

4. If necessary, **click** on the **Alignment tab**. The Alignment tab will come to the top.

5. Click the **Vertical drop-down menu**. A list of options will appear.

6. Click an alignment **option**. The option will be selected.

7. Optionally, **select** an **orientation**, and if you want the text to be displayed at an angle, select the angle degrees.

8. Click on **OK**. The selections will be applied to the highlighted cells.

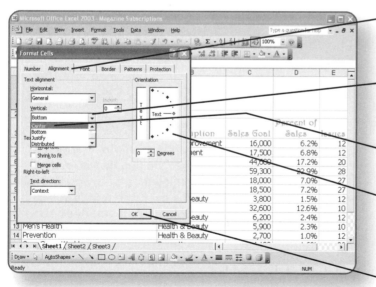

Centering Headings

You can also center text across a group of columns to create attractive headings.

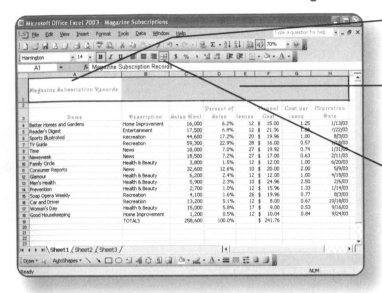

1. **Type** the heading **text** in the first column of the worksheet body. This is usually column A.

2. **Select** the **heading cell and the cells** you want to include in the heading. The cells will be highlighted.

3. **Click** on the **Merge and Center button**. The title will be centered.

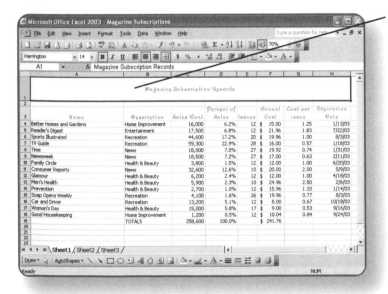

Notice the gridlines have disappeared and the cells appear to be joined together.

NOTE

In this example, it appears that the heading is located in Columns B, C, and D; however, the text is still in Column A. If you need to change the text, be sure to select Column A, not Column B, C, or D.

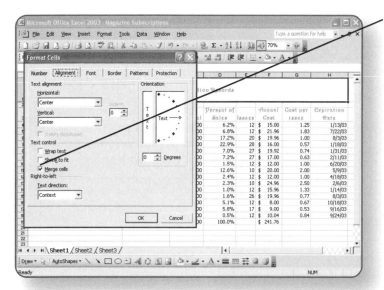

Remove the Merge and Center option through the Format Cells dialog box.

Adding Cell Borders

You can add border lines to individual cells and groups of cells. A border can appear around all sides of the cell or only on certain sides, such as the top or bottom. Unlike an underline, which runs directly under letters and numbers, a border includes the entire width or height of a cell.

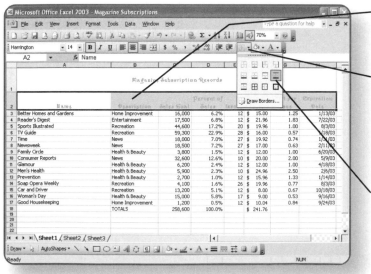

1. Select the **cells** you want to format. The cells will be highlighted.

2. Click on the **down arrow** next to the Borders button. The Borders palette will appear with icons displaying how the borders will be applied to a selected range.

3. Click on the desired **format**. The Borders palette will close.

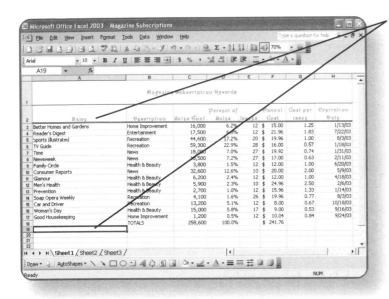

4. Deselect the **cells** to easily see the border.

TIP

You can select additional border options through the Border tab on the Format Cells dialog box.

Adding Background Color

Adding a background color to a cell or group of cells can make your worksheet more interesting and can call attention to specific areas of the worksheet. Excel calls the background color the Fill color.

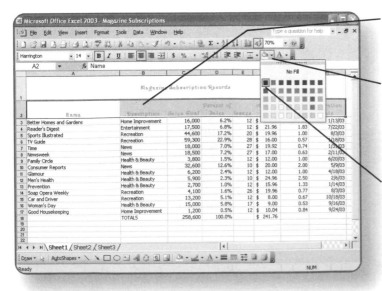

1. Select the **cells** you want to format. The cells will be highlighted.

2. Click on the **down arrow** next to the Fill Color button. The Fill Color palette will appear with icons displaying a selection of colors.

3. Click on the desired **color**. The Fill Color palette will close and the color will be applied to the selected cells.

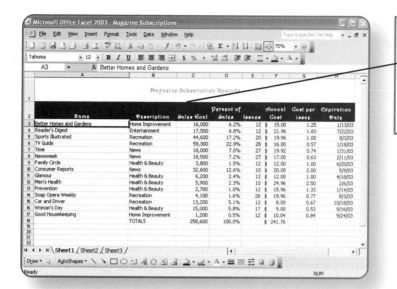

TIP

For a nice effect, use a dark background in combination with a light font color.

Using Cell Patterns

You can use a pattern instead of a single color as a background to your cells. A pattern uses two colors, arranged in some design, such as stripes or dots. Each pattern has both a background and a foreground color. The background color is the base color, whereas the foreground color is the color of the stripes or dots. Be careful using patterns because they can be distracting to the reader.

1. Select the **cells** you want to format. The cells will be highlighted.

2. Click on **Format**. The Format menu will appear.

3. Click on **Cells**. The Format Cells dialog box will open.

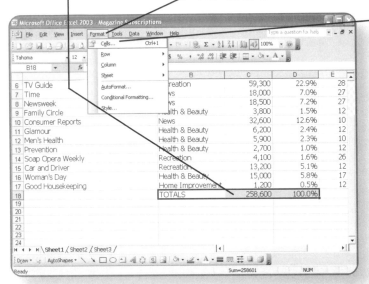

4. Click on the **Patterns tab**. The Patterns tab will appear in front.

5. Click on the Pattern **drop-down menu**. A palette of patterns and colors will appear.

6. Click on a **pattern** at the top of the list. The pattern and color palette will close.

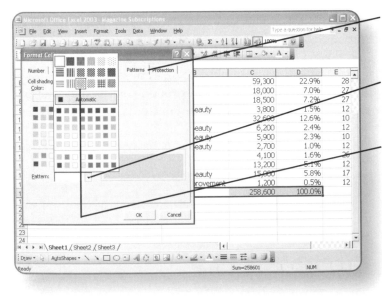

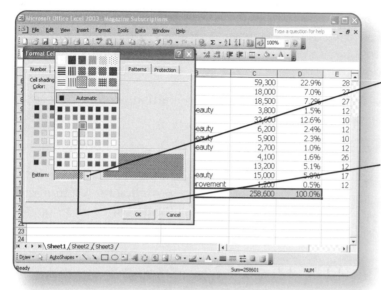

By default, the patterns are black and white, but you can change the colors.

7. Optionally, **click** on the Pattern **drop-down menu** again. A palette of patterns and colors will appear.

8. **Click** on a **color**. The pattern and color palette will close.

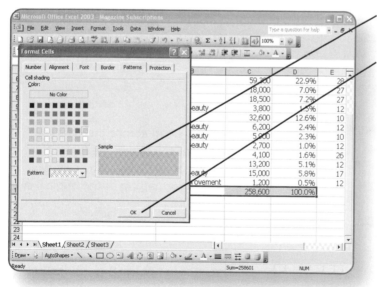

A sample will appear in the sample box.

9. **Click** on **OK**. The Format Cells dialog box will close and the selected cells will have the pattern selection.

Copying Cell Formatting

Sometimes it takes a lot of time and effort to get the formatting of a cell just the way you want it. Rather than duplicate all those steps for another cell, Excel includes a

Format Painter feature which copies formatting from one cell to another. Copied formatting includes font size, color, style attributes, shading, and alignment. When you copy the formatting, the values in the cells are not affected.

1. Select a **cell** containing the formatting you want to copy. The cell will be highlighted.

2. Click on the **Format Painter button**.

The mouse pointer will turn into a paintbrush with a plus sign.

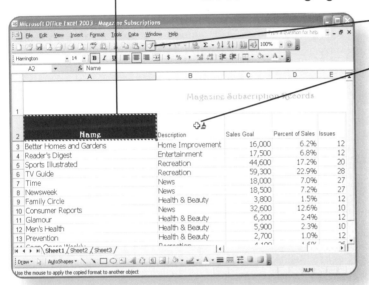

3. Drag across the **cells** you want to contain the formatting. Excel will "paint" the cells with the formatting of the original cell.

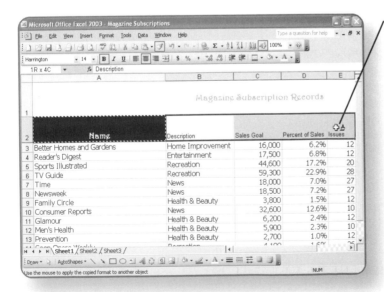

5

Selecting Printing Options

Before you print your worksheet, you can adjust the printing options. In addition, Excel can save you time and money by letting you see exactly what you're going to print before you use any paper.

In this chapter, you'll learn how to:

- Set up page margins
- Specify page orientation and size
- Create a header or footer
- Adjust printing size
- Use Print Preview
- Print the worksheet

Setting Up the Pages

With a single click, you can print your worksheet. But before you print your worksheet, you might want to specify what paper size to use, how large to make the margins, and whether to print the gridlines. You also might want to specify to print only a portion of the worksheet instead of printing it in its entirety.

Setting Up Margins

By default, Excel uses a top and bottom margin of 1 inch and left and right margins of .75 inch. You can change these margins to meet your needs.

1. **Click** on **File**. The File menu will appear.

2. **Click** on **Page Setup**. The Page Setup dialog box will open.

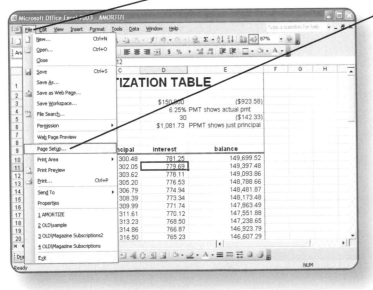

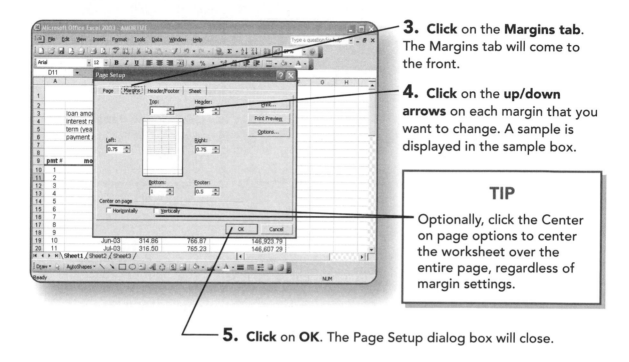

3. Click on the **Margins tab**. The Margins tab will come to the front.

4. Click on the **up/down arrows** on each margin that you want to change. A sample is displayed in the sample box.

TIP

Optionally, click the Center on page options to center the worksheet over the entire page, regardless of margin settings.

5. Click on **OK**. The Page Setup dialog box will close.

Setting Page Orientation and Size

If your worksheet uses quite a few columns, you might want to change the orientation or paper size. The default size is 8-½ x 11-inch paper in portrait orientation—the short side at the top and bottom. Changing to landscape orientation will print with the long edge of the paper at the top and bottom.

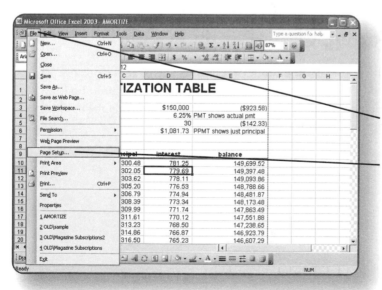

1. Click on **File**. The File menu will appear.

2. Click on **Page Setup**. The Page Setup dialog box will open.

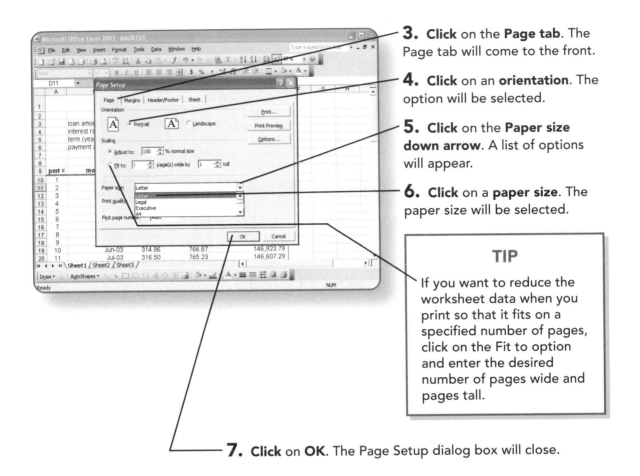

3. **Click** on the **Page tab**. The Page tab will come to the front.

4. **Click** on an **orientation**. The option will be selected.

5. **Click** on the **Paper size down arrow**. A list of options will appear.

6. **Click** on a **paper size**. The paper size will be selected.

TIP

If you want to reduce the worksheet data when you print so that it fits on a specified number of pages, click on the Fit to option and enter the desired number of pages wide and pages tall.

7. **Click** on **OK**. The Page Setup dialog box will close.

Setting Other Printing Options

Although you see them on your screen, Excel does not, by default, print the gridlines or the row and column headings. You can indicate you want Excel to print those items through the Page Setup dialog box.

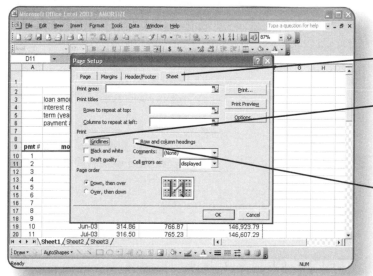

1. Open the **Page Setup** dialog box.

2. Click on the **Sheet tab**. The Sheet tab will come to the front.

3. Click on **Gridlines** if you want Excel to print the gridlines. A check mark will appear in the selection box.

4. Click on **Row and column headings** if you want Excel to include the headings when printing. A check mark will appear in the selection box.

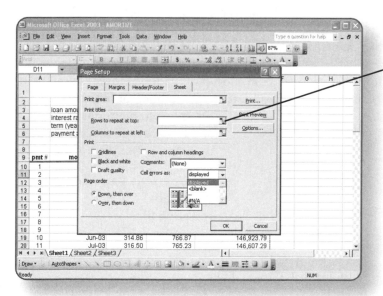

TIP

If your worksheet will be more than one printed page in height or width, you may want to print a particular column or row on each page, sort of as a title for each page. Click on the worksheet icon on the Rows or Columns to select which rows or columns to repeat.

In some worksheets, especially those that include formulas, you may see an error message. An example might be when a formula divides a cell by zero; the resulting answer displays as #DIV/0! in the worksheet cell. You can tell Excel to print the error messages as displayed, print N/A, print two dashes (--), or print nothing at all, leaving the cell blank when printing. (You will learn more about formulas in Chapter 6, "Working with Formulas.")

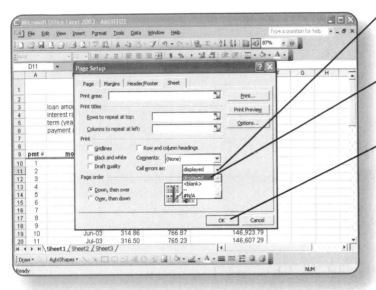

5. **Click** the **Cell errors as drop-down menu**. A list of options will appear.

6. **Click** an **option**. The selection will appear in the Cell errors as box.

7. **Click** on **OK**. The Page Setup dialog box will close.

Creating a Header or Footer

Headers and *footers* are simply text that appears either at the top (header) or bottom (footer) of every page. The types of information you might include in a header or footer might be a report title, the current date, page number, or file name. Like other printing options, headers and footers are created through the Page Setup dialog box.

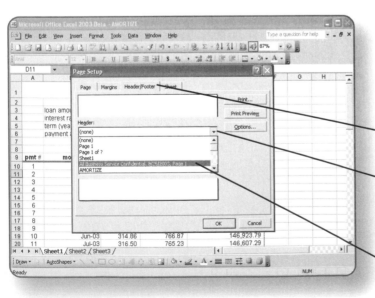

1. **Open** the **Page Setup** dialog box. The Page Setup box will appear.

2. **Click** on the **Header/Footer tab**. The tab will come to the front.

3. **Click** on the **Header** or **Footer drop-down menu**. A list of predefined headers or footers will appear.

4. **Click** a predefined **header or footer**. The header or footer will appear in the sample box.

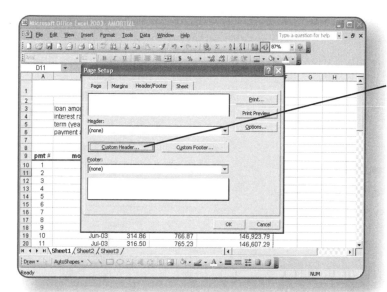

If none of the predefined headers or footers meets your needs, you can create your own.

5. Click on **Custom Header** or **Custom Footer**. The Header or Footer dialog box will open.

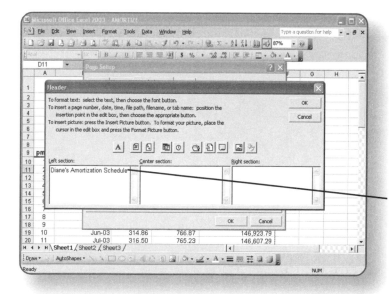

Headers and Footers are divided into three areas of the page: the left side, the center, or the right side.

6. Click in the Left, Center, or Right section **text box**. A blinking insertion point will appear in the section you selected.

7a. Type any **text** you want to appear in the header or footer. The text you type will appear in the section box.

AND/OR

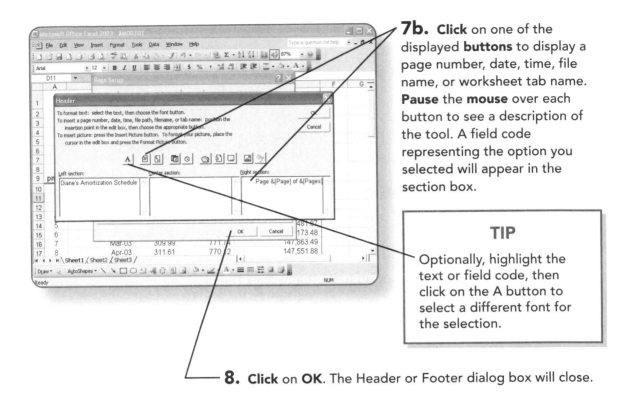

7b. Click on one of the displayed **buttons** to display a page number, date, time, file name, or worksheet tab name. **Pause** the **mouse** over each button to see a description of the tool. A field code representing the option you selected will appear in the section box.

TIP

Optionally, highlight the text or field code, then click on the A button to select a different font for the selection.

8. Click on **OK**. The Header or Footer dialog box will close.

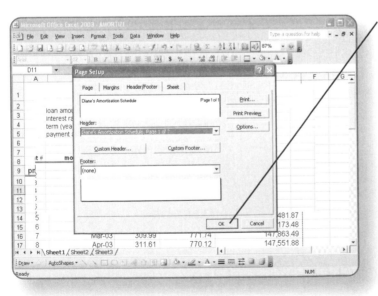

9. Click on **OK**. The Page Setup dialog box will close.

Selecting a Print Area

Excel assumes you want to print the entire worksheet, but you may only want to print a portion of the sheet. You can specify a specific print range for Excel to print.

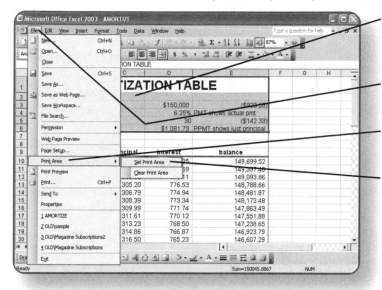

1. **Select** the **cells** you want to print. The cells will be highlighted.

2. **Click** on **File**. The File menu will appear.

3. **Click** on **Print Area**. The Print Area submenu will appear.

4. **Click** on **Set Print Area**. Excel will display a dotted line around the area you selected.

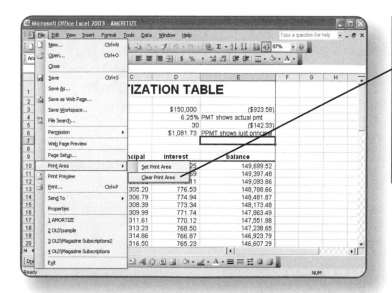

TIP

To clear the print area so Excel will print the entire worksheet or so you can define a different print area, select Clear Print Area from the File, Print Area menu.

Printing a Worksheet

Once you have specified any print specifications and options, you can print the worksheet. You may want to preview the worksheet on the screen before you print, just to make sure you have all the options set correctly.

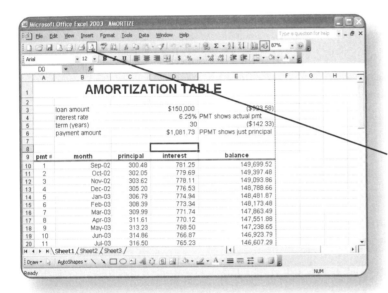

Using Print Preview

Using the Print Preview feature can save lots of paper by allowing you to see the worksheet on your screen before actually printing it to paper.

1a. **Click** on the **Print Preview button**. The Print Preview window will open.

OR

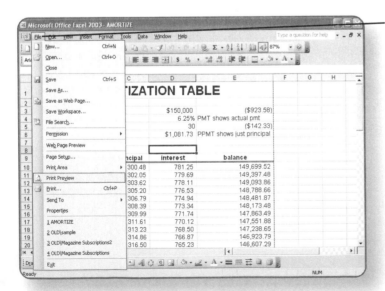

1b. **Click** on **File**. The File menu will appear. Then **click** on **Print Preview**. The Print Preview window will open.

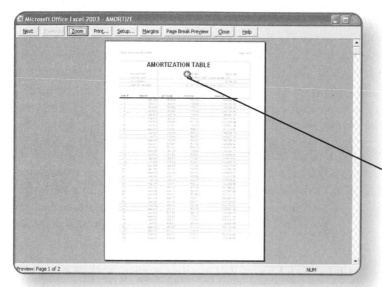

Don't strain your eyes trying to read the text in the Preview window. You are looking at the overall perspective here, not necessarily the individual cell contents. You cannot edit the worksheet cell contents while in Preview mode.

Your mouse pointer is a magnifying glass while in Print Preview.

2. Click on the **worksheet** to zoom in on a specific area. The worksheet will be magnified.

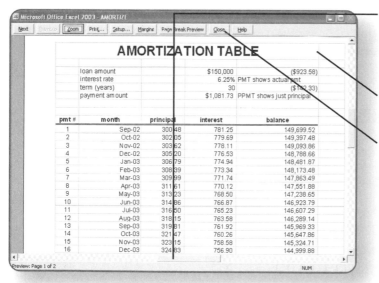

While zoomed in on the worksheet, you can use the scroll bars to view different areas of the worksheet.

3. Click on the **worksheet** again. The worksheet will shrink.

4. Click on the **Close button**. The view will return to the actual worksheet.

Printing the Worksheet

Typically, the end result of creating a worksheet is to get the information onto paper. Now that you've checked all your printing options, you are ready to print. You can print from the toolbar, or specify additional printing options through the Print dialog box.

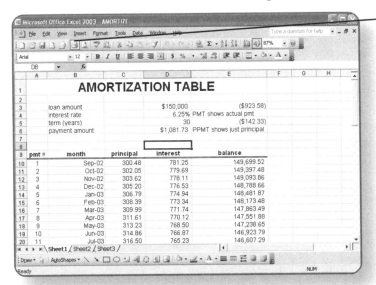

1a. **Click** on the **Print button**. The worksheet will print to your default printer with the options you specified in the Page Setup box. No dialog box will appear.

OR

1b. **Click** on **File**. The File menu will appear. Then **Click** on **Print**. The Print dialog box will open.

2. Click on any desired **options** from the Print dialog box, including:

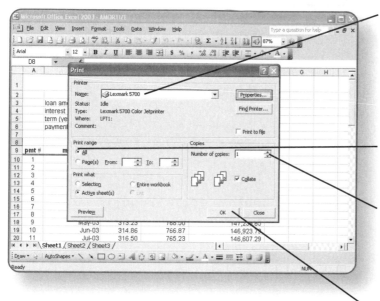

- **Printer name.** If you have access to more than one printer, you can choose which printer to use for this print job. Click on the Name drop-down menu and select the printer you want to use.

- **Print range.** Choose which pages of your document you want to print.

- **Number of copies.** Select the number of copies you want to print by clicking on the up/down arrows in the Number of copies list box.

3. Click on **OK**. The document will print.

Part I Review Questions

1. When you first open Excel, which task pane does it display?
   See 'Changing Task Panes' in Chapter 1

2. Which two keys do you press to quickly move to Cell A1?
   See 'Using the Keyboard' in Chapter 1

3. What three components make up spreadsheet data? *See 'Entering Data' in Chapter 2*

4. Where do you click to select (highlight) an entire column?
   See 'Learning Selection Techniques' in Chapter 3

5. What do you click to reverse your previous action? *See 'Undoing the Previous Step' in Chapter 3*

6. If you type the name of a month in a cell, then use the fill handle to drag down 4 cells, what will Excel do when you release the mouse? *See 'Using the Fill Feature' in Chapter 3*

7. What does AutoFormat do? *See 'Using AutoFormat' in Chapter 4*

8. What is the difference in the dollar sign placement between the currency and accounting styles? *See 'Formatting for Currency' in Chapter 4*

9. What are the default margins in an Excel worksheet? *See 'Setting Up Margins' in Chapter 5*

10. What option can you select to tell Excel to print the page on a specified number of pages wide or tall? *See 'Setting Page Orientation and Size' in Chapter 5*

P A R T I I

Working with Formulas and Larger Worksheets

6

Working with Formulas

Many people use a worksheet to perform mathematical calculations. By using formulas, if a value in a referenced cell changes, any formula based on the cell automatically adjusts to accommodate the new value. Excel can accommodate both simple formulas, such as adding two values together, and complex formulas, such as adding two values together and multiplying the result by another number. In addition, Excel can include the values from many different worksheet cells.

In this chapter, you'll learn how to:

- Create simple and compound formulas
- Edit formulas
- Copy formulas
- Create an absolute reference in a formula
- View formulas in the worksheet
- Understand common formula error messages

Creating Formulas

All formulas must begin with the equal (=) sign, regardless of whether the formula consists of adding, subtracting, multiplying, or dividing. Formulas can reference either a static value or the value in a referenced cell.

Creating a Simple Formula

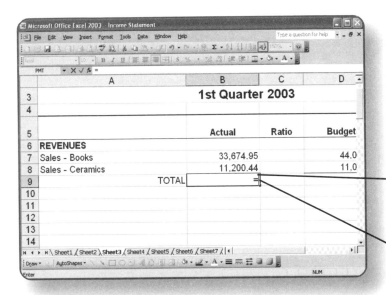

An example of a simple formula is to add two cell values together. For example, you could elect to add the values of B7 and B8.

1. Click on the **cell** in which you want to place the result. The cell will be selected.

2. Type an **equal (=) sign** to begin the formula. The symbol will display in the cell.

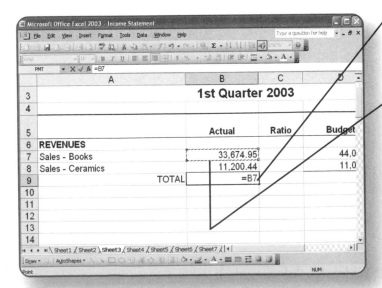

3. Type the **cell address** of the first cell to be included in the formula. This is called the cell reference.

Excel references the cell address in color and places a matching color box around the referenced address.

NOTE

Worksheet formulas are not case sensitive. For example, B7 is the same as b7.

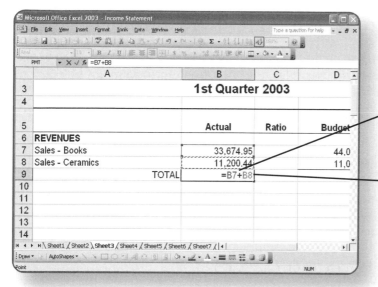

A formula needs an operator to suggest the next action to be performed. Operators are plus (+), minus (-), multiply (*), or divide (/) symbols.

4. **Type** the **operator**. The operator will display in the formula.

5. **Type** the **reference** to the second cell of the formula. The reference will display in the cell.

Excel references the second cell address in a different color and places a matching color box around the referenced address.

6. **Press** the **Enter key**. The result of the calculation will appear in the cell.

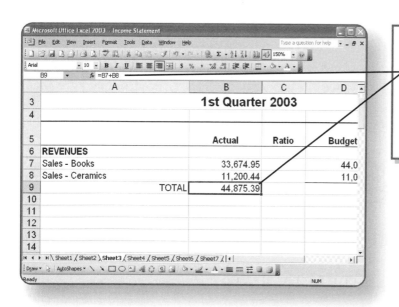

NOTE

Notice how the result appears in the cell, but the actual formula, =B7+B8, appears in the Contents box of the Edit line.

Creating a Compound Formula

You use compound formulas when you need more than one operator. Examples of a compound formula might be =B7+B8+B9+B10 or =B11-B19*A23.

> ## NOTE
>
> When you have a compound formula, Excel will do the multiplication and division first, then the addition and subtraction. If you want a certain portion of the formula to be calculated first, put it in parentheses. Excel will do whatever is in the parentheses before the rest of the formula. For example, the formula =B11-B19*A23 will give a totally different answer than =(B11-B19)*A23.

1. Click on the **cell** in which you want to place the formula answer. The cell will be selected.

2. Type an **equal sign (=)** to begin the formula. The symbol will display in the cell.

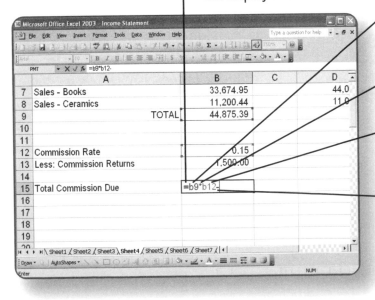

3. Type the **reference** to the first cell of the formula. The reference will display in the cell.

4. Type the **operator**. The operator will display in the cell.

5. Type the **reference** to the second cell of the formula. The reference will display in the cell.

6. Type the next **operator**. The operator will display in the cell.

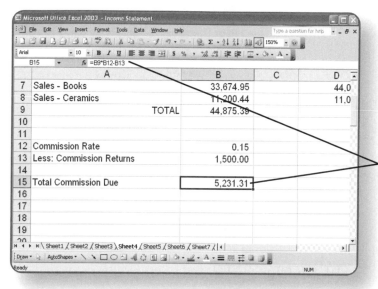

7. Type the **reference** to the third cell of the formula. The reference will display in the cell.

8. Repeat steps 6 and 7 until the formula is complete, adding the parentheses wherever necessary.

9. Press the **Enter key** to accept the formula. The calculation answer will be displayed in the cell and the formula will be displayed in the content bar.

Try changing one of the values you originally typed in the worksheet and watch the answer to the formula change.

NOTE

Excel also provides more complex formulas, called Functions, that can perform statistical, financial, mathematical, and many other types of calculations. You'll learn about Functions in Chapter 7, "Using Excel Functions."

Editing Formulas

Excel provides several methods for editing an incorrect cell, whether it's a label, a value, or a formula. One method involves simply retyping the desired data in the correct cell. When you press Enter, the new data replaces the old data. If, however, the data is complex or lengthy, you might want to edit only a portion of the existing information. You can make changes to a cell entry directly in the cell.

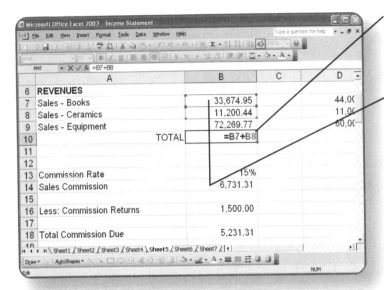

1. Double-click on the **cell** you want to modify. The blinking insertion point will appear in the cell.

When editing formulas, Excel color codes each cell address to its corresponding cell.

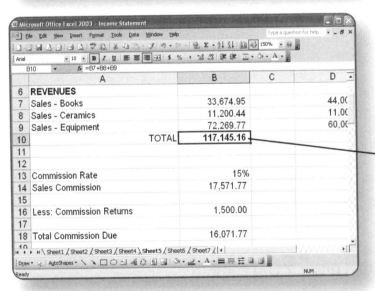

2. Type any **corrections**. You may need to use the keyboard arrow keys to move the insertion point to the position of the incorrect data. The changes will appear in the cell and on the Formula line.

3. Press the **Enter key**. The change will be accepted and if the data was a formula, the answer will be recalculated.

Copying Formulas

Now that you've created a formula, there's no reason to type it repeatedly for subsequent cells. Let Excel copy the formula for you! When you copy a formula, the formula changes depending on where you put it. It is said, therefore, to be *relative*—relative to the position of the original formula.

Copying Using the Fill Feature

If you're going to copy a formula to a surrounding cell, you can use the Fill method. You first learned about the Fill command in Chapter 3, "Editing a Worksheet."

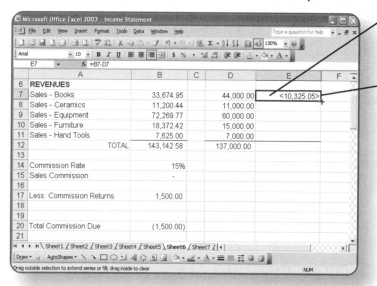

1. **Click** on the **cell** that has the formula. The cell will be selected.

2. **Position** the **mouse pointer** on the lower-right corner of the beginning cell. The mouse pointer will become a black cross.

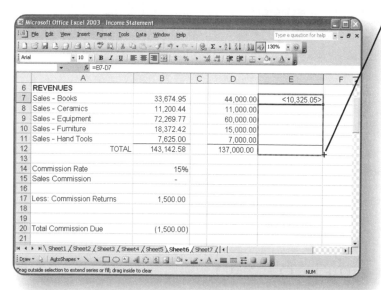

3. **Press and hold** the **mouse button and drag** to select the next cells to be filled in. The cells will be selected.

4. **Release** the **mouse button**. The formula will be copied.

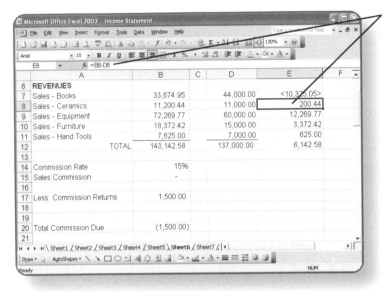

When Excel copies a formula, the references change as the formula is copied. If the original formula was =B7-D7 and you copied it to the next cell down, the formula would read =B8-D8. Then, if you copied it down again it would be =B9-D9, and so on.

Copying with Copy and Paste

If the originating cells and the recipient cells are not sequential, you can use copy and paste. You first learned about copy and paste in Chapter 3, "Editing a Worksheet."

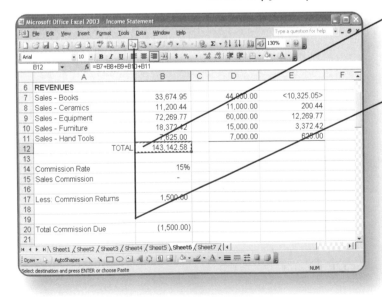

1. **Select** the **cell** with the formula that you want to duplicate. The cell will be selected.

2. **Click** on the **Copy button**. Marching ants will appear around the copied cells.

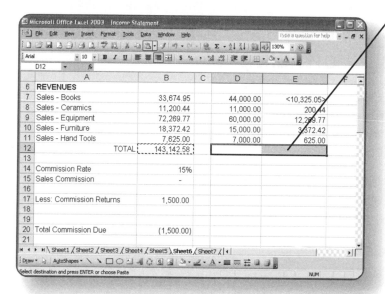

3. Highlight the **cells** in which you want to place the duplicated formula. The cells will be selected.

4. Press the **Enter key**. The formula will be copied to the new location.

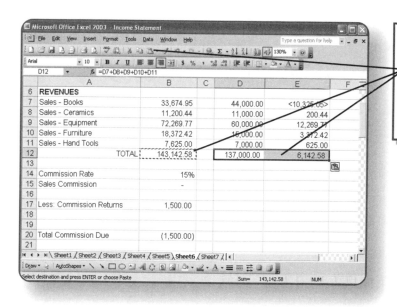

TIP

Optionally, click on the Paste button and then press Esc to cancel the marching ants.

Creating an Absolute Reference in a Formula

Occasionally when you copy a formula, you do not want one of the cell references to change. That's when you need to create an *absolute reference*. To indicate an absolute reference, use the dollar sign ($).

It's called an absolute reference because when you copy it, it absolutely and positively stays that cell reference and never changes. An example of a formula with an absolute reference might be =B22*B24. The reference to cell B24 will not change when copied.

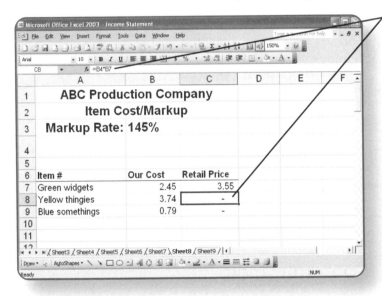

This figure shows a formula that is supposed to take the cost of an item and multiply it to the mark up rate. The result is the retail cost of the item. The first formula is fine, but as you can see, when the formula is copied or filled down, the other products display an erroneous cost. The original formula was B3*B6, where B3 is the mark up percentage rate. When the formula is copied down to the next cell, it becomes B4*B7, and the cell in B4 is not the mark up percentage rate cell.

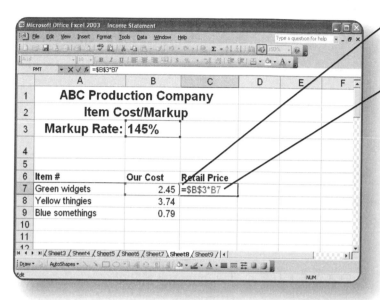

1. **Click** on the **cell** in which you want to place the formula answer. The cell will be selected.

2. **Type** the **formula.** If any references are to be an absolute reference, add dollar signs ($) in front of both the column reference and the row reference.

3. **Press** the **Enter key.** The answer will display in the cell.

NOTE

Compound formulas can also have absolute references.

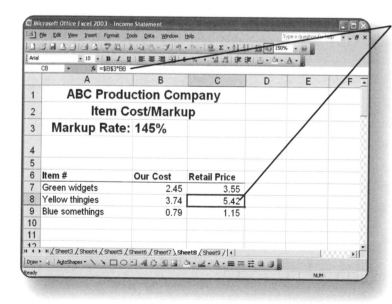

4. **Copy** the **formula** to the adjacent cells using one of the methods in the preceding section.

Viewing Formulas

As you've already seen, when you create formulas, the result of the formulas is what Excel displays in the worksheet. Although the Edit bar displays the actual formula, you can only view one formula at a time. Excel provides a method to view the formulas in the cells. Having the formulas display is a wonderful tool for proofing and troubleshooting formula errors in your worksheet.

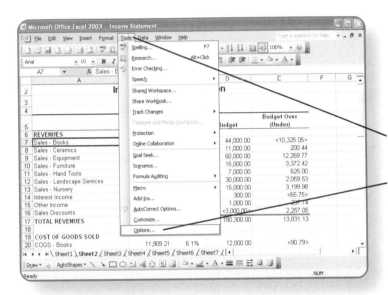

1. **Click** on **Tools**. The Tools menu will appear.

2. **Click** on **Options**. The Options dialog box will open.

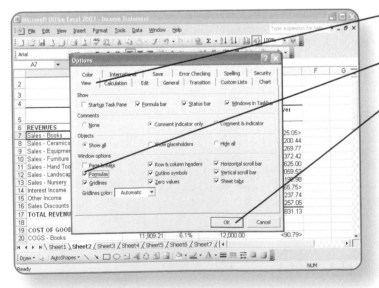

3. **Click** on the **View tab**. The View tab will come to the front.

4. **Click** on **Formulas**. A check mark will display in the option.

5. **Click** on **OK**. The dialog box will close.

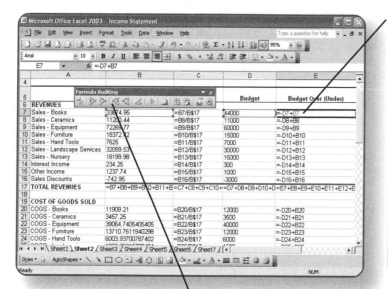

The formulas will be displayed in each cell instead of the formula result. Each cell reference in a formula is assigned a color and a corresponding colored box surrounds the referenced cell.

NOTE

If you print the worksheet while the formulas are displayed, the formulas will print, not the formula results.

The Formula Auditing toolbar may appear to assist you in tracing through formulas. You may find the Auditing toolbar handy when resolving worksheet errors. The Formula Auditing toolbar can display tracer arrows, which are arrows that show the relationship between the active cell and its related cells. It traces Dependents, which are cells that contain formulas that refer to other cells, and Precedents, which are cells that are referred to by a formula in another cell.

6. Repeat steps 1-5 to turn off the formula display.

Understanding Common Formula Error Messages

There are a number of error messages that may appear when you type a formula. Some are typing mistakes and some may be a result of a cell value.

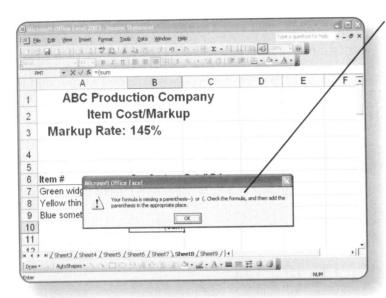

Often when you enter a formula with an error, Excel notifies you of the error and attempts to correct the error for you or offers suggestions on correcting the error.

Other errors may appear in the formula result cell. Following are a few of the more common error messages:

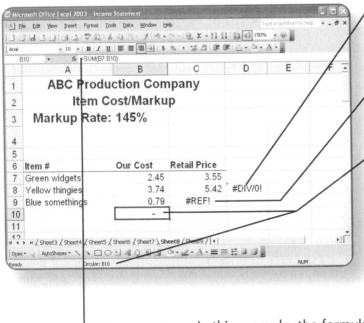

#DIV/0!. This means that the formula is trying to divide by either an empty cell or one with a value of zero.

#REF!. This may mean that the formula includes an invalid cell reference.

Circular. This means that a formula in a cell refers to the same cell. Excel displays a circular reference notation in the status bar. Excel may also display an error box and display a Circular Reference toolbar to assist you in locating the erroneous formula.

In this example, the formula in B10 is trying to add itself to the total, thereby creating the circular reference.

7

Using Excel Functions

While creating a formula provides mathematical calculations, Excel includes a much more powerful feature called functions. Functions are basically a fast way to enter a complex formula. Excel has over 230 different functions you can use, and it groups them together by categories such as mathematical, statistical, logical, or date and time. Using functions can save considerable room in the Formula bar and cuts down on typographical errors that are so easy to make when typing formulas.

In this chapter, you'll learn how to:

- Understand function requirements
- Use the SUM function and AutoSum button
- Work with numerical functions
- Create statistical, date, and logical functions

Understanding Function Syntax

Functions consist of several different parts. Like a formula, a function begins with an equal (=) sign. The next part is the function name, which might be abbreviated to indicate what the function does. Examples of a function name might be SUM, AVERAGE, or COUNT. After the name, you enter a set of parentheses and enter *arguments* within those parentheses. Arguments are additional pieces of information that clarify how you want the function to behave. Arguments can consist of one or more components, ranging from cell addresses such as D13 or a range of cell addresses like D13:D25, to other variables such as a number of digits you want Excel to do something to. With only a few exceptions, all functions in Excel must follow that pattern. This function structure is called the *syntax*. Here are a few examples of function syntax. You'll learn throughout this chapter what these functions do.

> **NOTE**
>
> Function names are not case sensitive.

- =SUM(B3:B21)

- =AVERAGE(F1:G6)

- =IF(B3>B4,"yes", "no")

Creating a Total with the SUM Function

The most commonly used function in Excel is the SUM function, which adds two or more values together and displays the total in the current cell. If any of the values change, the SUM total will automatically update. There are a number of different methods to enter the SUM function, but the following section describes two of the most common ways. The syntax for the SUM function is =SUM(*range of values to total*).

Entering a SUM Function

One way to enter a SUM function is to type the function in its syntax directly into a cell where you want the answer. Like other formulas, Excel will display the answer in the current cell, but display the actual function in the Formula bar.

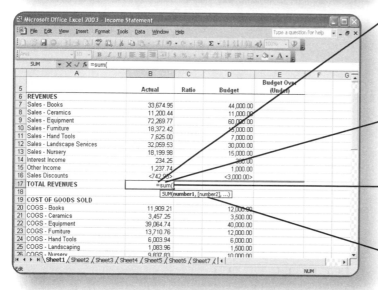

1. Enter some **values** in two or more cells. The values display in the cells.

2. Click in the **cell** where you want the total of the values to display. The cell will be selected.

3. Type an **equal sign (=)**. The blinking insertion point will appear after the equal sign. (Do not press the Enter key until the function is complete.)

4. Type the word **SUM**. The word SUM will appear after the equal sign.

5. Type an **opening parenthesis**. The (character will appear after the function name.

The arguments for a SUM function require that you enter the cell addresses you want to add. You can enter the cell addresses using the keyboard or the mouse. The next two sections will show you both methods.

Entering an Argument with the Keyboard

When you enter function arguments with the keyboard, you type the cell addresses you want to add. If the cell addresses are adjacent to each other, you separate them with a colon (:). For example, typing B2:B5 will add the values in B2 plus B3 plus B4 plus B5. If the cell addresses you want to add are not adjacent, you separate them with a comma. For example, B2, B5, B13 will add the values in cells B2 and B5 and B13 but not the value of any cells in between. You can also combine adjacent and non-adjacent cells, such as B2, B5, B13:B15 which would add the values in the cells B2 and B5 and B13, B14, and B15.

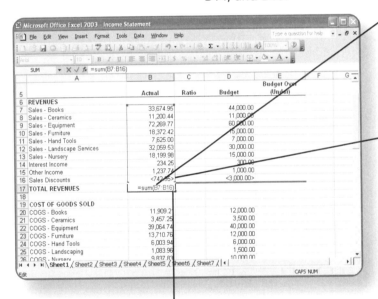

1. After you type the opening parenthesis, **type** the **cell addresses** you want to add together, using the colon or comma to separate the addresses.

As you type the cell addresses, Excel puts a border around the cells so you can quickly see if you typed the correct cell address.

NOTE

When typing a cell address, the address is not case-sensitive, but you must remember to type the column letter first, followed by the row number.

2. **Type** a **closing parenthesis**. A) character will appear after the cell addresses.

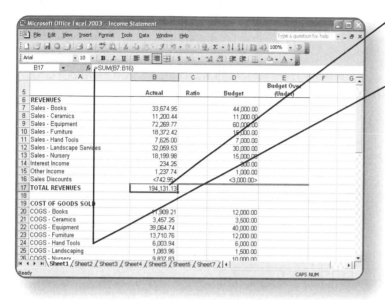

3. **Press** the **Enter key**. The resulting value will appear in the cell.

The Formula bar still reflects the function and its options.

Entering an Argument with the Mouse

Instead of typing cell addresses, you can use your mouse to highlight the desired cells. Highlighting the cells instead of typing them makes it easier to see that you have selected the correct cells.

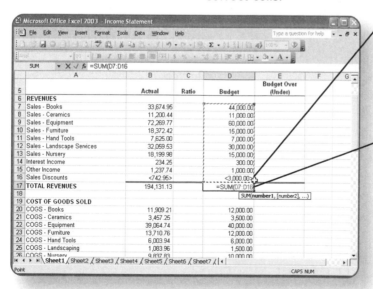

1. After you type the opening parenthesis, **click and drag** the **mouse** around the cells you want to add. A marquee of marching ants will appear around the selected cells.

The cell addresses appear in the function cell.

TIP

If you have a non-adjacent range to select, separate them with a comma so Excel will let you continue to the next selection.

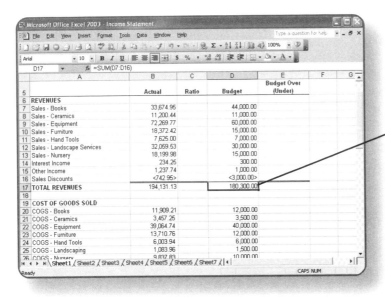

2. Type a **closing parenthesis**. A) character will appear after the cell addresses, and the selected cells will have a temporary border surrounding them.

3. Press the **Enter key**. The resulting value will appear in the cell.

Using the AutoSum Button

Since the SUM function is the function used most, Microsoft includes a button for it on the standard Excel toolbar. This makes creating a simple addition formula a mouse click away!

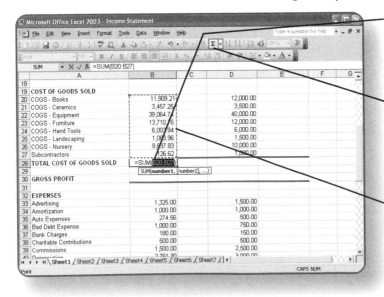

1. Click on the **cell** below or to the right of the values you want to total. The cell will be selected.

2. Click on the **AutoSum button**. The cells to be totaled are highlighted.

NOTE

Excel will suggest the values above it first. If no values are directly above the current cell, Excel will look for values in the cells to the left.

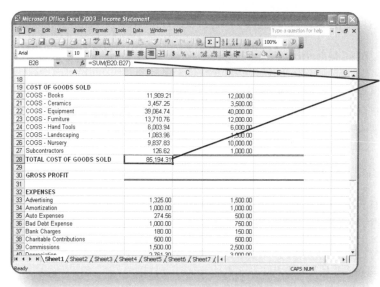

If you want to total different cells than Excel has highlighted, select them with your mouse.

3. Click the **AutoSum button** again **or press** the **Enter key**. Excel will enter the total value of the selected cells.

Using Other Functions

As mentioned at the beginning of this chapter, Excel includes over 230 different built-in functions that are divided into categories according to the function's purpose. The SUM function, for example, is considered a mathematical function.

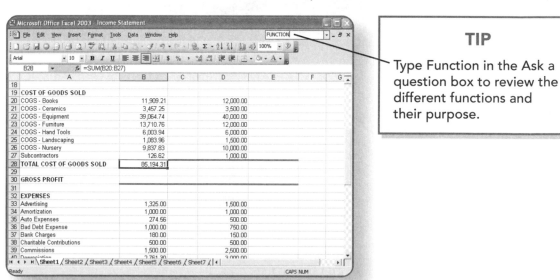

TIP

Type Function in the Ask a question box to review the different functions and their purpose.

Calculating with Mathematical Functions

You have learned how to create a mathematical function to add a series of numbers together by using the SUM function. Excel includes many other mathematical functions, including some for complex trigonometry calculations. The next section illustrates a couple of other commonly used mathematical functions.

Using the INT Function

The INT function rounds a number down to the nearest integer. The number can be a specific number you type or, more commonly, the reference to a specific cell. The syntax is =INT(*cell address or number*). For example, to find the integer of cell B3, you would enter =INT(B3).

TIP

Functions can be nested. For example, to find the integer of the SUM of a range of cells, you might type =INT(=SUM(B3:B10)). Excel will add each cell and round down the total.

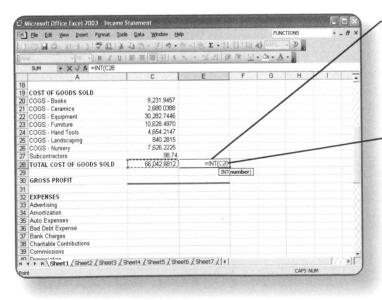

1. Type =INT(in the cell you want to place the integer. Excel will immediately identify the entry as a function and will display a tip box with the function syntax.

2. Type or click on the **cell** you want to reference. The referenced cell will have a border surrounding it.

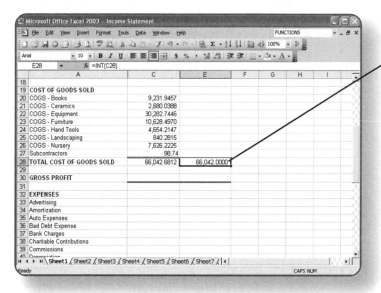

3. **Type** a **closing parenthesis**. The symbol will display in the cell.

4. **Press** the **Enter key**. The integer value of the referenced cell will display. The result will contain the same number of decimal points as the referenced cell.

Using the ROUND Function

Whereas the INT function displays whole numbers for you, the ROUND function takes a value and rounds it to a specified number of digits. The ROUND function contains two different arguments; one to specify which cell you want to round and the second to tell Excel how many decimal places you want to display. The syntax is =ROUND(*number,num of digits*). For example, if cell B10 has a value of 79.3264 and you want it rounded to two decimal places, you would enter =ROUND(B10,2); then Excel would display the answer of 79.3300.

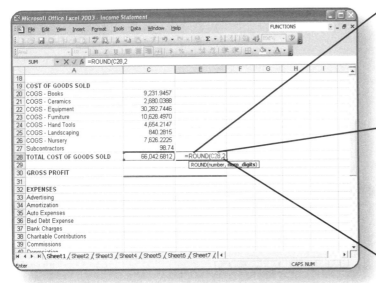

1. **Type =ROUND(** in the cell you want to place the integer. Excel will immediately identify the entry as a function and display a tip box with the function syntax.

2. **Type or click** on the **cell** you want to reference. The referenced cell will have a border surrounding it.

3. **Type** a **comma**. The comma divides the arguments.

4. **Type** the number of **decimal places** you want in the result. You can enter from 0 to 15 as the number of decimal places.

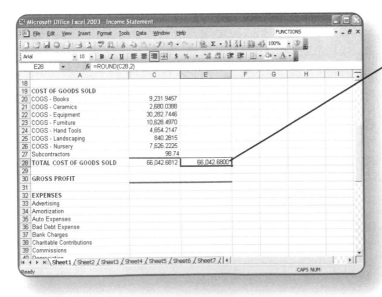

5. **Type** a **closing parenthesis**. The symbol will display in the cell.

6. **Press** the **Enter key**. The rounded value of the referenced cell will display.

Analyzing with Statistical Functions

Statistical-based functions provide a means for analysis of data. Statistical analysis helps you explore, understand and visualize your data.

Using the AVERAGE Function

The AVERAGE function finds an average of a range of values. The syntax for this function is =AVERAGE(*range of values to average).* An example might be =AVERAGE(B7:D7), which would add the values in the three cells B7, C7, and D7, then divide that total by three to get the average value.

1. Type =AVERAGE(in the cell you want to place the averaged result. Excel will immediately identify the entry as a function and display a tip box with the function syntax.

2. Type or highlight the **cells** you want to add together and average. A colored border will appear around the selected cells.

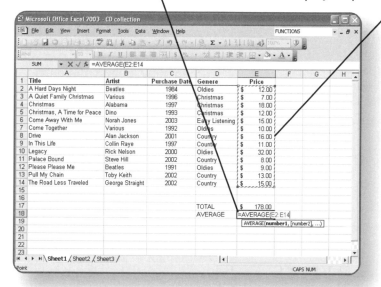

3. Type a **closing parenthesis**. The symbol will display in the cell.

4. Press the **Enter key**. Excel will add the referenced cells and display an average of those numbers.

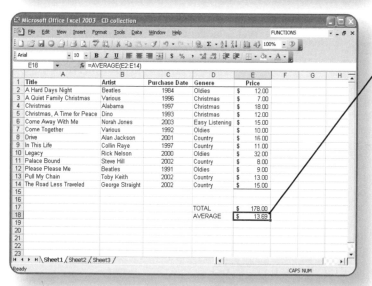

Using the MAX and MIN Functions

Two other common statistical functions are the MAX and MIN functions. The MAX function will display the largest value in a range of cells, whereas the MIN function will display the smallest value in a range of cells. The syntax is =MAX(*range of values*) or =MIN(*range of values*).

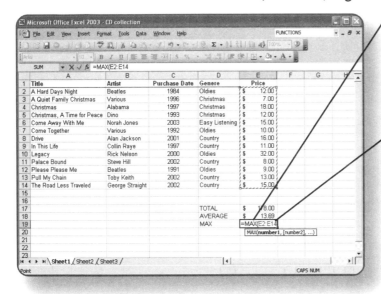

1. **Type =MAX(** or **=MIN(** in the cell where you want the result to be displayed. Excel will immediately identify the entry as a function and display a tip box with the function syntax.

2. **Type or highlight** the **cells** you want to analyze. A colored border will appear around the selected cells.

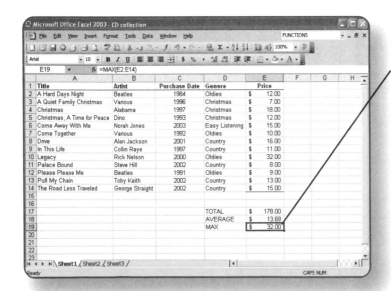

3. **Type** a **closing parenthesis**. The symbol will display in the cell.

4. **Press** the **Enter key**. If you typed =MAX in step 1, the largest number in the referenced area will display.

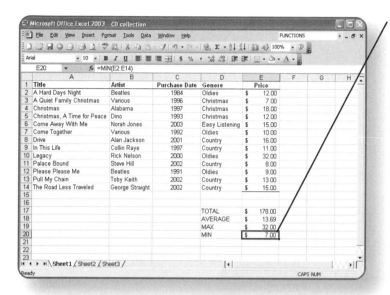

If you typed =MIN in step 1, the smallest number in the referenced area will display.

Using the COUNT and COUNTA Functions

The COUNT function is handy to find out how many numerical entries are in a specified area. The COUNTA function is similar except it is not limited to numerical entries; it will count any non-blank cell, no matter what type of information the cell contains. The syntax of these functions is very similar: =COUNT(*range of cells to count*) and =COUNTA(*range of cells to count*).

1. **Type =COUNT(** or **=COUNTA(** in the cell where you want the result to be displayed. Excel will immediately identify the entry as a function and display a tip box with the function syntax.

2. **Type or highlight** the **cells** you want to count. A colored border will appear around the selected cells.

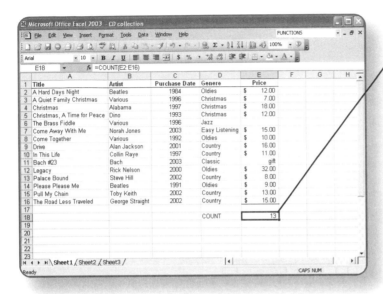

3. **Type** a **closing parenthesis**. The symbol will display in the cell.

4. **Press** the **Enter key**. If you typed =COUNT in step 1, the number of cells containing numerical entries in the referenced area will display.

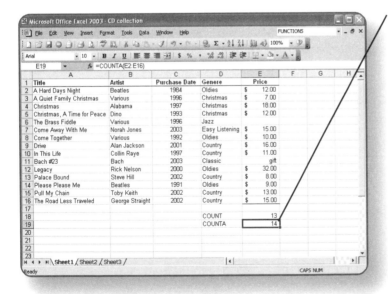

If you typed =COUNTA in step 1, Excel will count all the non-blank entries in the referenced area.

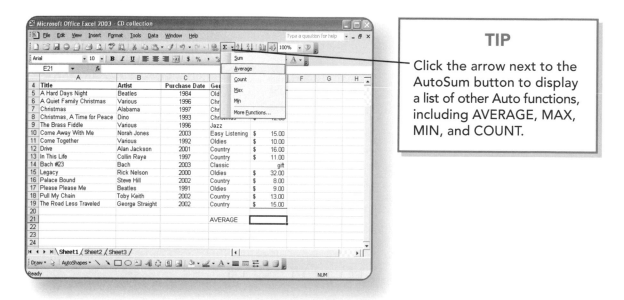

TIP

Click the arrow next to the AutoSum button to display a list of other Auto functions, including AVERAGE, MAX, MIN, and COUNT.

Using Date Functions

Date functions are commonly used to enter the current date into a worksheet, or to calculate the difference between two or more dates. Excel stores dates as sequential serial numbers so they can be used in calculations. By default, January 1, 1900 is serial number 1, and September 16, 2003 is serial number 37880, because it is 37,880 days after January 1, 1900. When you type a date in Excel, it will display the date in a regular date format, such as 9/16/2003, but behind the scenes Excel still considers that date a serial number.

Because dates and times are values, they can be added, subtracted, and included in other calculations.

Using the NOW Function

If you enter the NOW function in a cell, Excel will display the current date and time. The date and time are dynamic in that the current date and time will change whenever you recalculate anything in the worksheet. By default, Excel recalculates the worksheet whenever any changes, additions, or deletions are made. The NOW function does not contain any arguments, so the syntax is =NOW().

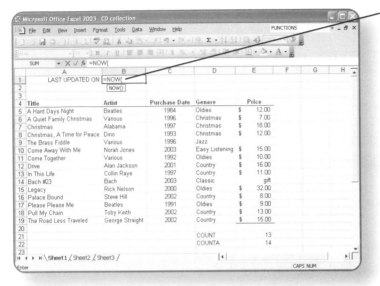

1. Type =NOW(in the cell where you want the current date and time to display. Excel will immediately identify the entry as a function and display a tip box with the function syntax.

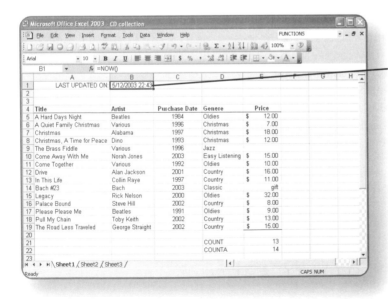

2. Type a **closing parenthesis**. The symbol will display in the cell.

3. Press the **Enter key**. The cell will display the current date and time.

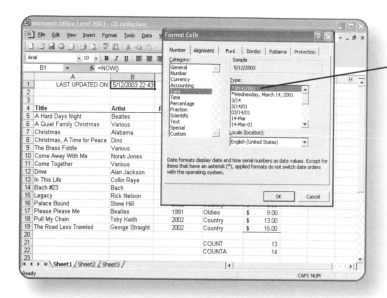

TIP

You can change the date and time display through the Format Cells dialog box.

Finding the Difference between Two Dates

A very popular use for entering dates in an Excel worksheet is to find the number of days between two dates. Since Excel stores dates as serial numbers, you can create a simple mathematical function to figure the number of days between two dates. While this is more of a formula instead of an Excel function, the mathematical calculation can include a cell with a date function, such as =NOW.

1. Enter a **date** in a cell. Excel will display the date you entered. In the example you see here, the current date was entered in cell A1 with the =NOW function.

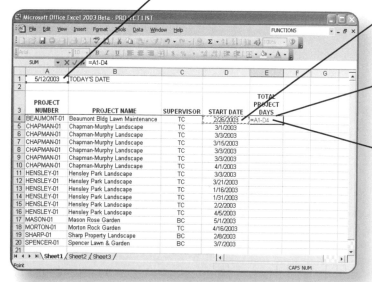

2. Enter another **date** in a different cell. Excel will display the date you entered.

3. Click in the **cell** where you want the difference stored. The cell will be selected.

4. Enter a **formula** to subtract the older date from the newer date.

The example you see here is a formula to subtract the project start date from today's date, so the formula is A1-D4.

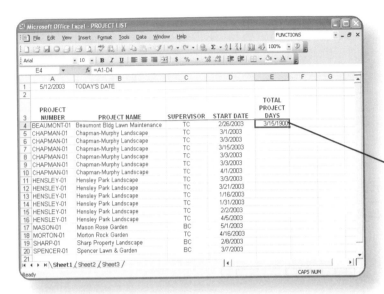

NOTE

You cannot subtract a date that is later than another date, or the error #### appears in the cell.

5. Press the **Enter key**. Excel will calculate the difference.

Since both of the original dates are in a date format, Excel will display the difference in a date format. You will need to tell Excel to display that value as a number.

6. Click on the **Comma style button**. The value is displayed in numeric format with two decimal points. The decimal points represent the portion of the day.

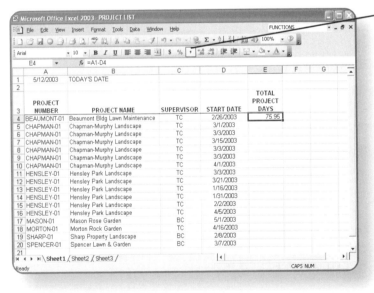

TIP

Unfortunately, there is no *easy* method to calculate the exact difference in years. While you can change the mathematical formula to divide the total by 365, this calculation does not take into account leap years. It will, however, give a pretty close calculation of years.

Figuring with Financial Functions

Financial functions perform elaborate calculations such as returns on investments or cumulative principal or interest on loans. Functions exist to calculate future values or net present values on investments or to calculate amortization.

Using the PMT Function

The PMT function calculates the payment for a loan based on a constant interest rate. You will need to enter the interest rate, the number of payments, and the amount of the loan. The syntax is =PMT(*rate,nper,pv,fv,type*) where *rate* is the interest rate, *nper* is the number of payments and *pv* is the loan amount. There are two other optional arguments, including *fv*, (future value),which Excel assumes to be zero unless you enter an *fv*. The other optional argument is for *type*, which refers to when the payment is due.

TIP

Be uniform about the units you use for specifying *rate* and *nper*. If you make monthly payments on a six-year loan at an annual interest rate of 8 percent, use 8%/12 for *rate* and 6*12 for *nper*. If you make annual payments on the same loan, use 8 percent for *rate* and 6 for *nper*.

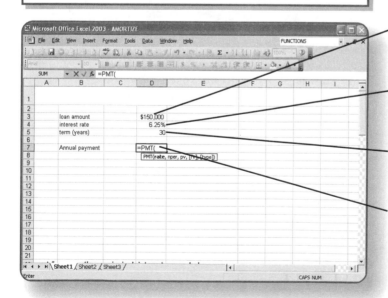

1. Enter a **loan amount** in a worksheet cell. The value will appear in the cell.

2. Enter an **interest rate** in a worksheet cell. The value will appear in the cell.

3. Enter the **number of payments** you intend to make. The value will appear in a cell.

4. Type =PMT(in the cell where you want to display the payment amount. Excel will immediately identify the entry as a function and display a tip box with the function syntax.

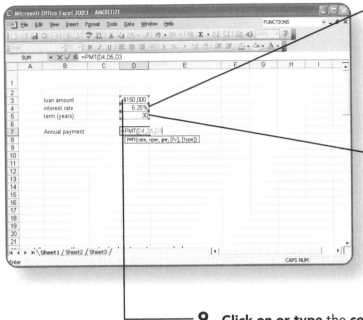

5. **Click on or type** the **cell address** you entered in step 2, which is the interest rate. The referenced cell will have a border around it.

6. **Type** a **comma**. Excel uses a comma to separate arguments

7. **Click on or type** the **cell address** you entered in step 3, which is the number of payments. The referenced cell will have a border around it.

8. **Type** another **comma**. The comma will precede the next argument.

9. **Click on or type** the **cell address** you entered in step 1, which is the value of the loan. The referenced cell will have a border around it.

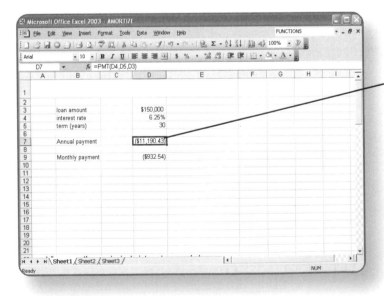

10. **Type** the **closing parenthesis**. The symbol will display in the cell.

11. **Press** the **Enter key**. Excel will calculate and display the payment amount.

NOTE

The payment amount returned by PMT includes principal and interest only

Understanding Logical Functions

You have seen that most functions work in basically the same way. You enter the equal sign, enter the function name, and then tell the function which data to use. Most functions involve some sort of mathematical calculation. Logical functions are different in that they use operators such as equal to (=), greater than (>), less than (<), greater than or equal to (>=), less than or equal to (<=), and not equal to (<>).

Using the IF Function

The IF function is a logical function that evaluates a condition and returns one of two answers, depending on the result of the evaluation. The IF function has three parts. The first part determines if a situation is true or false; the second part determines the result to display if the first part is true; and the third part determines the result to display if the first part is false. It's really not as confusing as it may sound. The syntax is =IF(*item to test, value if true, value if false*).

For example, in cell C1 you want to find out if the value in cell B5 is greater than the value in cell B6. If B5 *is* larger than B6 (true), you want to enter "Yes" in cell C1; if B5 is not larger than B6 (false), you want the answer "No" in cell C1. You would enter the function as =IF(B5>B6,"Yes","No").

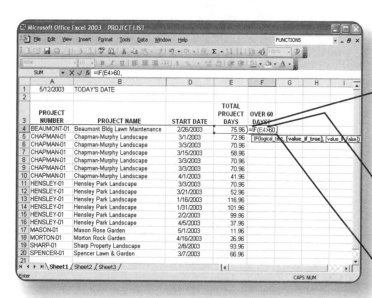

1. **Type =IF(** in the cell in which you want to display the answer. Excel will immediately identify the entry as a function and display a tip box with the function syntax.

2. **Type** the **first argument** including an operator. This is the condition you want Excel to evaluate.

3. **Type** a **comma**. This will begin the second argument.

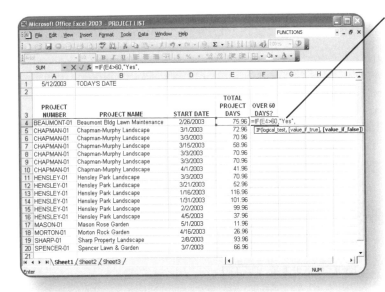

4. **Type** the **result** you want if the evaluation is true. The true result can be a value, a calculation, or text.

TIP

If you want the result to be text, the result must be enclosed in quotation. The quotation marks will not be displayed in the answer. No quotation marks are needed if the result is numeric.

---

5. **Type** a **comma**. This will begin the third argument.

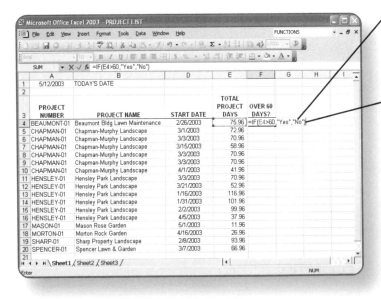

6. **Type** the **result** you want if the evaluation is false. The false result can also be a value, a calculation, or text.

7. **Type** the **closing parenthesis**. The symbol will display in the cell

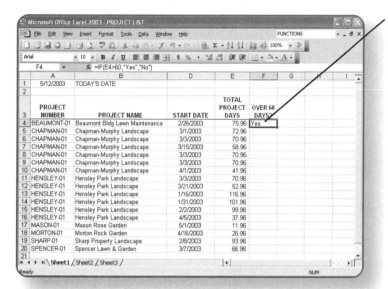

8. Press the **Enter key**. Excel will calculate and display the evaluation result.

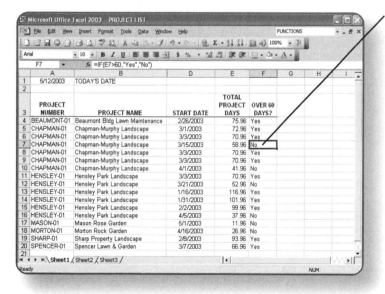

In this example, the IF function checks if the total job days is greater than 60 days. If it is, Yes is displayed; if not, No is displayed.

Getting Help with Excel Functions

With each Excel function having a different syntax, it becomes almost impossible to remember the syntax of each function. You've already seen that when you begin typing the function and the open parenthesis, Excel displays a tooltip to help you, but you can get even more help with functions by using the Insert Function dialog box.

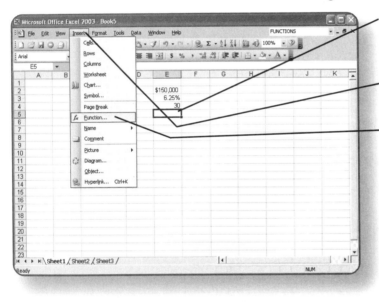

1. **Click** in the **cell** where you want to enter a function. The cell will be selected.

2. **Click** on **Insert**. The Insert menu will appear.

3. **Click** on **Function**. The Insert Function dialog box will open.

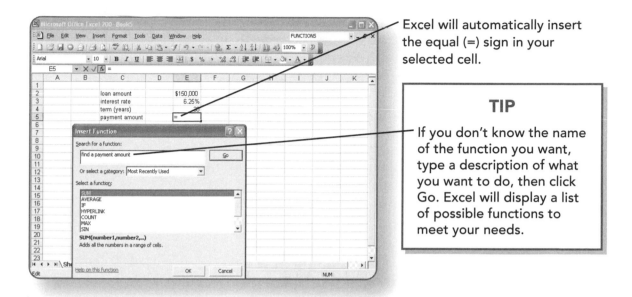

Excel will automatically insert the equal (=) sign in your selected cell.

TIP

If you don't know the name of the function you want, type a description of what you want to do, then click Go. Excel will display a list of possible functions to meet your needs.

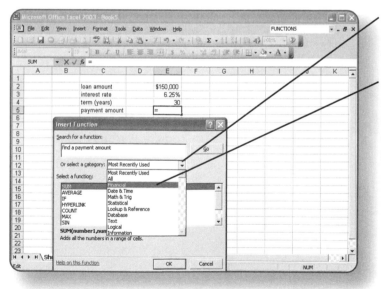

4. Click on the **Or select a category down arrow**. A list of function categories will appear.

5. Click on the **function category** you want to use. A list of available functions under that category will appear in the Select a function list.

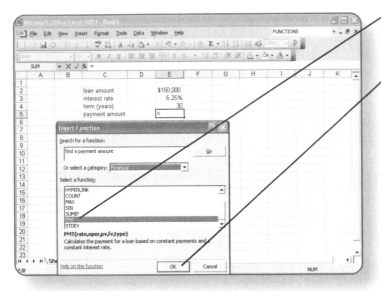

6. **Click** on a **function**. The function syntax and a description of the function will display.

7. **Click** on **OK**. The Function Arguments dialog box will open.

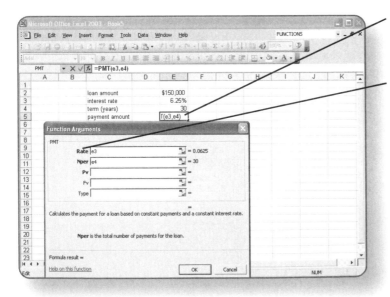

Excel will insert the Function name and the parentheses in the selected cell.

Some function arguments are optional. In the Function Arguments dialog box, Excel lists the required arguments in bold.

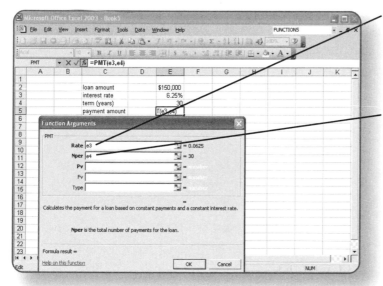

8. Type the **cell address, actual value, or click on the cell** that contains the argument. The argument box will contain the cell reference or value.

9. Click in the **next argument and repeat** step 8. The argument box will contain the cell reference or value.

As you click in each argument, a description will appear.

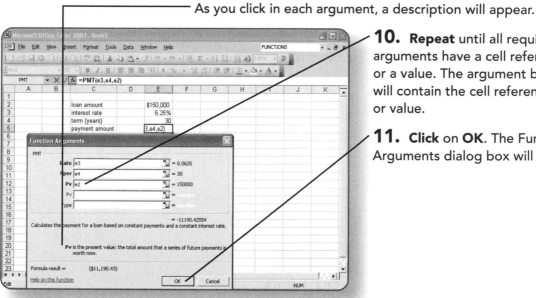

10. Repeat until all required arguments have a cell reference or a value. The argument box will contain the cell reference or value.

11. Click on **OK**. The Function Arguments dialog box will close.

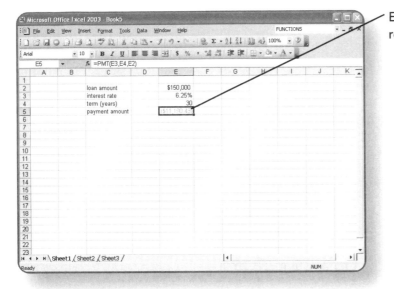

Excel will display the function result in the selected cell.

8

Working with Larger Workbooks

A single Excel file can have multiple worksheets—up to 256—in a single file. And since each worksheet has 256 columns and 65,536 rows, that's a potential for 4,294,967,296 cells of information in a single Excel file! Technically, Excel calls files with multiple sheets *workbooks*.

In this chapter, you'll learn how to:

- Move between worksheets
- Insert and name a worksheet
- Hide a worksheet
- Delete a worksheet
- Create a reference to another worksheet
- Link to other workbooks

Moving from Worksheet to Worksheet

By default, a new blank worksheet includes three worksheets named Sheet1, Sheet2, and Sheet3. You can move from worksheet to worksheet using the mouse or the keyboard.

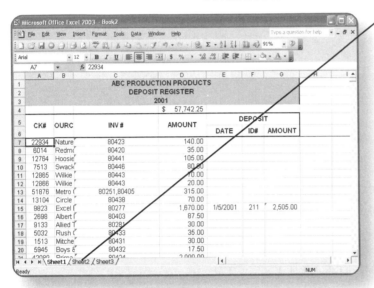

1. Click on the desired **worksheet tab**. That worksheet will come into view.

TIP

If you cannot see the tab for the desired worksheet, click on the sheet navigation arrows to move other sheets into view.

You also can use the keyboard to move from worksheet to worksheet.

2. Press either **Ctrl + Page Up** or **Ctrl + Page Down**. The cell pointer will move to the preceding or next sheet.

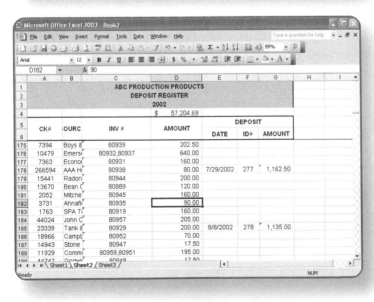

Inserting Worksheets

If you need extra worksheets in your workbook, you can easily add them through the Insert menu. Whenever you save your Excel file, all worksheets in the workbook are saved.

1. Click on **Insert**. The Insert menu will open.

2. Click on **Worksheet**. Excel will insert another worksheet.

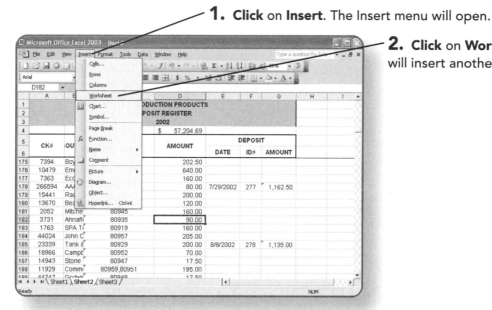

The new sheet is named with the next sequential number, such as Sheet4.

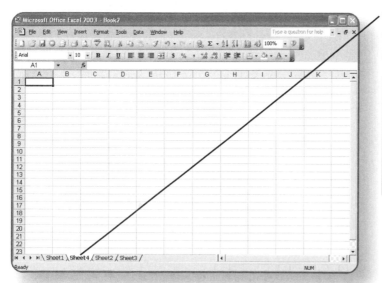

TIP

You can rearrange the order of the tabs on the screen by dragging the tab to the desired position.

Naming Worksheets

Since Excel uses the rather generic name scheme of Sheet1 or Sheet2, you can more easily identify the type of data each worksheet contains if you give the worksheets more descriptive names. Names for sheets can be up to 31 characters long and are not case sensitive; however, a worksheet name cannot be left blank and cannot include a few special characters—namely * / \ ? : [ ]

1. Double-click on the **tab** of the sheet you want to rename. The sheet name will become highlighted and a blinking insertion point will appear.

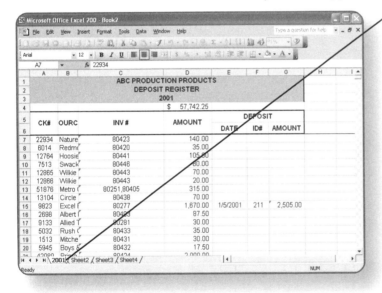

2. Type a new **name** for the sheet. The name you type will replace the default Excel name.

TIP

Optionally, right-click on a worksheet tab and select Rename.

---

3. Press the **Enter** key. The worksheet will be renamed.

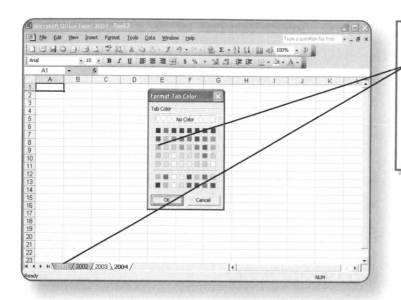

TIP

Color-code sheet tabs for easier identification by clicking on the sheet you want to color code and clicking Format, Sheet, then Tab Color.

Hiding a Worksheet

A worksheet can be hidden from view but still contain active working formulas and data.

1. Click anywhere on the **worksheet** you want to hide.

2. Click on **Format**. The Format menu will appear.

3. Click on **Sheet**. The Sheet menu will appear.

4. Click on **Hide**. The current worksheet will be hidden from view.

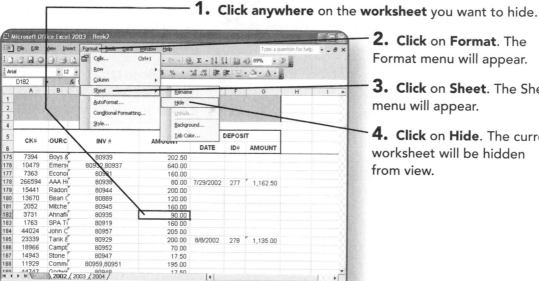

Notice in this example, the sheet named 2002 is not visible.

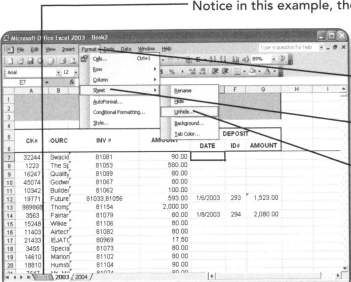

You can just as easily redisplay any hidden worksheets.

5. Click on **Format**. The Format menu will appear.

6. Click on **Sheet**. The Sheet menu will appear

7. Click on **Unhide**. The Unhide dialog box will appear showing a list of all hidden worksheets.

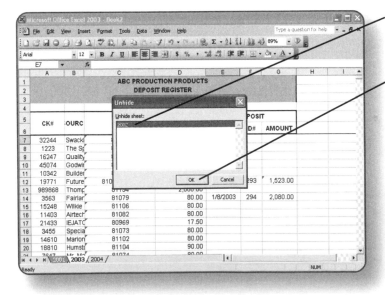

8. Click on the **sheet you want to unhide**. The worksheet name will be highlighted.

9. Click on **OK**. The Unhide dialog box will close and the worksheet will be redisplayed.

Deleting Worksheets

If you have created a worksheet in an Excel file that you no longer need, you can delete it. Deleting unnecessary worksheets can save on file size and make the file quicker to open and close.

1. **Click anywhere** on the **worksheet** you want to delete.

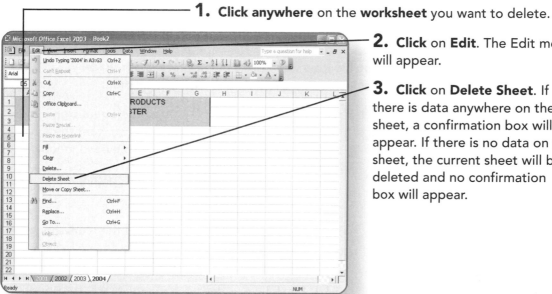

2. **Click** on **Edit**. The Edit menu will appear.

3. **Click** on **Delete Sheet**. If there is data anywhere on the sheet, a confirmation box will appear. If there is no data on the sheet, the current sheet will be deleted and no confirmation box will appear.

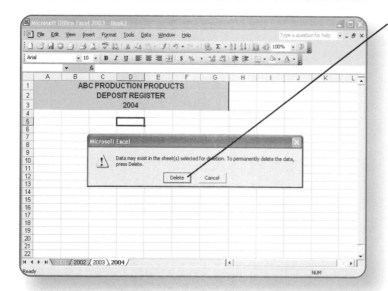

4. **Click** on **Delete**. The current worksheet will be deleted.

CAUTION

Use extreme caution here! When you choose to delete a sheet, the sheet is deleted permanently. You will not be able to undo the deletion.

Creating a Reference to Another Worksheet

Sometimes you need to refer to information stored in another worksheet. For example, if you have a workbook with sheets for each month's sales information, along with a worksheet that totals the monthly worksheets, you can create a reference in the Totals worksheet that instructs Excel to reference the data in the various monthly worksheets. When you create a reference to a different sheet, Excel will use the name of the sheet first, then the cell location.

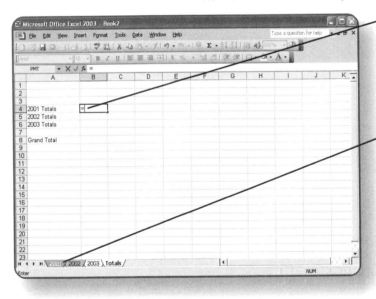

1. **Type** the **equal sign** in the cell where you want the cross reference (the destination cell). This will instruct Excel to take the value of whatever you type or click on next.

2. **Click** on the **worksheet tab** that contains the cell you want to reference.

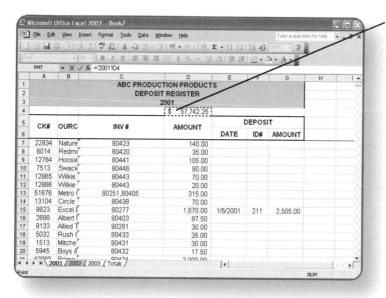

3. **Click** on the **cell** you want to reference. A marquee will surround the selected cell.

4. **Press** the **Enter key**. The reference is complete.

Excel will return you to the original worksheet with the value displayed.

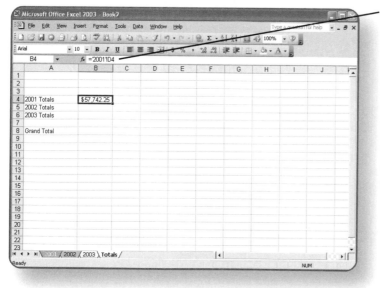

The answer is displayed in the worksheet, but on the Edit line, the originating cell location is displayed. The linked reference is the sheet name followed by an exclamation point and the cell location.

If the value in the originating cell changes, the value in the cross reference cell will also change.

Creating Links to Other Workbooks

Similar to creating a link to a different worksheet in the current workbook, you can also create links to specific locations in other workbooks. The easiest method to create a workbook link is to have both the origination and the destination workbooks open.

1. Type the **equal sign** in the cell where you want the cross reference (the destination cell). This will instruct Excel to take the value of whatever you type or click on next.

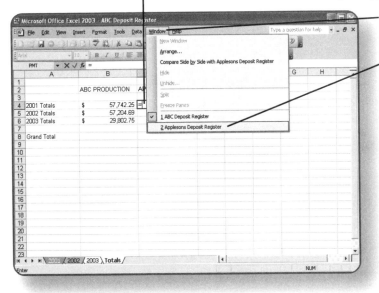

2. Click on the **Window menu**. The Window menu will appear.

3. Click on the **file** that contains the data you want to reference. Excel will switch to the selected file.

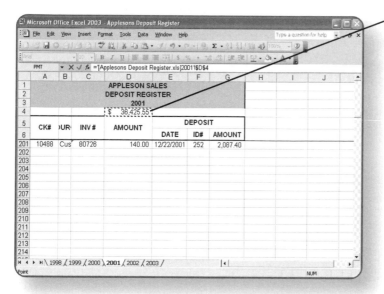

4. Click on the **cell** you want to reference. A marquee will surround the selected cell.

5. Press the **Enter key**. The reference is complete.

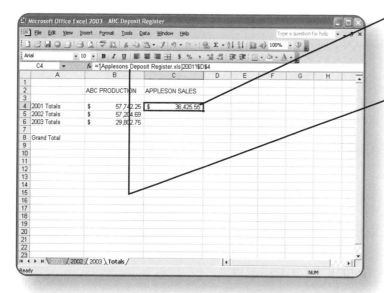

Excel will return you to the destination worksheet with the cross-referenced value displayed.

Excel will display the result in the worksheet, but on the Edit line, the originating cell location is displayed. The linked reference is the data path, the Excel file name (in brackets), then the sheet name, an exclamation point, and the cell location.

When you reopen the current workbook, Excel will prompt you whether to check for changes in the linked workbook.

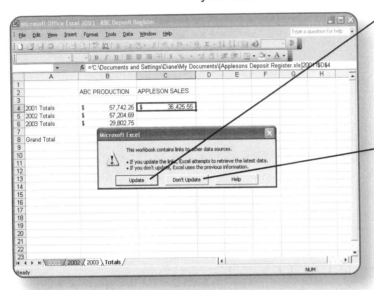

6a. **Click** on **Update**. Excel will check the linked workbook for changes in the cross-referenced cell, and if needed, update the current workbook.

OR

6b. **Click** on **Don't update**. Excel will display the data that was in the cell the last time the workbook was saved.

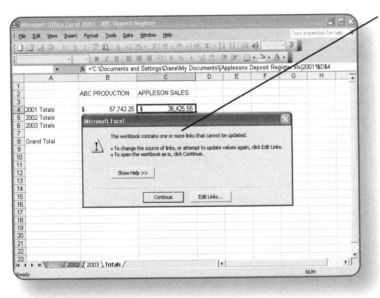

If, when updating links, the originating workbook was renamed, deleted, or moved, an information dialog box will appear notifying you it could not update the link. You have the option of continuing, leaving the data as it was last saved, or clicking an Edit Links button to change the link references.

9

Managing Larger Worksheets

Because workbooks can get very large, it sometimes becomes difficult to maneuver around the workbook efficiently. You may find yourself bouncing from one part of the worksheet to another. Excel contains several tools to aid navigation and viewing of worksheets.

In this chapter, you'll learn how to:

- Hide and display parts of a worksheet
- Split a window
- Freeze window planes
- Zoom in and out of a worksheet
- Work with ranges
- Use the Find and Replace feature

Modifying Worksheet Views

When working with a larger worksheet, it can become difficult to see the entire worksheet on the screen. As you scroll down or across the worksheet, you may lose track of which column or row of data you are entering. Excel contains several tools to help you view your worksheet from different perspectives.

Hiding Rows and Columns

If you have rows or columns you don't really need to see, or that you don't want to print, you can hide them from view. Hiding them doesn't delete them or make their data inaccessible; it only keeps them out of view. When you hide rows or columns, Excel is actually changing the row height or column width to zero.

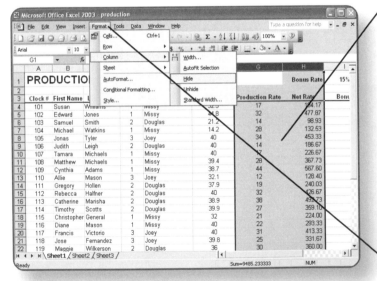

1. Select the **columns or rows** you want to hide. The columns or rows will be highlighted.

NOTE

You can hide multiple columns at one time or multiple rows at one time, but do not try to hide both columns and rows in a single step.

2. Click on **Format**. The Format menu will appear.

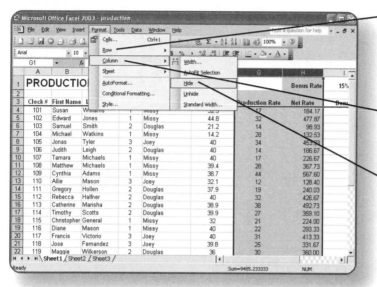

3a. **Click** on **Row** if you want to hide rows. The Row menu will appear.

OR

3b. **Click** on **Column** if you want to hide columns. The Column menu will appear.

4. **Click** on **Hide**. The selected columns or rows will be hidden from view.

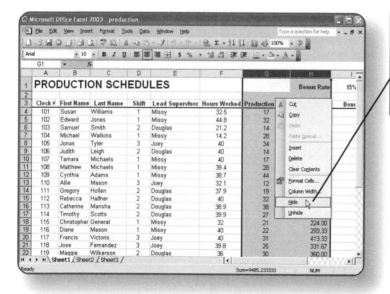

TIP

Optionally, right-click over a selected column or row and choose Hide.

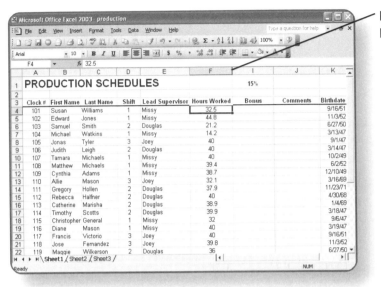

In this example, columns G and H are hidden.

If you need to see the hidden rows or columns, you can easily make them redisplay in the worksheet.

5. **Select** the **rows or columns** on both sides of the hidden rows or columns. The rows or columns will be highlighted.

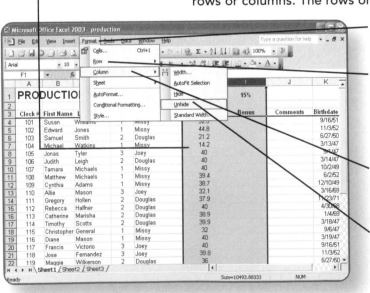

6. **Click** on **Format**. The Format menu will appear.

7a. **Click** on **Row** if you want to unhide rows. The Row menu will appear.

OR

7b. **Click** on **Column** if you want to unhide columns. The Column menu will appear.

8. **Click** on **Unhide**. The previously hidden rows or columns will redisplay.

TIP

Optionally, right-click over a selected column or row and choose Unhide.

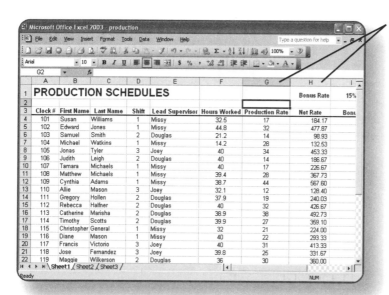

In this example, columns G and H are redisplayed.

Splitting a Window

Sometimes you need to see two or more different sections of your worksheet at the same time, but your worksheet is too large to view both sections. Excel includes a feature which allows you to split a window into four sections which you can move independently of each other.

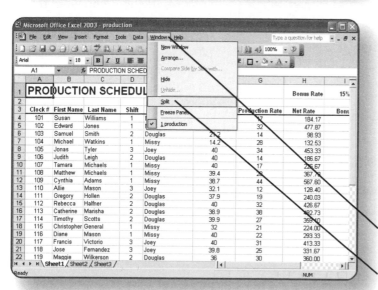

1. Click on **Window**. The Window menu will appear.

2. Click on **Split**. Split bars will appear on the worksheet.

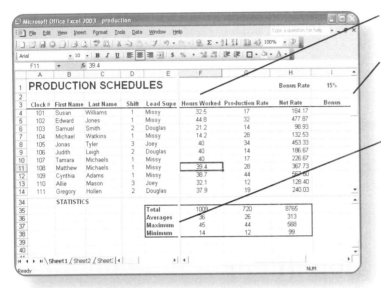

The current worksheet will be divided into four panes.

Each section has its own scroll bar.

TIP

Click and drag the split bars until the panes are the size you want.

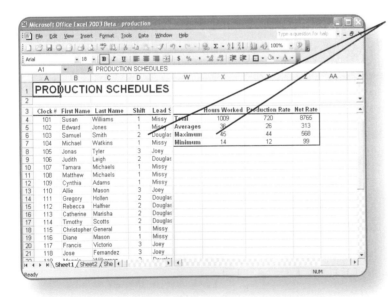

3. Scroll through the different **panes** until you see the sections of the worksheet you want to compare.

When you are finished working in the split view, you can easily return the worksheet to a single panel.

4. **Click** on **Window**. The Window menu will appear.

5. **Click** on **Remove Split**. The split bars will disappear.

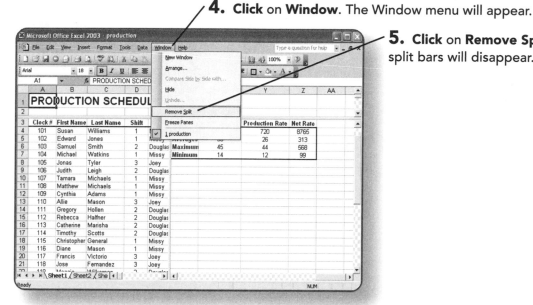

Freezing Panes

When working with a long or wide list, as you add more data, you might lose track of which column or row you are entering data into. It would be helpful if you could see which column or row label you are working with. You can freeze the column headings and row labels so they remain visible no matter where you are working in your worksheet.

1. Click on the desired **cell**:

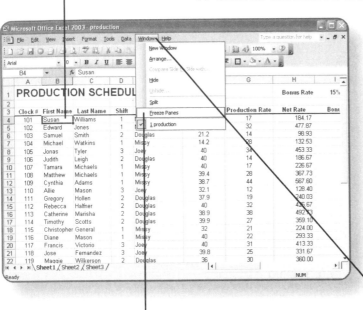

- To freeze columns, click the mouse one cell to the right of the columns you want to freeze.

- To freeze rows, click the mouse one cell below the rows you want to freeze.

- To freeze both columns and rows, click the mouse in the cell below the rows, hold down the Ctrl key, and click to the right of the columns you want to freeze.

2. Click on **Window**. The Window menu will appear.

3. Click on **Freeze Panes**. A black line will appear below the column labels and to the right of the row labels.

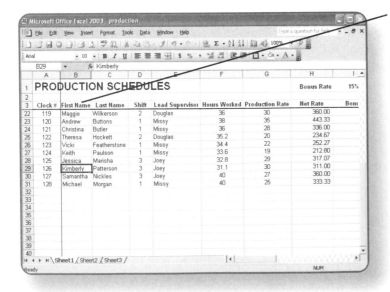

As you scroll through your worksheet, the column and row headings will remain visible.

NOTE

Typically, when you press the Home key, Excel takes you to cell A1, but when you have the Freeze Panes feature active, Excel will take you to the cell just below and to the left of the frozen headings.

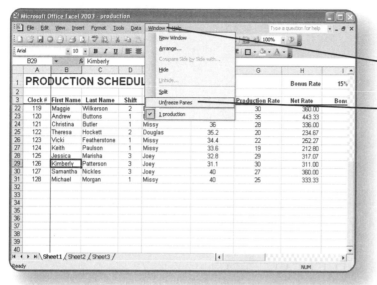

You can easily remove the freeze from row and column headings.

4. Click on **Window**. The Window menu will appear.

5. Click on **Unfreeze Panes**. The black divider lines will disappear and the heading columns and rows will scroll with the rest of the worksheet.

Using Zoom

The Zoom feature enlarges or shrinks the display of your worksheet to allow you to see more or less of it. Excel can zoom your worksheet in percentages, with the normal display of your worksheet being 100%. Zooming in or out does not affect printing.

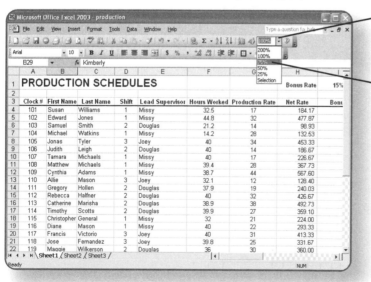

1. Click on the **Zoom button down arrow**. A list of magnifications will display.

2. Click on a magnification **percentage**. The higher the number, the larger the cells will appear on your screen and less of your worksheet will be visible.

TIP

Optionally, type your own magnification percentage.

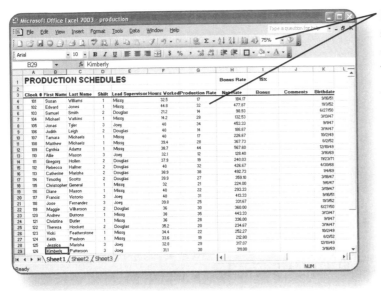

In this example, the zoom was set to 75% which allowed more of the worksheet to display on the screen.

To reset the display to normal, change the zoom to 100%.

Working with Ranges

A *range name* is basically a descriptive name for an area of the worksheet. Range names are much easier to remember than actual cell addresses. You can use range names in formulas or commands such as Go To.

Creating Range Names

Giving cells recognizable range names makes locating data easier. It also can help make formulas more logical and easier to understand.

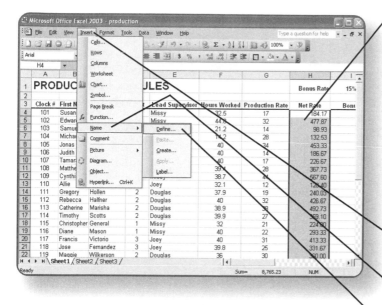

1. Select the **cells** you want to name. The cells will be highlighted.

TIP

Ranges can be a single cell, a contiguous group of cells, entire rows, or entire columns.

---

2. Click on **Insert**. The Insert menu will appear.

3. Click on **Name**. The Name submenu will appear.

4. Click on **Define**. The Define Name dialog box will open.

5. Type the **range name** you want to use. If you have text in the first selected cell, Excel will suggest that as the range name. There are several caveats about creating range names:

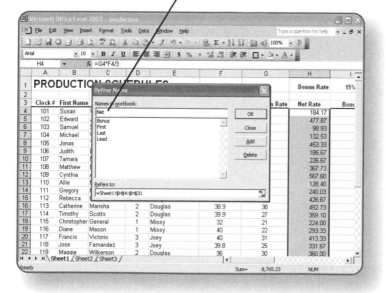

- Range names must begin with a letter or the underscore character.

- Range names cannot include a space or a hyphen.

- Range names are not case sensitive. You can use uppercase or lowercase letters.

- Range names can be up to 255 characters, but shorter is better.

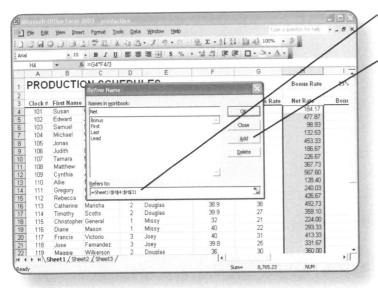

Excel displays the selected cell addresses.

6. Click on **Add**. The range name will appear in the Define Name dialog box.

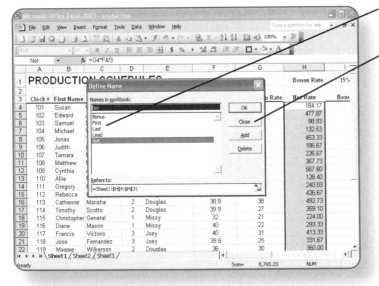

List of range names in the workbook.

7. Click on **Close**. The Define Name dialog box will close.

Using Range Names

Range names can help you jump quickly to specific areas of your worksheet. You can also use range names when creating Excel formulas.

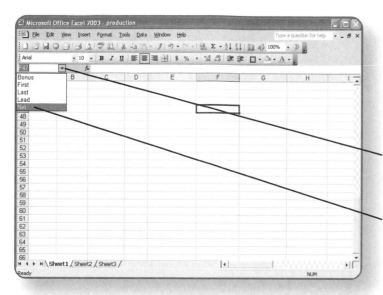

Excel provides a convenient drop-down menu that you can use to quickly move around in your worksheet. Moving to remote areas of your worksheet can be a mouse click away using range names.

1. Click the **Name box drop-down menu.** A list of range names will appear.

2. Click on the **range name** you want to locate.

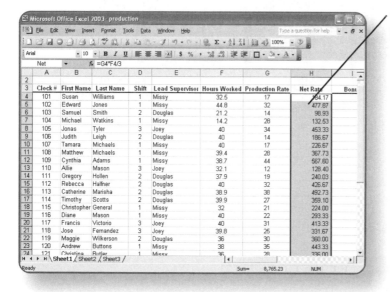

The range will become highlighted.

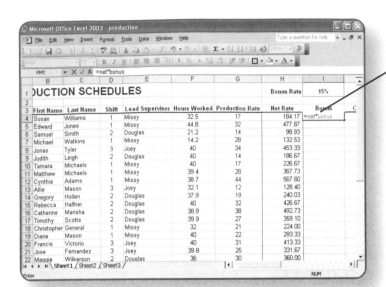

TIP

Using a range name in a formula makes creating formulas much easier to understand. For example, it is easier to identify a formula that is =Income-Expenses than it is to comprehend one that says =SUM(B6:B16)-SUM (B20-B54).

Using Find and Replace

The Excel Find and Replace feature lets you locate specific text or formulas in your worksheet and optionally replace the found data with something different.

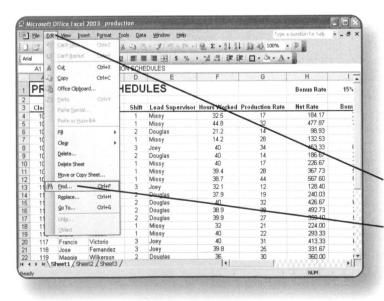

Locating Data with Find

When you have large workbooks, sometimes it's difficult to locate specific entries. You can let Excel locate the data automatically for you.

1. Click on **Edit**. The Edit menu will appear.

2. Click on **Find**. The Find and Replace dialog box will open.

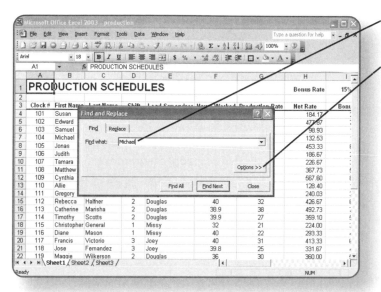

3. Type the **word, phrase, or number** you want to find.

4. Click on the **Options button**. The Find and Replace dialog box will expand to display additional options.

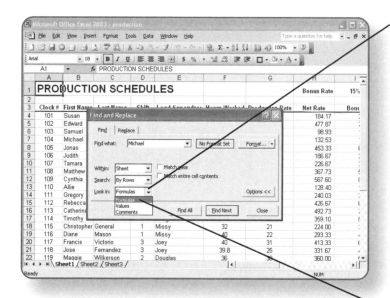

5. Click on the **drop-down menu** next to the Look in list box. A list of options will appear.

The Find feature can search through formulas, values, or comments. If you select formulas, the Find feature will look through both the underlying formulas and the values for the selected data. If you select values, Excel will look only in the results, not in the formulas. If you select comments, Excel will look only in comments.

6. Click on the **type of data** you want to search for. The option will be selected.

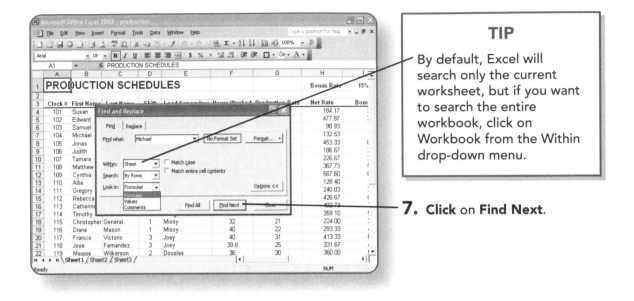

TIP

By default, Excel will search only the current worksheet, but if you want to search the entire workbook, click on Workbook from the Within drop-down menu.

7. Click on **Find Next**.

Excel will find the first occurrence of the word or number.

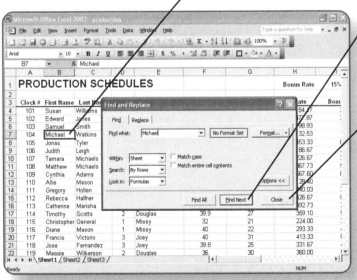

8. Click on **Find Next** if this is not the occurrence you were looking for. Excel will find the next occurrence of the specified data.

9. Click on **Close**. The Find dialog box will close.

Replacing Entries

Excel can locate specific data for you and automatically replace it with different data.

1. Click on **Edit**. The Edit menu will appear.

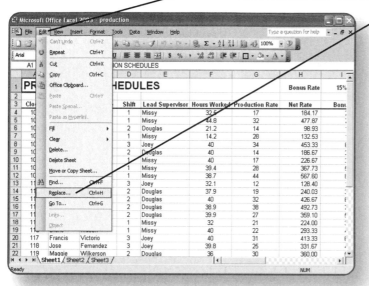

2. Click on **Replace**. The Find and Replace dialog box will open.

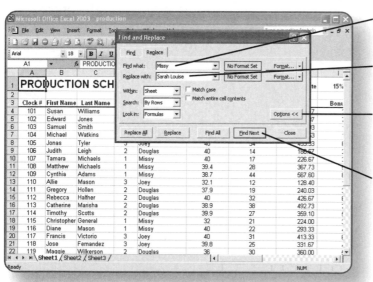

3. Type the **data** you want to replace in the Find what text box.

4. Type the **replacement data** in the Replace with text box.

The Replace box also has options similar to the Find dialog box.

5. Click on **Find Next**. Excel will locate the first occurrence of the selected text.

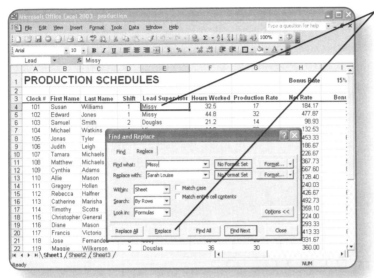

6. Click on **Replace** if you want to replace the found data with the replacement data. Excel will make the replacement and proceed to the next occurrence.

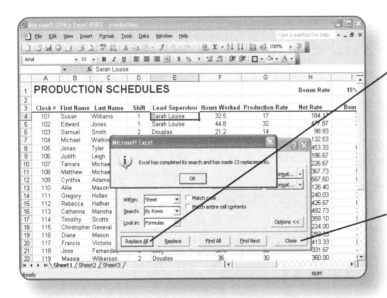

TIP

You can click on Replace All to have Excel replace all occurrences of the original data with the replacement data. Excel will notify you of the total number of occurrences.

7. Click on **Close**. The Find and Replace dialog box will close.

Part II Review Questions

1. What key must you press to begin an Excel formula? *See 'Creating Formulas' in Chapter 6*

2. When might you want to use an absolute reference in a formula? *See 'Creating an Absolute Reference in a Formula' in Chapter 6*

3. When does Excel display #DIV/0! in a cell? *See 'Understanding Common Formula Error Messages' in Chapter 6*

4. What are Excel functions? *See 'Using Excel Functions' in Chapter 7*

5. What are function arguments? *'See 'Understanding Function Syntax' in Chapter 7*

6. Which Excel function displays the current date in a cell? *See 'Using the NOW Function' in Chapter 7*

7. What does Excel call a file with multiple worksheets? *See 'Working with Larger Workbooks' in Chapter 8*

8. What does Excel do when you first open a workbook with a link to another workbook? *See 'Creating Links to Other Workbooks' in Chapter 8*

9. What can you do so the row and column headings always remain visible as you move through a large worksheet? *See 'Freezing Panes' in Chapter 9*

10. Why might you give a group of cells a range name? *See 'Creating Range Names' in Chapter 9*

PART III

Adding Visual Interest

10

Working with Art Images

In a world where everyone is frantically busy, you need to communicate your ideas quickly. Graphic images help you do this. No time or talent to draw? That's not a problem. Excel contains a number of tools to assist you in placing images into your worksheet.

In this chapter, you'll learn how to:

- Insert clip art and other images
- Move and size the art object
- Adjust the contrast and brightness
- Wrap text around an image
- Create WordArt

Inserting Images

There are a number of different types of images, ranging from photographs to drawn art images, to text that takes on artistic shapes. Excel art is considered an *object* which means that you can easily move it, resize it, or modify it.

Inserting Clip Art

Excel comes with a wide variety of clip art. *Clip art* is simply a collection of computer pictures or graphics that are ready to use. You just select an appropriate picture and insert it in your worksheet.

1. Click the **mouse pointer** approximately where you want to insert your image. Don't worry if you choose the wrong area; you will later learn how to move your graphic image.

2. Click on **Insert**. The Insert menu will appear.

3. Click on **Picture**. The Picture menu will appear.

4. Click on **Clip Art**. The Insert Clip Art task pane will open.

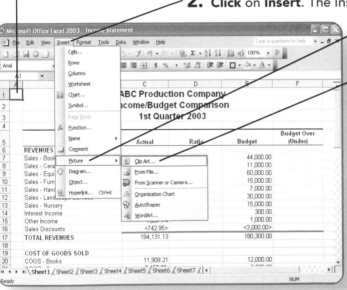

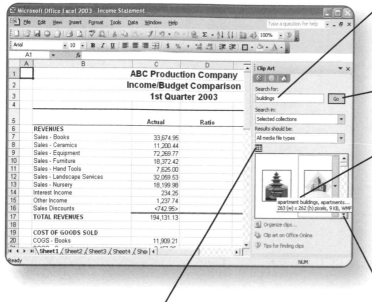

5. Type a **description** of the clip art you want. Excel will look for any clip art matching your description.

6. Click on **Go**. Excel will search for clip art located on your hard drive.

7. Pause the **mouse** over a picture. The selected picture will have a frame around it, an arrow on the right side, and a tip box that will describe the selected image.

8. Use the **scroll arrow** when available to preview more images.

TIP

Click on the Expand Results button to display more images at a time.

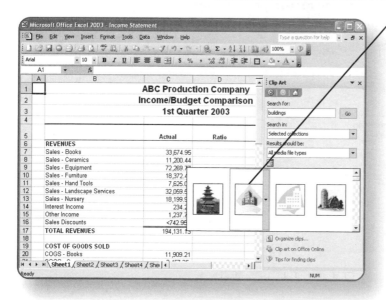

9. Click on the desired **image**. Excel will insert the clip into your worksheet.

You will learn in a later section how to move, resize, and adjust any image you insert into your worksheet.

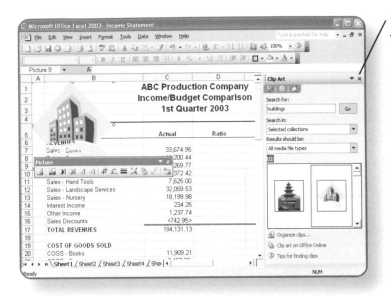

10. **Click** on the **Close button**. The Clip Art task pane will close.

Inserting Saved Images

You can easily insert your own artwork into an Excel worksheet, whether it's a photograph, scanned image, logo, or other type of artwork.

1. **Click** the **mouse pointer** approximately where you want to insert your image.

2. **Click** on **Insert**. The Insert menu will appear.

3. **Click** on **Picture**. The Picture menu will appear.

4. **Click** on **From File**. The Insert Picture dialog box will open.

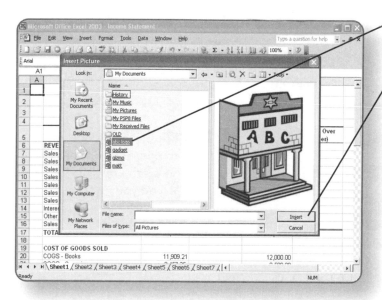

5. Locate and click on the **image** you want to insert. The image will be selected.

6. Click on **Insert**. The image will be inserted into your current worksheet and the picture toolbar will appear.

You'll learn in a later section how to move, resize, and adjust any image you insert into your worksheet.

Inserting Images from Your Camera

Although you will probably want to use the Windows XP Camera and Scanner Wizard or other software to download a batch of images from your digital camera, you can download images directly from your camera into your Microsoft Excel worksheet. So go ahead, take those pictures of your inventory items and insert them directly into your worksheet.

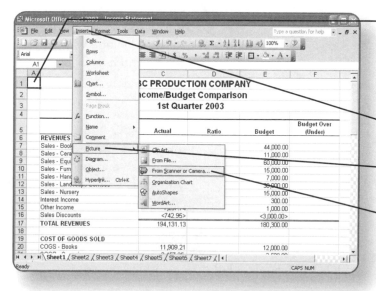

1. Click the **mouse pointer** approximately where you want to insert your image. The blinking insertion point will appear.

2. Click on **Insert**. The Insert menu will appear.

3. Click on **Picture**. The Picture menu will appear.

4. Click on **From Scanner or Camera**. A dialog box will open prompting you to specify the device you want to acquire the images from.

NOTE

Your camera must be installed and properly configured with Windows XP.

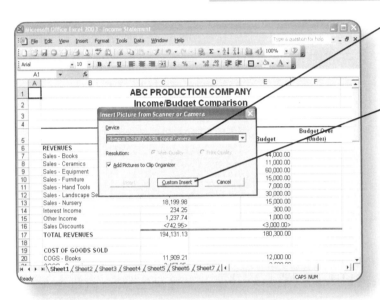

5. Click on the **device** you want to use. Your options will depend on the devices you have installed on your system.

6. Click on **Custom Insert**. The Which pictures do you want to copy? dialog box will open.

The images stored on your camera will appear as thumbnails.

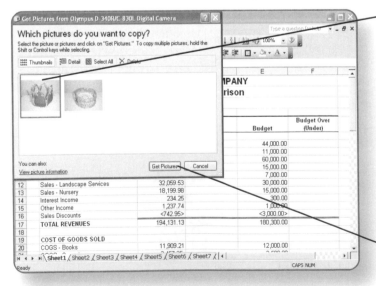

7. Click on the **image** you want to insert into your worksheet. The selected image will have a border around it.

TIP

If you want to insert multiple images, hold down the Ctrl key and select the additional images.

8. Click on **Get Pictures**. Excel will insert the selected images into your worksheet.

You'll learn in the next section how to move, resize, and adjust any image you insert into your worksheet.

Customizing Art

After the image is in your worksheet, you can make adjustments to it so that it blends well with your worksheet. You can move it, change its size, adjust the brightness and contrast, and wrap text around it or over it.

Resizing Images

The image might not fit on the page exactly as you had envisioned it. You can easily make the image smaller or larger.

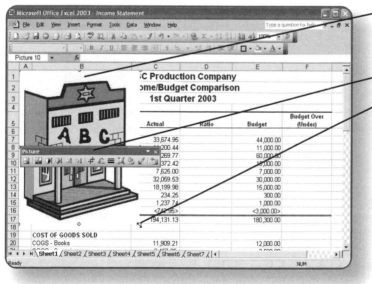

1. Click on the **image**. The image will be selected and eight small handles will appear.

The picture toolbar will appear.

2. Position the **mouse pointer** over one of the handles. The mouse pointer will turn into a double-headed arrow.

3. Press and hold your **mouse button** down on one of the selection handles. The pointer will turn into a plus sign.

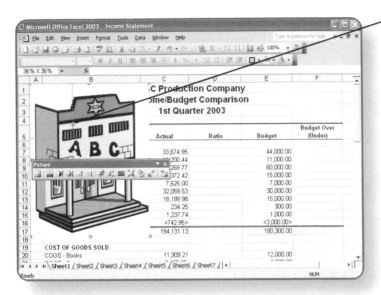

4. **Drag** the **selection handle** out to make the picture larger, or in to make it smaller. A dotted box will indicate the new size.

> ### NOTE
>
> Dragging on any corner handle will resize the height and width of the object at the same time; dragging on any side handle will resize the image in a single direction.

5. **Release** the **mouse button**. The image will remain at the new size.

Moving Art

The picture you choose might need to be moved. As the image is inserted into the worksheet, surrounding text adjusts to make room for it. When you position an image in an Excel worksheet, it automatically aligns (or snaps) to an invisible grid, which helps keep everything lined up.

1. **Click** on the **art image**. The image will be selected.

2. **Position** the **mouse pointer** anywhere inside the frame of the graphic. Do not position it over one of the selection handles.

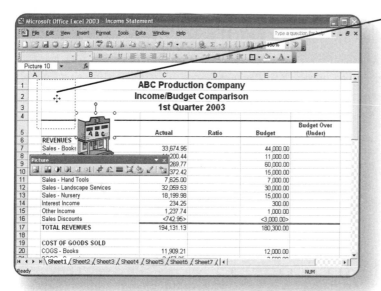

3. Press and hold the **mouse button** and **drag** the insertion point (in the form of a gray dotted line) to the new location. The mouse pointer will be a four-headed arrow.

4. Release the **mouse button**. The graphic will be in the new location.

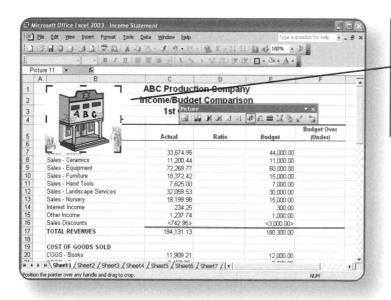

TIP

Click anywhere outside of the image to deselect it. The Picture toolbar will also close.

Cropping an Image

You might want to use just a portion of the entire picture you've selected. You can easily modify the picture size and content by using the Cropping tool.

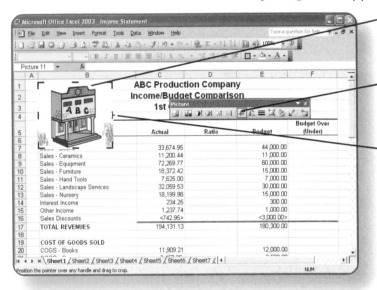

1. Click on the **image**. The image will be selected and the Picture toolbar will display.

2. Click on the **Crop button**. The pointer will change to the Cropping tool.

3. Position the **mouse pointer** over one of the selection handles. The Cropping tool will display over the handle.

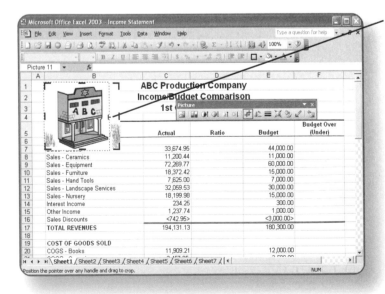

4. Press and hold the **mouse button** and **drag** toward the center of the graphic. The pointer will change to a plus sign, and a dashed line will form a box. The edges of this box form the new edges of the picture, with only the portion inside the box remaining uncropped.

5. Release the **mouse** button. The image will be cropped.

6. Repeat steps 4 and 5 to crop as many sides as needed until the picture displays only the portion of the image you want.

7. Click on the **Crop button** again. The Cropping tool will be turned off.

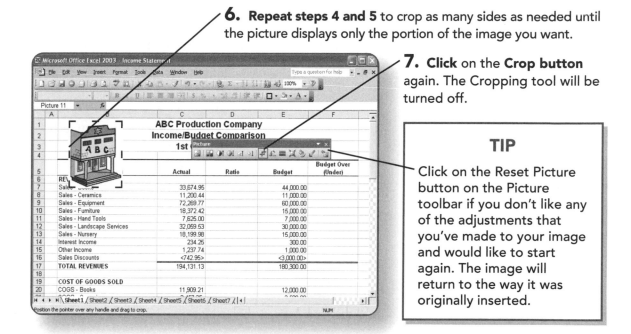

TIP

Click on the Reset Picture button on the Picture toolbar if you don't like any of the adjustments that you've made to your image and would like to start again. The image will return to the way it was originally inserted.

Adding WordArt

Adding clip art to a worksheet is one way to add visual excitement, but if you're the creative type, you might want to draw your own pictures using Excel's drawing tools. If you want your text to have more impact, WordArt might be your solution. With WordArt, you can take headings or key words and add decorative color schemes, shapes, and special effects.

1. **Click** on **Insert**. The Insert menu will appear.

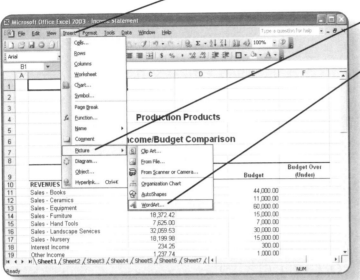

2. **Click** on **Picture**. The Picture submenu will appear.

3. **Click** on **WordArt**. The WordArt Gallery dialog box will open, containing predefined styles in which formats such as shape, color, or shadows are used to enhance text.

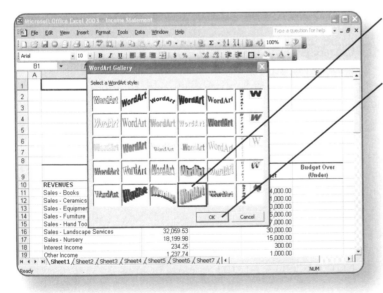

4. **Click** on a WordArt **style**. The selection will have a box around it.

5. **Click** on **OK**. The Edit WordArt Text dialog box will open.

A placeholder in the Text box will say, "Your Text Here."

6. Type the **text** that you want to appear as WordArt. Your text will replace the highlighted text.

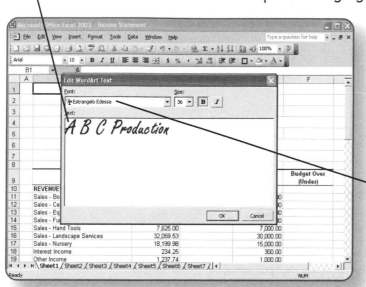

NOTE

Limiting WordArt to a single line of text is a good idea; the elaborate formatting can make lengthier text difficult to read.

---

7. Select a **font**. The preview box will display your text in the selected font.

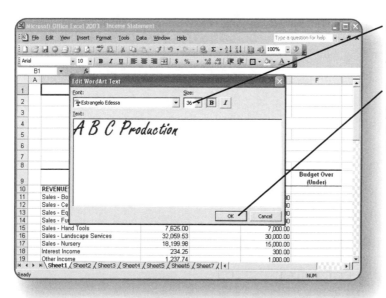

8. Select a **font size**. The preview box will display your text in the selected font size.

9. Click on **OK**. The text that you typed with the WordArt style you selected will be inserted in the worksheet.

Making Adjustments to the WordArt

Even though it looks as though you've made a very specific design selection in the WordArt dialog box, you can actually make lots of adjustments to your selection. You can move and resize a WordArt object in the same manner you learned earlier in this chapter.

Editing WordArt Text

If you made a typing error or you want to adjust the size or font of the text, you can easily open the WordArt feature again.

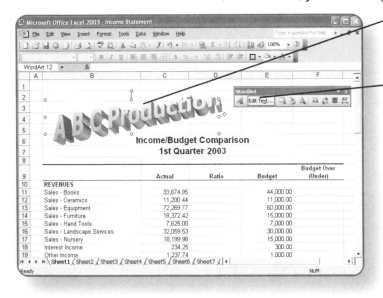

1. **Click** on the WordArt **object**. The object will be highlighted with selection handles.

2. From the WordArt toolbar, **click** on the **Edit Text button**. The Edit WordArt Text dialog box will open.

TIP

Optionally, double-click the WordArt object to display the Edit WordArt Text dialog box.

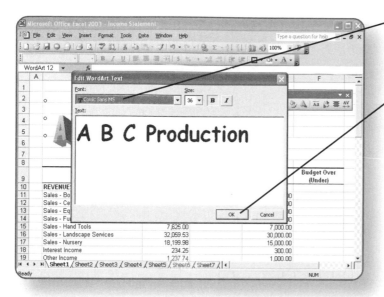

3. **Select** a new **font, font size, or modify** the **text.** The preview box will display your text in the newly selected settings.

4. **Click** on **OK.** The WordArt object will reflect your changes.

Changing WordArt Style

When you created the WordArt object, you selected a style from the WordArt Gallery, which contained styles such as shape, color, or shadows that were used to enhance your text. If you want a different WordArt style, you can easily access the WordArt Gallery to select a different style.

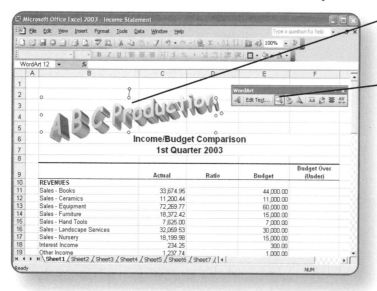

1. **Click** on the WordArt **object.** The object will be highlighted with selection handles.

2. **Click** on the **WordArt Gallery button** on the WordArt toolbar. The WordArt Gallery dialog box will open.

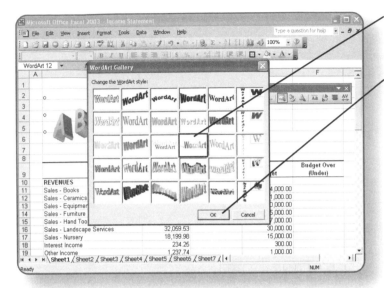

3. Click on a WordArt **style**. The selection will have a box around it.

4. Click on **OK**. The WordArt Gallery dialog box will close.

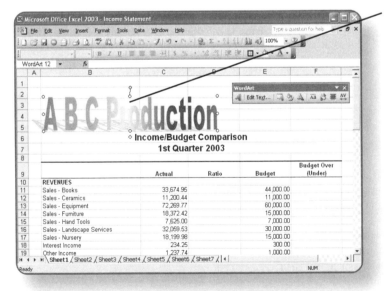

The existing WordArt object will change to the new style.

Reshaping WordArt

In addition to changing the size and style of the WordArt text, you can also change the shape of the WordArt object. The WordArt shape options include placing the WordArt object in a circular or semi-circular pattern, or even waves, triangles, or octagonal shapes.

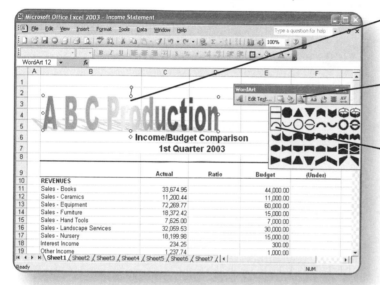

1. **Click** on the **WordArt object**. The object will be highlighted with selection handles.

2. **Click** on the **WordArt Shape button** on the WordArt toolbar. A palette of shapes will appear.

3. **Click** on a **shape**. Your WordArt will change to the shape you selected.

NOTE

Some shapes will make your text hard to read, while others will add an exciting or fun tone to your words. You may have to experiment with the different choices to select the shape to best fit your text.

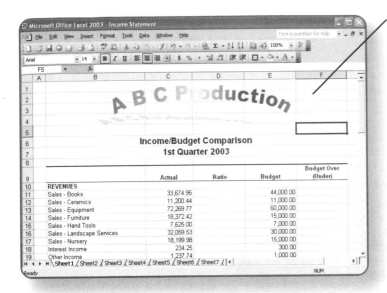

4. Click anywhere in the **worksheet** outside of the WordArt object. The WordArt object will be deselected.

Deleting an Art Image

Whether it's clip art, logos, photographs, or WordArt, it's easy to delete any unwanted art from your worksheet. You must first select the item you don't want, then press the Delete key.

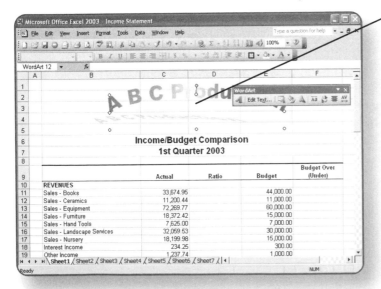

1. Click on the **image**. The image will be selected.

2. Press the **Delete key**. The image will be deleted.

11

Creating Charts from Excel Data

A chart is an effective way to illustrate the data in your worksheet. It can make relationships between numbers easier to see because it turns numbers into shapes, and the shapes can then be compared to one another.

In this chapter, you'll learn how to:

- Create a chart
- Modify a chart
- Delete a chart

Creating a Chart

Creating a chart is a simple process using the Excel Chart Wizard. You first decide what data you want to chart and how you want it to look.

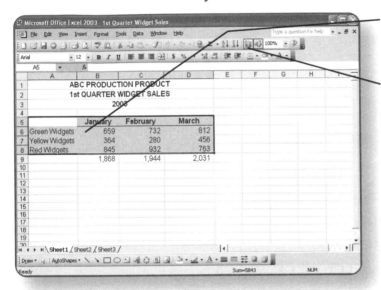

1. **Select** the **range** that you want to chart. The range will be highlighted.

2. **Click** on the **Chart Wizard button**. Step 1 of the Chart wizard will display on-screen.

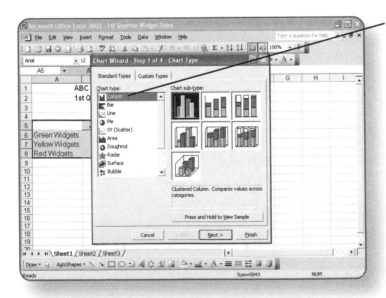

3. **Click** on a **Chart type**. A selection of chart subtypes will be displayed.

NOTE

Traditionally, bar charts compare item to item, pie charts compare parts of a whole item, and line charts show a trend over a period of time.

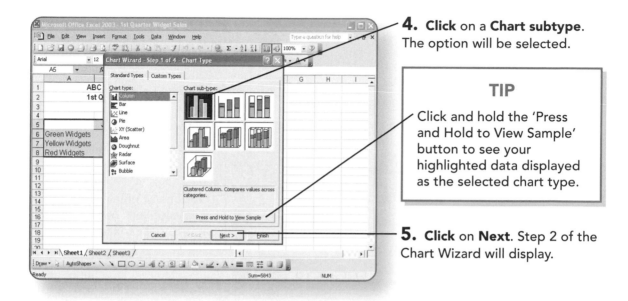

4. **Click** on a **Chart subtype**. The option will be selected.

TIP

Click and hold the 'Press and Hold to View Sample' button to see your highlighted data displayed as the selected chart type.

5. **Click** on **Next**. Step 2 of the Chart Wizard will display.

Next, Excel will try to determine the direction of the data—whether the values to be plotted are in rows or columns.

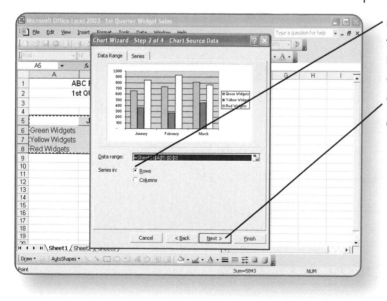

6. **Click** on **Rows or Columns** to display the data series in rows or columns. Your data will appear in the preview box.

7. **Click** on **Next**. Step 3 of the Chart Wizard will display.

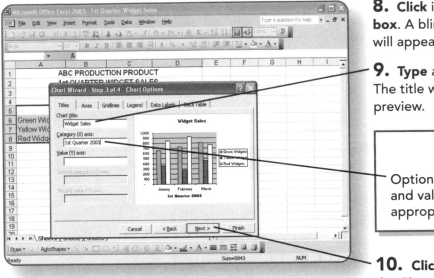

8. **Click** in the **Chart Title text box**. A blinking insertion point will appear.

9. **Type** a **title** for your chart. The title will appear in the chart preview.

TIP

Optionally, enter category and value axis titles in the appropriate text boxes.

10. **Click** on **Next**. Step 4 of the Chart Wizard will display.

You must now choose whether you want the chart to display on its own sheet or to appear on the same sheet as the data.

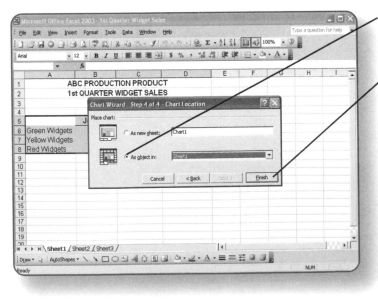

11. **Click** on a **Place Chart option button**. The option will be selected.

12. **Click** on **Finish**. The Wizard will close. The chart will be displayed either as a new sheet or below the existing data.

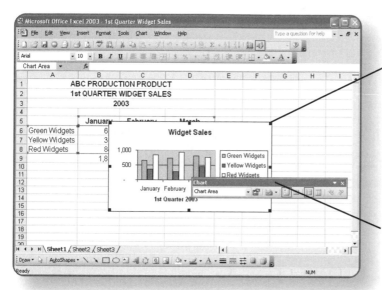

NOTE

When a chart is on the same page as the data, the chart is selected when eight black handles appear around the outer edge of the chart. Click outside of the chart to deselect it, or click on the chart to select it.

The Chart toolbar also appears.

The data from the selected cells of the worksheet is plotted in a chart. If the data in the worksheet changes, the chart will also change automatically.

In the next section, you'll learn how to change the size and look of your chart.

TIP

A quick way to create an Excel chart is to highlight the chart data and press the F11 key.

Modifying a Chart

Creating a chart is so simple that it probably made you want to enhance the chart to improve its appearance. Items you can change include the size, style, color, and placement.

Resizing a Chart

When a chart is inserted on the worksheet page, it will probably be too small for you to read the data correctly. You can use your mouse to resize it.

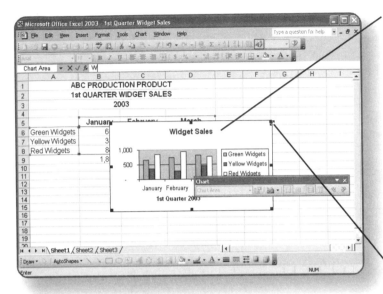

1. If necessary, **click** on the **chart** to select it. The chart will have eight small handles around it.

NOTE

If your chart is on its own page, you don't need to click on the chart to select it. Just having the chart displayed makes it eligible for modification.

2. Position the **mouse pointer** over one of the handles. The mouse pointer will change to a double-headed arrow.

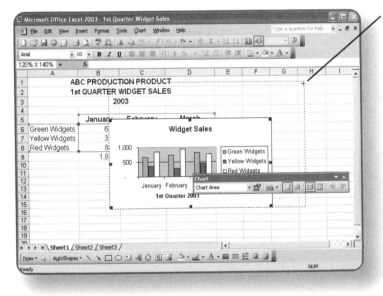

3. Press the **mouse button** and **drag** the **black handle**. A dotted line will indicate the new chart size.

4. Release the **mouse button**. The chart will be resized.

Moving a Chart

When a chart is inserted on the worksheet page, you can easily move it to any location on the page.

1. If necessary, **click** on the **chart** to select it. The chart will have eight small handles around it.

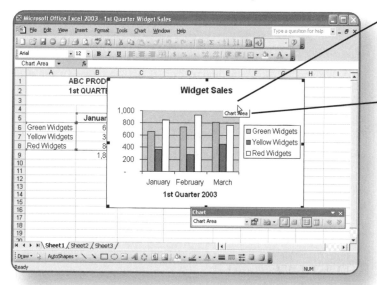

2. Position the **mouse pointer** anywhere over a blank area of the chart. The mouse pointer will be a left-pointing, white arrow.

You will also see a yellow tooltip indicating that you're pointing to the chart area.

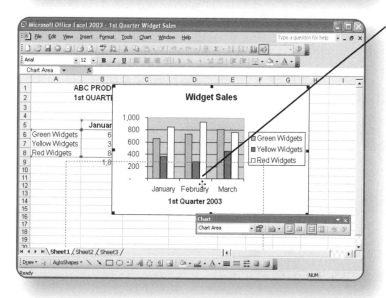

3. Press the **mouse button** and **drag** the **chart** to the new location. The mouse will turn into a four-headed arrow and a dotted-line box will indicate the new position.

4. Release the **mouse button**. The chart will move to the new position.

Changing a Chart Style

If you want to change the style of the chart, you can select a bar, area, pie, line, or a number of other style charts. Most of these charts can also be 3-D.

1. If necessary, **click** on the **chart**. The chart will be selected.

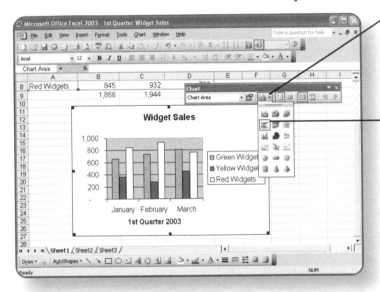

2. Click on the **drop-down menu** to the right of the Chart Type button on the Chart toolbar. A list of chart types will display.

3. Click on a **chart type**. The chart will change to the selected type.

TIP

Use 3-D charts lightly. Adding the extra dimension might make the chart look nice, but can also make the data difficult to read.

Editing the Series Appearance

If you do not like the default colors or patterns assigned to a chart, you can change them for any series.

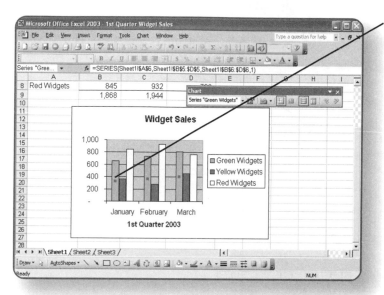

1. Double-click on any colored **bar, line, or series item**. A small black square will appear in all items in the selected series and the Format Data Series dialog box will open.

2. Click on **Patterns**. The Patterns tab will come to the front.

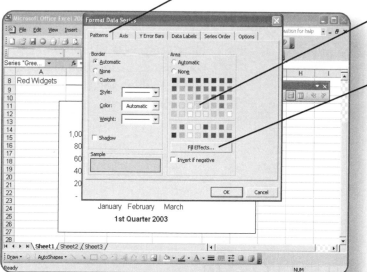

3. Click on a **color** for the selected series. The color will be highlighted.

4. Click on **Fill Effects**. The Fill Effects dialog box will open.

5. Click on the **Gradient, Texture, or Pattern tab**. The tab will come to the front with its available options.

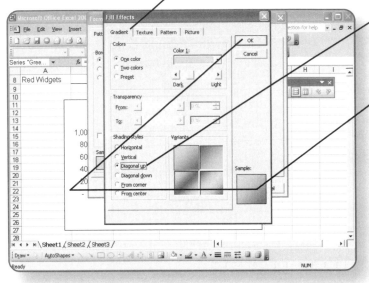

6. Click on any desired **gradient, texture, or pattern options** for the selected series. The pattern will be highlighted.

7. Click on **OK**. The Fill Effects dialog box will close.

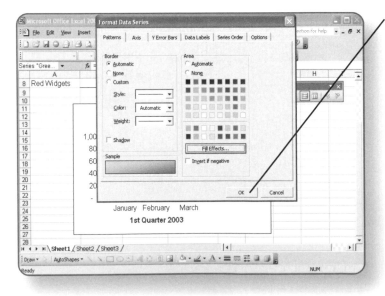

8. Click on **OK**. The Format Data Series dialog box will close and the series will change to the selected options.

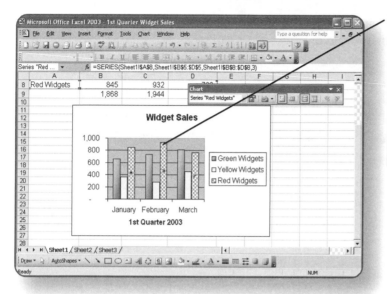

9. Repeat the previous **steps** for each series to be modified.

TIP

Double-click on any section of the chart to edit options for that section.

Modifying Chart Text

You can add or modify any text font, size, color, or border by double-clicking on the text.

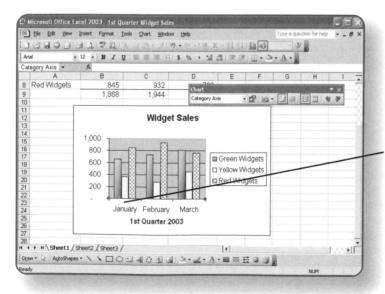

Working with Labels

Labels are the descriptive text you add, including the chart title or labels for the x or y axis of the chart. The legend is also made of labels.

1. Double-click on the **text** you want to modify. The Format dialog box for that section will open.

For example, here the Format Axis dialog box appeared, because the axis text was selected.

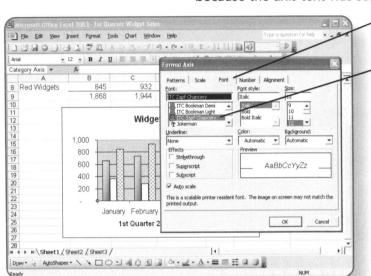

2. **Click** on the **Font tab**. The Font tab will be on top.

3. **Click** on any desired **font changes**. The options will be selected.

You can modify the alignment of your labels, including rotating them.

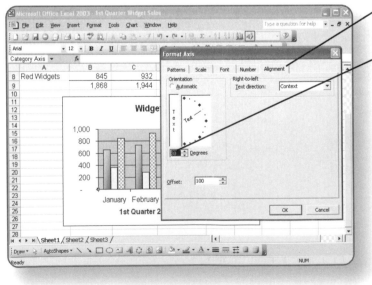

4. **Click** on the **Alignment tab**. The Alignment tab will be on top.

5. **Click** on any alignment **options**. The options will be selected.

You also might want to apply a number format to your y axis, which displays the values in your chart. The same number formats available in an Excel worksheet are available for an Excel chart.

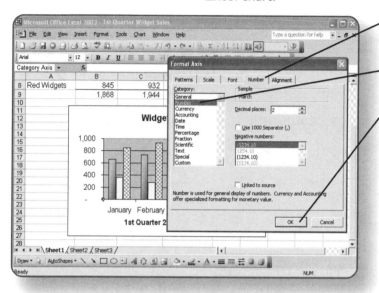

6. Click on the **Number tab**. The Number tab will be on top.

7. Click a number **format** including decimal point options.

8. Click on **OK**. The dialog box will close and the font changes will take effect.

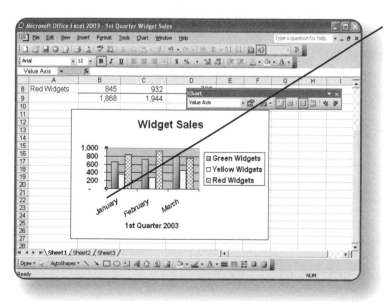

9. Repeat for any text you want to modify. The chart will display the changes you selected.

Placing the Legend

You can move the legend box, which is the key describing your y axis data, anywhere on the chart. Additionally, you can modify the legend box color and style. You cannot, however, modify the legend data since the legend is tied to the data series.

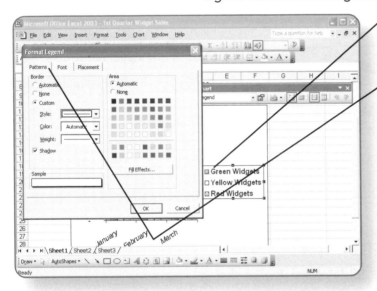

1. **Double-click** anywhere on the **legend**. The Format Legend dialog box will open.

The Patterns tab allows you to select a border and fill color for the legend box.

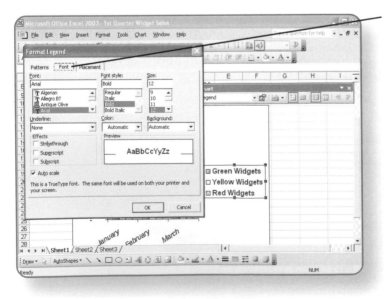

The Font tab allows you to select font, font size, and color for the legend text.

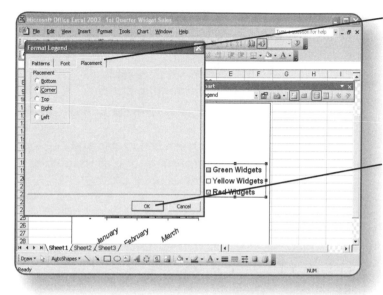

The Placement tab allows you to select a position for the legend, which is by default on the right side of the chart.

2. Make any desired **selections**. The options will be selected.

3. Click on **OK**. The Format Legend dialog box will close.

TIP

You can also click and drag the legend to any desired location.

Displaying the Data Table

A data table is a grid that contains the numeric data used to create the chart. You can add a data table to your chart; it is usually attached to the category axis of the chart. The data table will also display the legend for your chart.

1. Click the **Data Table button** on the Chart toolbar. The chart will display a data table.

Since the data table will contain a legend, you should turn off the legend display.

2. Click the **Legend button**. The Legend will be hidden.

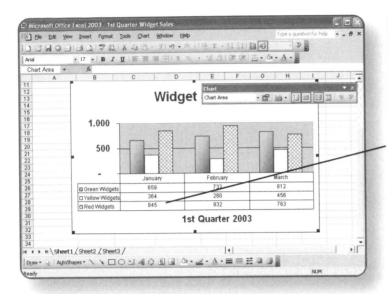

TIP

Double-click the data table to set data table formatting options.

Both the Data Table and Legend buttons are toggles to turn the features on or off.

Deleting a Chart

If you no longer want the chart created from your worksheet, you can delete it. The method you'll use to delete the chart depends on whether the chart is on the same sheet as the data or on a separate sheet.

Removing a Chart from a Data Sheet

If the chart is on the same sheet as the data, you'll delete it with the Delete key.

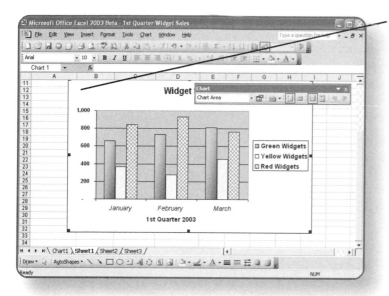

1. Click on the **chart**. The chart will be selected.

2. Press the **Delete key**. The chart will be deleted.

Deleting a Chart on Its Own Sheet

If the chart is on a separate sheet, you'll need to delete the entire sheet to delete the chart.

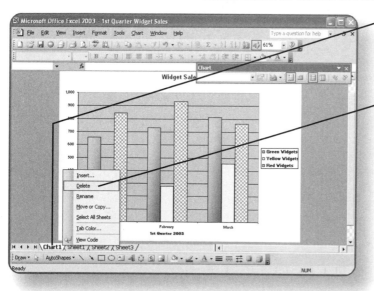

1. Right-click on the **sheet tab**. This tab is usually marked Chart1, Chart2, and so forth. A shortcut menu will appear.

2. Click on **Delete**. A confirmation message will appear.

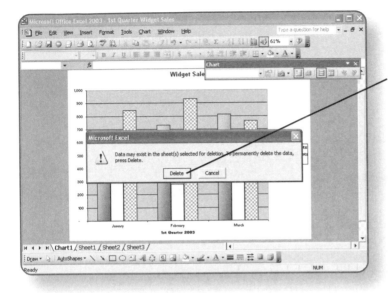

Note that deleting a chart sheet does *not* delete *any data* from the originating worksheet.

3. Click on **Delete**. The chart sheet will be deleted.

12

Using the Drawing Toolbar

Excel contains a complete set of drawing tools to help you create drawings, annotations, or diagrams. Also included for the less artistic is a set of predefined shapes called AutoShapes, which make the drawing process easier and faster. After creating your drawings, you can enhance them with special effects such as adding text or shadows.

In this chapter, you'll learn how to:

- Display the Drawing toolbar
- Draw AutoShapes
- Add text to a drawing
- Give shapes a shadow effect
- Make a shape 3-dimensional

Drawing Shapes

You don't have to be a gifted artist to draw lines, circles, squares, or any of a number of different shapes. Excel provides tools to assist you with all your drawing needs.

Displaying the Drawing Toolbar

Excel provides the drawing tools through the Drawing toolbar. You will find the drawing tools useful in many ways. Each button on the Drawing toolbar performs a specific function. Some tools draw lines or shapes; some tools help position the drawn objects on the screen; and you can use some drawing tools to change the color or appearance of a drawn shape or line.

1. **Click** on **View**. The View menu will appear.

2. **Click** on **Toolbars**. A list of available toolbars will display.

3. **Click** on **Drawing**. The Drawing toolbar will display at the bottom of your screen.

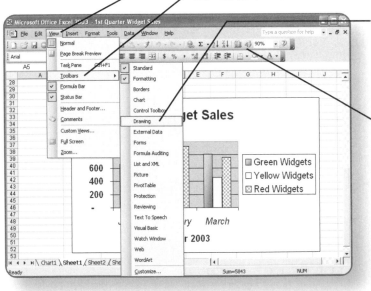

TIP

Optionally, click on the Draw button.

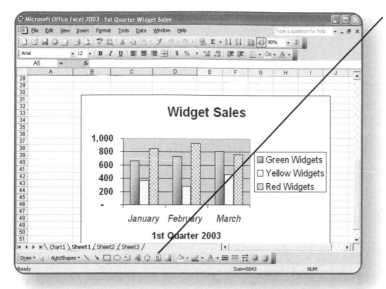

The Drawing toolbar

Creating Lines and Arrows

Two of the most commonly used drawing tools in an Excel worksheet are the line tools and arrow tools. With these tools, you can draw straight lines or angled lines, either of which can have an arrow head. The arrow tool is predefined with an arrow head that will appear at the end of your line. If you use the line tool, you can add the arrow head later.

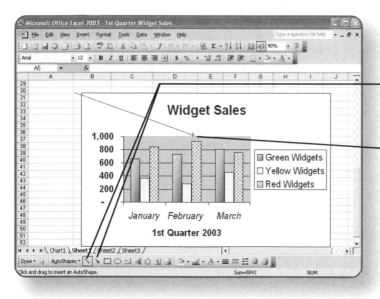

1. **Click** on the **Line tool or the Arrow tool**. The mouse pointer will become a small black cross.

2. **Click and drag** in the direction you want the line to go. A line will appear as you drag in the worksheet.

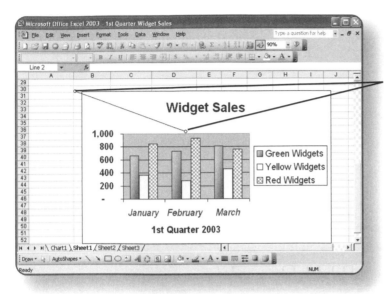

3. Release the **mouse button**. The line or arrow will be selected.

Line selection handles.

Choosing a Line Style

After you draw the line, you can make a number of changes to it, including adjusting the thickness of the line and choosing whether the line is a single line or a double line.

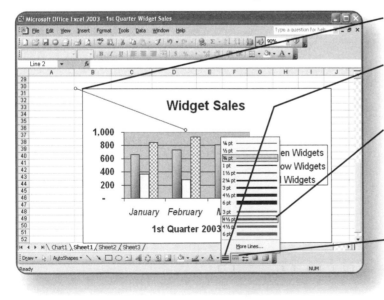

1. Click on the **line** you want to modify. The line will be selected.

2. Click on the **Line Style button**. A display of available line styles will appear.

3. Click on any line **style**. The selected line will change to the new style.

TIP

If you want the line to be a dashed or dotted line, select the line and make a selection from the Dash Style button.

Setting Arrow Heads

If you created a plain line and later determine you want arrow heads, or even if you want different arrow heads than you originally drew, Excel contains a tool to let you select from a variety of arrow heads.

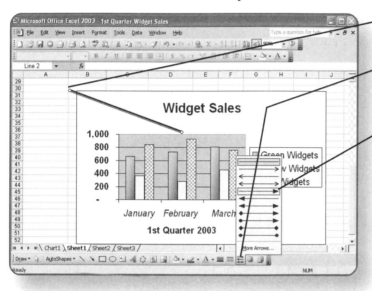

1. **Click** on the **line** you want to modify. The line will be selected.

2. **Click** on the **Arrow Style button**. A display of available arrow styles will appear.

3. **Click** on an arrow **style**. The selected line will change to the new arrow style.

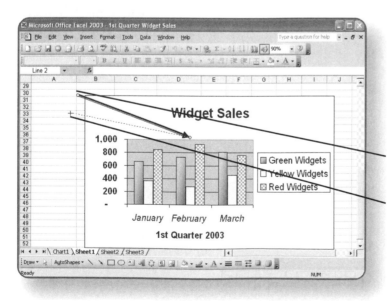

Rotating and Resizing Lines

After you draw the line, if you move your chart or data, you may need to move the line or arrow as well.

1. **Click** on the **line** you want to modify. The line will be selected.

2. **Click and drag** a selection **handle**. As you move the handle around, Excel will resize and rotate the line.

TIP

Position the mouse pointer over the center of a selected line to drag it to a new position.

3. **Release** the **mouse button**. The line will remain at the new size and rotation.

Adding Text Boxes

In Chapter 18, "Collaborating with Others," you will learn how to add comments to a worksheet. However, text boxes are different. You can draw text boxes to annotate and further explain data on your worksheet. Think of a text box as a "Post-it" note for your worksheet.

1. **Click** on the **Text box tool**. The mouse pointer will look like an upside down T.

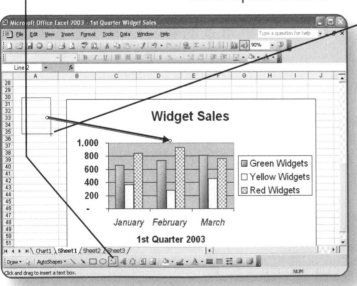

2. **Click and draw** a **box** approximately the size you want for the text you want to insert. A white box with a black border will appear along with a blinking insertion point.

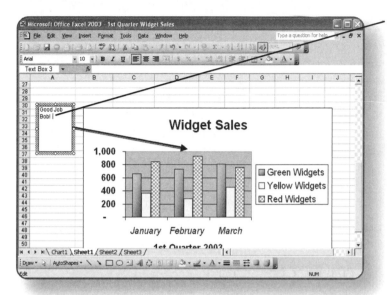

3. Type your **text**. The text will appear in the box.

TIP

Highlight and format the text as you would any text.

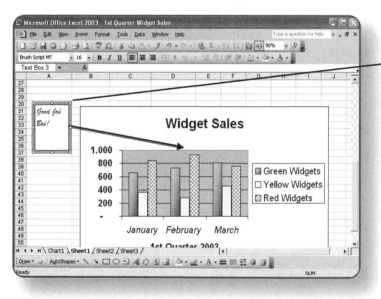

TIP

A text box, like other objects, can be resized by dragging any of the selection handles.

4. Click anywhere **outside** of the **text box**. The text box will be deselected.

Working with AutoShapes

Excel includes built-in images called *AutoShapes* that make it easy to click and drag to draw anything on your worksheet. AutoShapes are a group of ready-made shapes—from arrows, lines, stars, and banners, to basic shapes such as rectangles, ovals, or pyramids. Drawing an AutoShape is as easy as selecting a shape, then using your mouse to click and draw the shape in your worksheet.

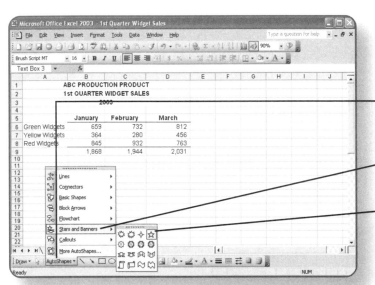

1. Click on the **AutoShapes button**. A list of AutoShapes categories will appear.

2. Click on a **category**. A selection of shapes will appear.

3. Click on a **shape**. The palette will close and your mouse pointer will turn into a small black cross.

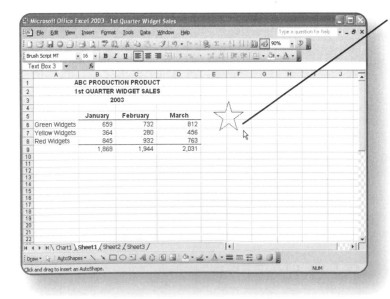

4. Click and drag the **mouse**. A shaped object will appear.

5. Release the **mouse button**. The new drawing shape will display with selection handles surrounding it.

TIP

To insert the same drawing object several times in your worksheet, double-click the Drawing Object button. The button stays selected or "sticky." When you're finished inserting the objects, click the Drawing Object button again, or press the Esc key.

Editing the Drawing Object

The same techniques you learned in Chapter 10, "Working with Art Images"—how to move, resize, and delete art images—are also used for objects you draw with the Drawing toolbar. Sometimes, however, you might want to change the color, line style, or other attributes of your drawing object.

NOTE

Some of the following features are not available with some types of objects.

Changing the Object Color and Fill

By default, when you draw an oval, rectangle, or other shape, the interior of the object is filled with solid white. You can change the fill color or you can make the fill area transparent so you can see your Excel data under it. Text boxes do not provide for object fill.

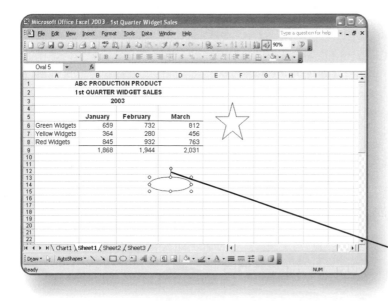

1. Double-click the **object** you want to change. The Format AutoShape dialog box will open.

NOTE

Even if you drew the selected oval or rectangle from the tools on the Drawing toolbar, Excel considers it an AutoShape.

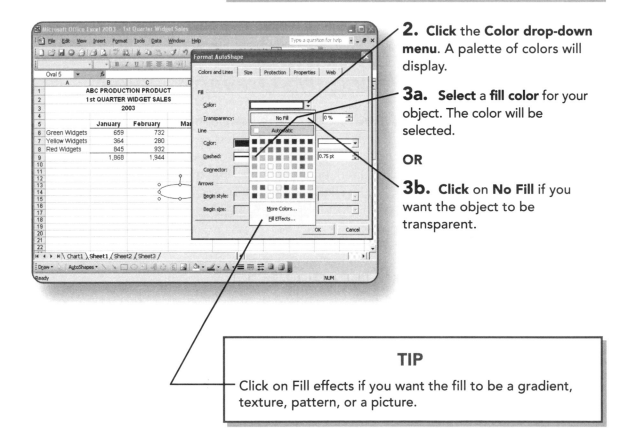

2. Click the **Color drop-down menu**. A palette of colors will display.

3a. Select a **fill color** for your object. The color will be selected.

OR

3b. Click on **No Fill** if you want the object to be transparent.

TIP

Click on Fill effects if you want the fill to be a gradient, texture, pattern, or a picture.

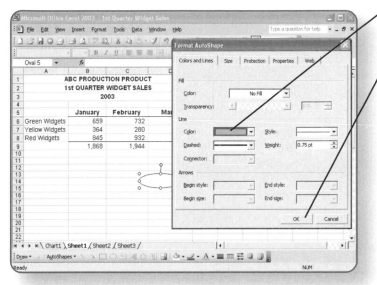

4. Select a **color** for the object border. The color will be selected.

5. Click on **OK**. The selected shape will take the new color attributes.

Adding Text to AutoShapes

When you create an AutoShape object, you can add text to it making it more informative and useful.

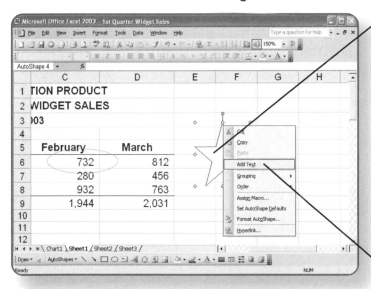

1. Right-click on the **drawn shape**. A shortcut menu will appear.

NOTE

If you selected an AutoShape from the Callouts category, the shape will be ready for text to be entered. You can skip steps 1 and 2.

2. Click on **Add Text**. The blinking insertion point will appear inside the AutoShape.

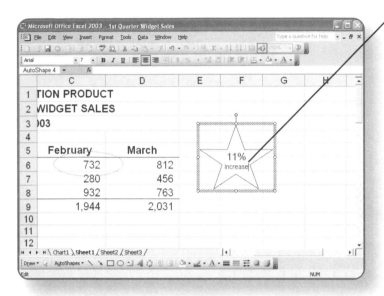

3. Type some **text**. The text will appear in the AutoShape object.

TIP

You can select and format the text font, size, color, or alignment in the same manner as any other worksheet text.

4. Click outside the **shape**. The blinking insertion point will disappear.

Creating Shadows

Shadows can add depth and visual interest to your AutoShape objects.

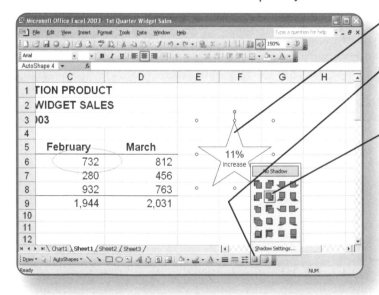

1. Click on the shape **object**. The object will be selected.

2. Click on the **Shadow Style button**. A palette with selections of shadows will appear.

3. Click on a shadow **option**. The shadow palette will close.

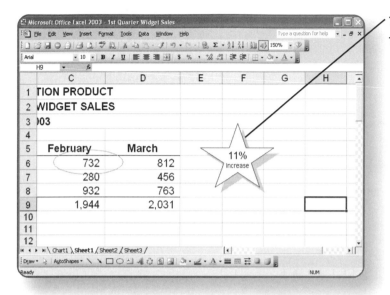

The shadow will appear around the shape.

Making Shapes 3-Dimensional

Make objects come alive by adding 3-dimensional effects! Some objects won't work with 3-dimensional shapes, so in those instances, the feature will not be available.

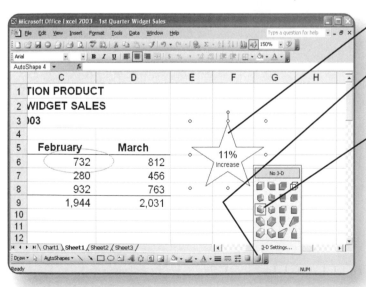

1. Click on the shape **object**. The object will be selected.

2. Click on the **3-D Style button**. A palette with selections of 3-D settings will appear.

3. Click on a 3-D **option**. The object will take on the added dimension.

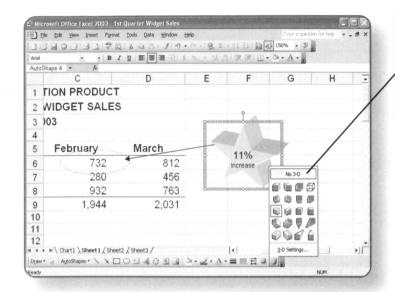

TIP

Remove 3-D settings by choosing No 3-D from the 3-D pallet.

Part III Review Questions

1. What is clip art? *See 'Inserting Clip Art' in Chapter 10*

2. Can you download images from your digital camera directly into an Excel worksheet? *See 'Inserting Images from Your Camera' in Chapter 10*

3. Why should you keep WordArt text to a single line of text? *See 'Adding WordArt' in Chapter 10*

4. What type of information do pie charts compare? *See 'Creating a Chart' in Chapter 11*

5. What are the two locations in a workbook where Excel can place a chart? *See 'Creating a Chart' in Chapter 11*

6. What are chart labels? *See 'Working with Labels' in Chapter 11*

7. What is a chart data table, and where does Excel place it? *See 'Displaying the Data Table' in Chapter 11*

8. What toolbar do you use to create drawn objects? *See 'Displaying the Drawing Toolbar' in Chapter 12*

9. What are AutoShapes? *See 'Working with AutoShapes' in Chapter 12*

10. What steps do you take to add text to an AutoShape? *See 'Adding Text to AutoShapes' in Chapter 12*

PART IV

Analyzing Data

13

Working with Data

Excel can store data that can be used in logical conditions such as sorting or filtering to locate specific pieces of information. This is called a *database*, and each row of related information is called a *record*. After you enter data into a worksheet, you may find it easier to locate particular pieces of information if the data were sorted. You can also create filters that specify to display only the data that meets certain criteria, and if you want, you can also stipulate that any data that meets the certain criteria be formatted in a specified pattern.

In this chapter, you'll learn how to:

- Sort data by rows and columns
- Filter your data for specific data
- Work with data subtotals
- Apply conditional formatting

Sorting

You can sort Excel data in ascending or descending order. In an ascending sort, Microsoft Excel sorts numbers first, then alphanumeric data. Ascending will sort alphabetically A through Z or numerically smallest to largest. Sorting descending will do just the opposite; it will sort alphabetically Z through A and numerically largest to smallest. Blank cells are always placed last, whether sorting in ascending or descending order.

Sorting with the Toolbar Buttons

Excel provides two buttons on the Standard toolbar to perform a simple sort, which is data sorted by a single column. If your data is in an inclusive arrangement, you can use the toolbar buttons to quickly sort by a specified column. One button, the AZ button, sorts the data in ascending order, and the other button, the ZA button, sorts in descending order.

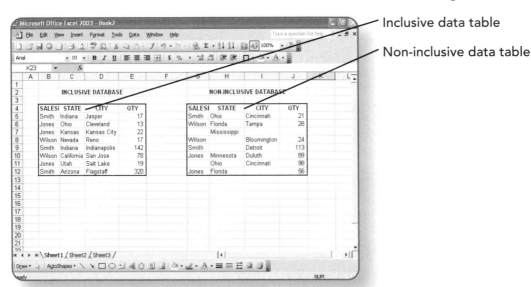

Inclusive data table

Non-inclusive data table

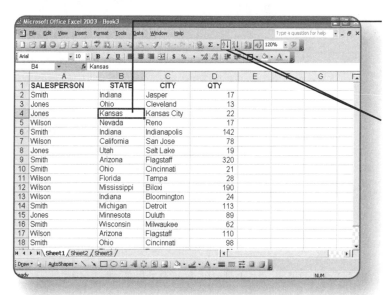

1. Click anywhere **in the column** you want to use to sort. Be sure only one cell is selected and not multiple cells—which can result in scrambled data.

2. Click on a **Sort button**. The table will be sorted.

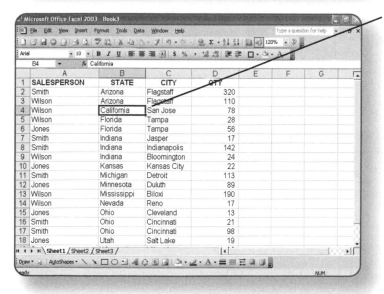

By sorting data in an inclusive arrangement, Excel knows to sort by the selected column, but also keep related data attached to the sorted data.

Sorting with the Sort Dialog Box

If you need to sort your data by more than a single column, you can use the Excel Sort dialog box. With the Sort dialog box, you can specify a column for a secondary or even a third sort. The most common sort is to sort the individual rows in a particular column. You create a secondary sort if two items in the first column are the same.

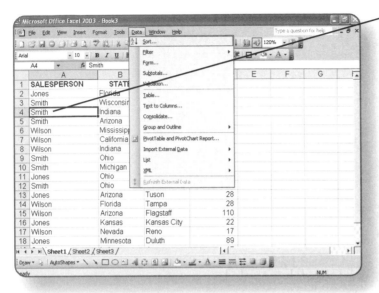

1. Click anywhere in the **data table or,** if the data is in a non-inclusive arrangement, **click and drag** to highlight all the **cells** you want to sort. Be sure to include any cells pertaining to the column you want to sort by. Any cell outside the selected area will not be included in the sort. If your data has a header row, select that data also.

TIP

If there is data in adjacent columns and you highlight only a portion of the data table, Excel will inquire if you meant to include the adjacent columns.

2. Click on **Data**. The Data menu will appear.

3. Click on **Sort**. The Sort dialog box will open.

The Sort dialog box provides the option to sort by three different fields.

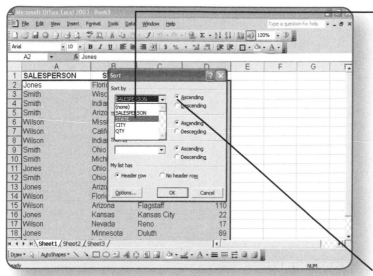

4. Select the **first column** you want to sort by. The column name will appear in the Sort by box.

NOTE

If your data has a header row, Excel will indicate the columns by the header explanation. If there is no header row, Excel will reference the columns by the column letter.

5. Click on **Ascending or Descending**. The option will be selected.

6. Select the **second field** you want to sort by if two or more items in the first column are the same.

7. Click on **Ascending or Descending**. The option will be selected.

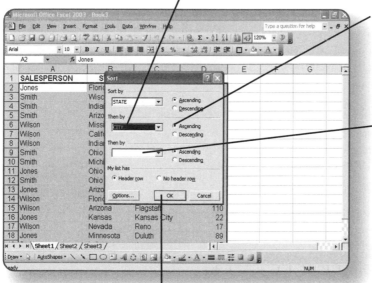

TIP

Optionally, you can specify a third method to sort by if two or more items are the same in both the first field and the second field. To sort by more than three fields, sort the list twice beginning with the least important field.

8. Click on **OK**. Excel will sort the data by the fields you specified.

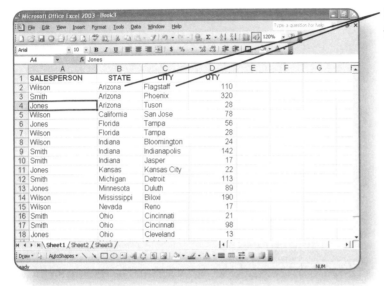

In this example, the data was first sorted by state, then by city.

Sorting by Dates

If you sort by a column of months, Excel will attempt to put them in alphabetical order—April, August, December, February, and so forth. You can, however, prompt Excel to recognize these cells as months and to sort them accordingly. You can also apply these same principles to sorting by days of the week.

There is a certain format dates must use when sorting. The months or days must be either spelled in their entirety or abbreviated with three characters and no period (such as Jan or Fri). Using any other abbreviation or punctuation will make the data sort incorrectly.

1. Select the **data table** you want to sort. The cells will be highlighted.

2. Click on **Data**. The Data menu will appear.

3. Click on **Sort**. The Sort dialog box will appear.

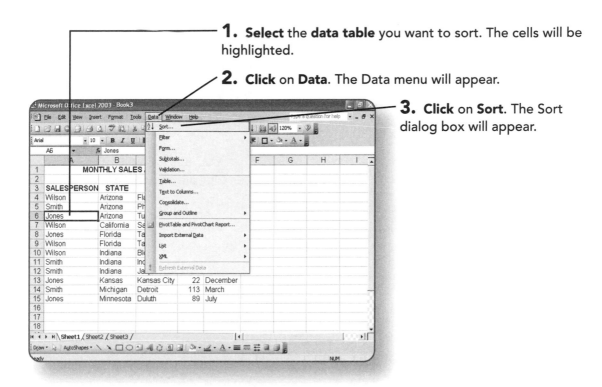

4. Select the **months column** as your primary sort field.

5. Select Ascending or Descending. The option will be selected.

6. Indicate whether your selection includes a **header row**. Header rows are not included in a sort.

7. Click on **Options**. The Sort Options dialog box will open.

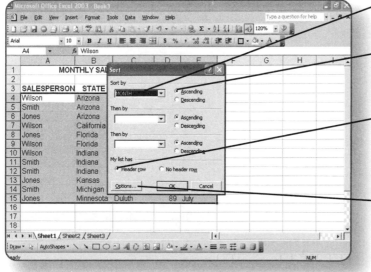

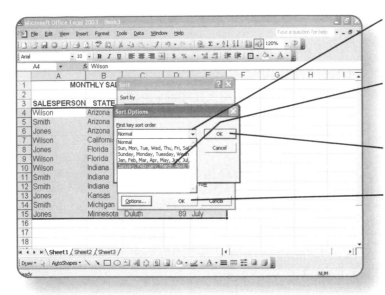

8. Click the **First key sort order drop-down menu**. A list of options will appear.

9. Click on the **pattern** you used for your data. The option will be selected.

10. Click on **OK**. The Sort Options dialog box will close.

11. Click on **OK**. The Sort dialog box will close.

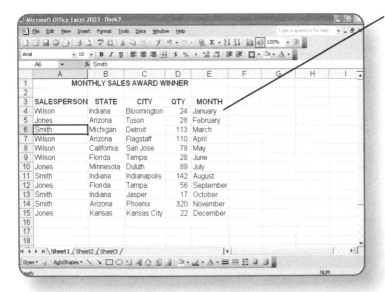

Excel will sort the data by month or day.

Using Filters

When you have a database of information, there are times when you do not want to see all the data you entered, only the data that meets criteria you specify. You can search for entries that match the criteria exactly or data that matches other operators, such as greater than, less than, begins with, or does not equal.

Working with AutoFilter

A very useful tool included with Excel is the *AutoFilter*, which can help you search and extract specific data from your worksheet.

1. **Click** on any **cell** of your database. The cell will be selected.

2. **Click** on **Data**. The Data menu will appear.

3. **Click** on **Filter**. The Filter submenu will appear.

4. **Click** on **AutoFilter**. Excel will display an AutoFilter arrow at the top of each column in your database.

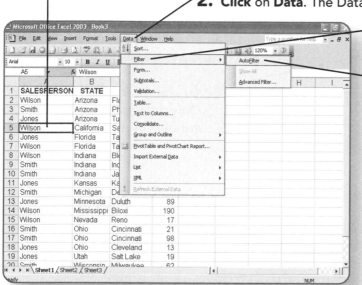

5. **Click** an **arrow**. Excel will display a list of options for that column.

The AutoFilter arrows at the top of each column allow you to select records from the following options:

- **All**. Displays all line items.

- **Top 10**. Displays the 10 most repeated or highest values in a field.

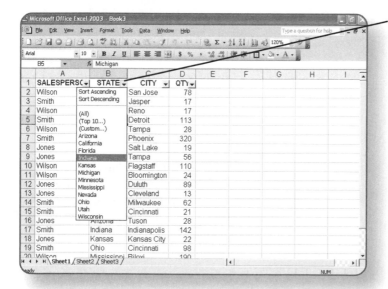

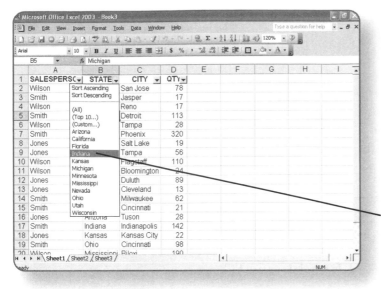

- **Custom**. Displays items that meet your specific requirements. You'll learn about custom filters in the next section.

- **Exact items**. Displays a complete list of the items in the column. You can click one, and only the records that contain that item will display.

6. Select an **item** from the list. Only the items that match the criteria you chose will appear.

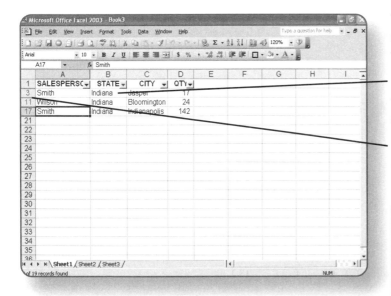

The arrows on a filtered column are displayed in a different color than the others.

In this example, only records from the State of Indiana are displayed.

Rows containing data that does not match your criteria are hidden.

TIP

To further isolate specific items, click the AutoFilter arrow in another column and select an item from the list.

You may want to redisplay all rows and perform a different filter.

7. Click on **Data**. The Data menu will appear.

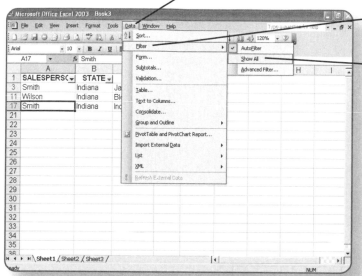

8. Click on **Filter**. The Filter submenu will appear.

9. Click on **Show All**. All the hidden rows become visible.

TIP

Click on AutoFilter again if you no longer want the AutoFilter feature active.

Creating Custom Filters

Using the AutoFilter Custom filter allows you to perform searches on your database for items with a range, or for items that meet a specific set of requirements.

You need the AutoFilter feature to be active to create the custom filter. If the AutoFilter is not active, follow the steps you learned in the previous section.

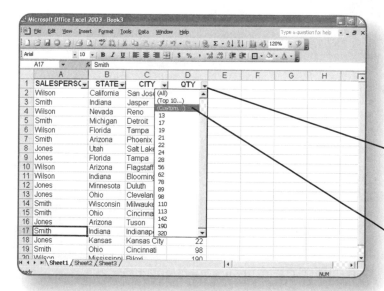

1. Click on the **AutoFilter arrow** at the top of the column you want to search. A list of options will appear.

2. Click on **Custom**. The Custom AutoFilter dialog box will open.

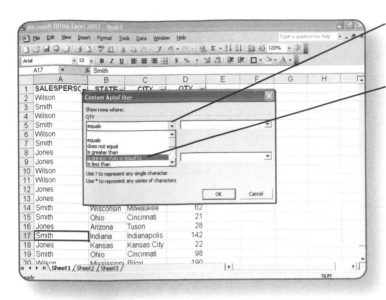

3. Click on the **first drop-down menu**. A list of operators will appear.

4. Click on the **operator** you want to use. The operator will appear in the box.

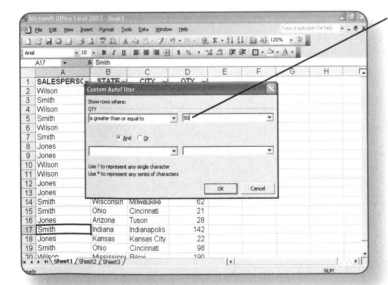

5. Enter the **value** you want to match the operator. The value will appear in the text box.

NOTE

Filter searches are not case sensitive and you can use a wildcard in the value box. Use a question mark (?) to represent a single character or the asterisk (*) to represent a group of characters. For example, entering I* in a box would find INDIANA, IOWA, ICE CREAM, and IDEA. If you typed D?N, Excel would find DAN, DON, or DEN.

If you specify a second filter, you need to specify the request with an AND or an OR option. If you select the AND option, the data must match both requirements you specify. If you select the OR option, the data must match one set or the other, but not necessarily both requirements.

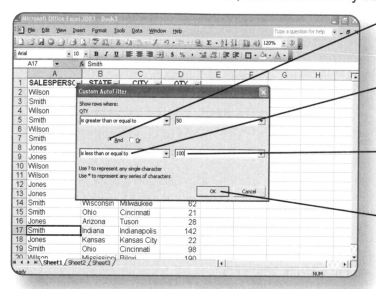

6. Select the **AND or** the **OR option**. The option will be selected.

7. Optionally, **select** a second filter **operator**. The operator will appear in the second box.

8. Enter the **value** you want to match the second operator. The value will appear in the text box.

9. Click on **OK**. Excel will filter the data according to your specifications.

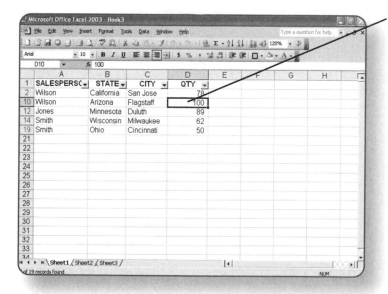

In this example, only those records with sales values between 50 and 100, inclusively, are displayed.

TIP

You can use the sort feature to sort any filtered list.

Data Subtotals

If your database contains numerical data, Excel can look at your database and create subtotals and grand totals, which can help you manage and analyze your data. Before creating subtotals, you must first sort the database by the field you want to subtotal. You can then calculate subtotals for any column that contains numbers.

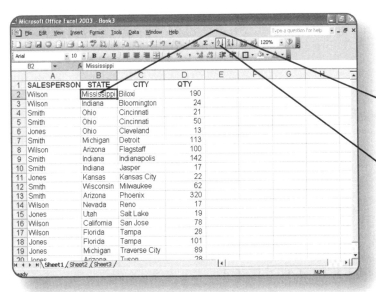

1. Click in the **column** you want to create subtotals. The cell will be selected.

2. Click on a **Sort button**. The sort can be ascending or descending.

3. Click on **Data**. The Data menu will appear.

4. Click on **Subtotals**. The Subtotal dialog box will open.

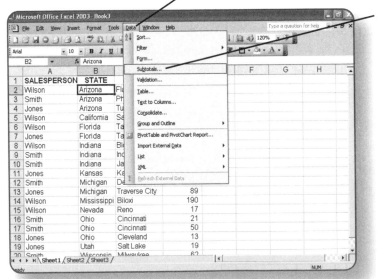

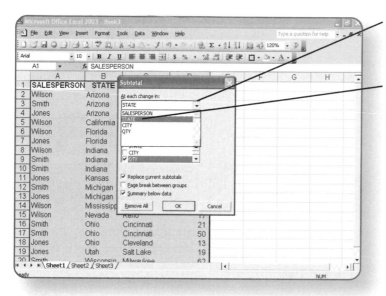

5. Click on the **At each change in drop-down menu**. A list of columns will appear.

6. Click on the **field** by which you want to create the subtotal break. This must be the field you sorted your data by.

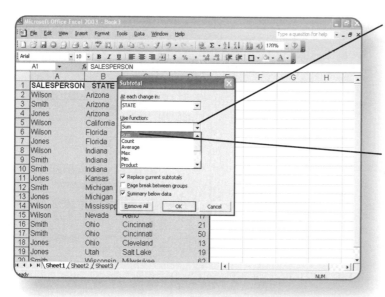

7. Click the **Use function drop-down menu**. A list of functions will appear.

You can create subtotals with a summary function, such as Sum, Average, Max, or Min.

8. Select the **summary function** you want to use.

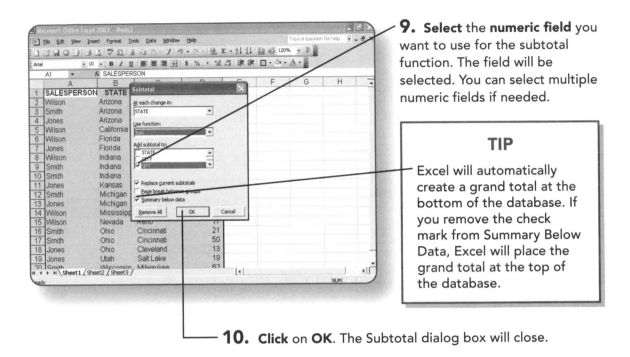

9. Select the **numeric field** you want to use for the subtotal function. The field will be selected. You can select multiple numeric fields if needed.

TIP

Excel will automatically create a grand total at the bottom of the database. If you remove the check mark from Summary Below Data, Excel will place the grand total at the top of the database.

10. Click on **OK**. The Subtotal dialog box will close.

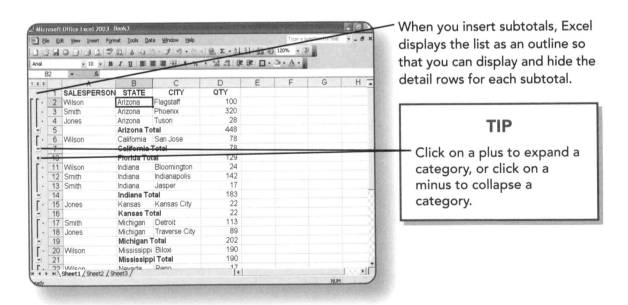

When you insert subtotals, Excel displays the list as an outline so that you can display and hide the detail rows for each subtotal.

TIP

Click on a plus to expand a category, or click on a minus to collapse a category.

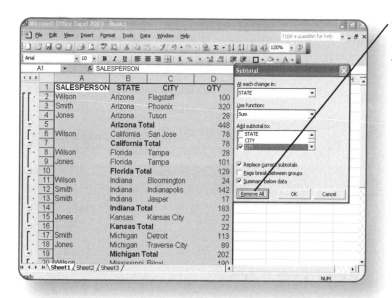

To remove the subtotals, click on the Remove All button from the Subtotal dialog box.

Conditional Formatting

When you use conditional formatting, you can instruct Excel to change the formatting for a cell if the cell's value meets a certain criteria. For example, if the sales for a particular salesperson meets a quota, you could have Excel add blue shading and a border to the cell.

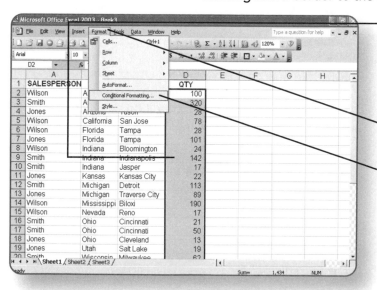

1. Select the **cell or multiple cells** with the contents you want to format with conditional formatting. The cell will be selected.

2. Click on **Format**. The Format menu will appear.

3. Click on **Conditional Formatting**. The Conditional Formatting dialog box will appear.

The second drop-down menu provides a list of operators such as greater than, less than, equal to, and between.

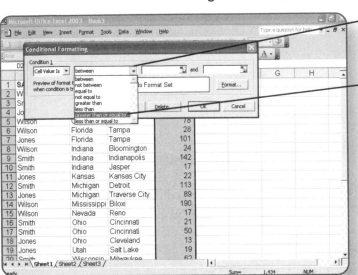

4. Click on the **operator drop-down menu**. A list of operators will appear.

5. Select the **operator** you want to use. Depending on which operator you select, you will see one or two more boxes to the right of the operator box. These are the value boxes.

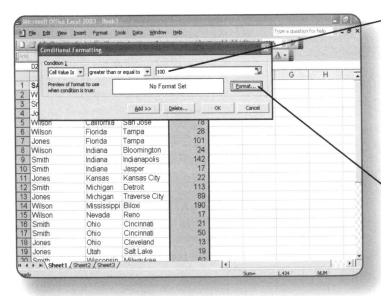

6. Enter the **value** you want to check in the value box. If there is a second box, enter a second value.

Now you must specify the formatting you want applied if the condition you just specified is met.

7. Click on the **Format button**. The Format Cells dialog box will open.

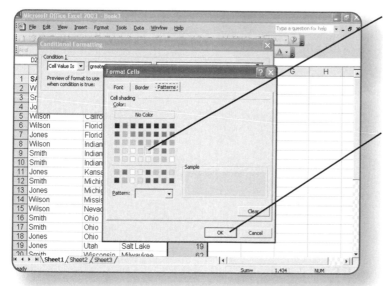

8. Specify the **formatting** you want Excel to apply if the condition is met. You can apply as many available attributes as you need. Font and font size changes are not permitted.

9. Click on **OK**. The Format Cells dialog box will close.

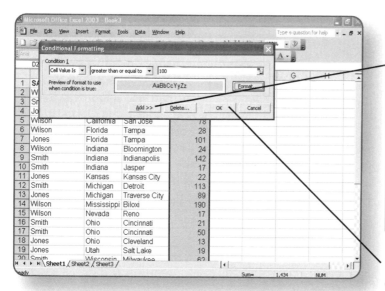

TIP

You can also specify a second or third condition. For example, if the sales quota is reached, the cell becomes yellow, but if the value reaches 125 percent of quota, the cell values become bold. Click on the Add button to add additional conditions.

10. Click on **OK**. Excel will check the cell for the conditions you specified.

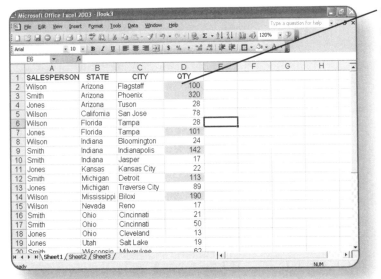

In this example, Excel placed shading on the cells with a value greater than or equal to 100.

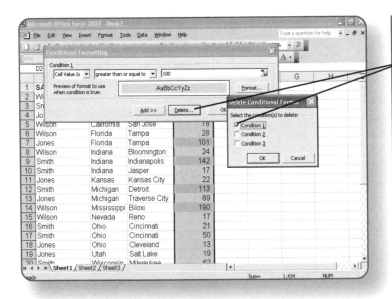

TIP

To remove conditional formatting, select the cells and reopen the Conditional Formatting dialog box. Click the Delete button, then select the conditions you want to delete.

14

Discovering Tools for Speed and Quality

Excel includes tools that help speed up the process of creating and editing spreadsheets, such as tools that locate mistakes and correct them automatically, tools that check your spelling, and—new to this version of Excel—the Research task pane which assists you, with the help of the Internet, in locating information about a specified topic.

In this chapter, you'll learn how to:

- Work with Excel's spell check feature
- Use AutoCorrect
- Discover the research tools
- Check the worksheet for errors
- Review smart tags

Checking the Spelling

Excel has a built-in dictionary that it uses to check your worksheet for misspellings. This feature isn't infallible; if you type air instead of err, Excel probably won't be able to tell you that you're wrong. However, combined with good proofreading, spell check can be very helpful.

TIP

Excel works best if you begin the spell check at the beginning of your worksheet—cell A1.

---

1. Click on **Tools**. The Tools menu will appear.

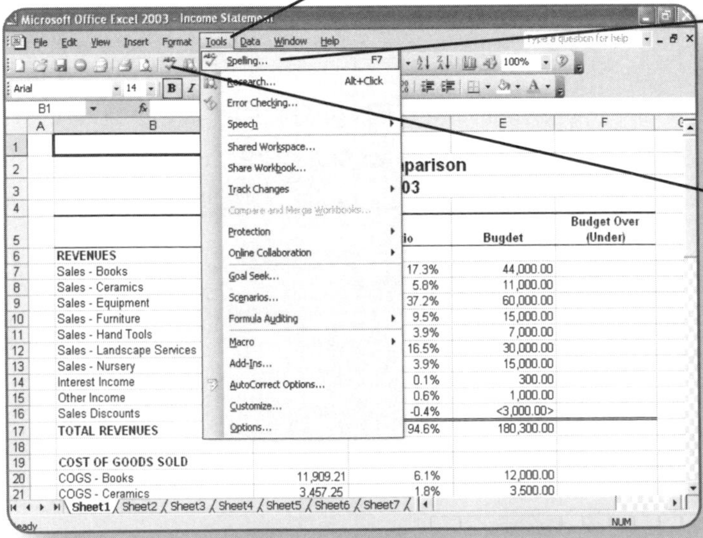

2. Click on **Spelling**. The Spelling dialog box will open.

TIP

Optionally, click on the Spelling button.

Excel will highlight the cell with the first potential misspelling and suggest changes.

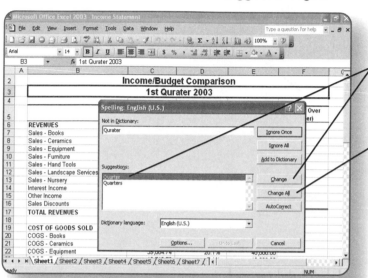

3. Select one of the following options:

- **Click** on a **suggestion, then click Change** to change just this incident of the spelling mistake.

- **Click** on **Change All** if you think you could have made the mistake more than once.

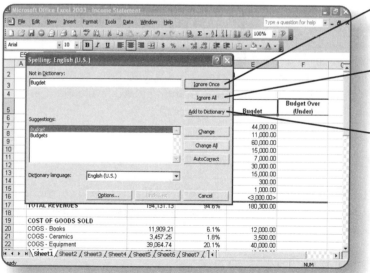

- **Click** on **Ignore Once** if you don't want to correct this instance of the spelling.

- **Click** on **Ignore All** if you don't want to correct any instances of the spelling.

- **Click** on **Add to Dictionary** to add a word, such as a proper name or legal term, to Excel's built-in dictionary so that it won't be flagged as an error in the future.

After you choose one of these actions, Excel will proceed to the next possible error.

When all potential mistakes have been identified, Excel will notify you that the spelling check is complete.

4. Click on **OK**. The message box will close.

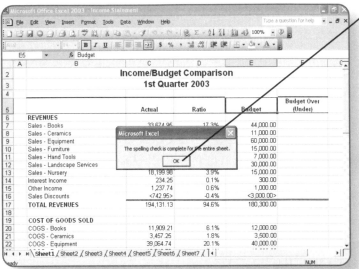

Working with AutoCorrect

AutoCorrect is a great feature. You type something wrong, and Excel automatically corrects it. Or, you type something like (c), and Excel understands that what you really want is a symbol for copyright, and it inserts ©.

Activating AutoCorrect Features

To take full advantage of this wonderful automatic correction feature, you have to understand how it works and how to customize it.

1. **Click** on **Tools**. The Tools menu will appear.

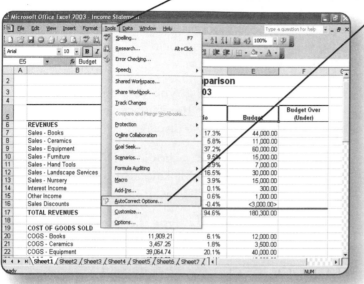

2. **Click** on **AutoCorrect Options**. The AutoCorrect dialog box will open with the AutoCorrect tab in front.

A check mark will appear next to the features that are activated.

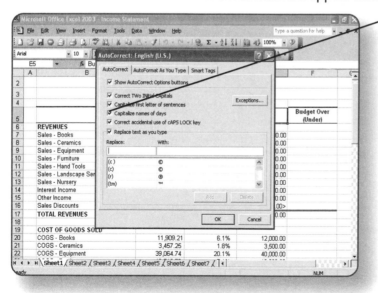

3. **Click** on an **option** to remove the check mark. The option will be turned off. If an option doesn't have a check mark next to it, **click** on the **option** to add a check mark. The option will be turned on.

Adding AutoCorrect Entries

If you know that you commonly make the same typing mistake, such as "clcik" when it should be "click," you can tell Excel to fix it for you.

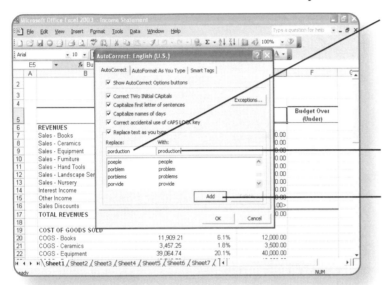

1. Type your **common mistake** in the Replace text box. The text will display.

2. Click in the **With text box**. A blinking insertion point will display.

3. Type the **correct version.** The text will display.

4. Click on **Add.**

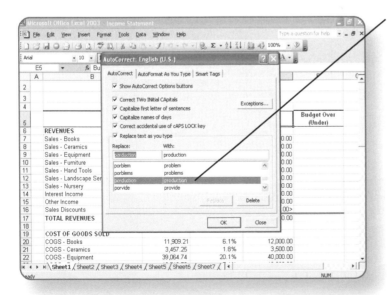

The word will be added to your permanent AutoCorrect list. Now, Excel will automatically correct your mistake each time you type it.

Deleting AutoCorrect Entries

What if you're entering data using a common term spelled slightly different? For example, you are entering data for a company called "ACN" and Excel thinks you meant "CAN." Or, you use "(c)" to indicate headings in a cell, and Excel keeps changing this to the copyright symbol? Just as easily as you could add an entry to the AutoCorrect list, you can delete entries as well.

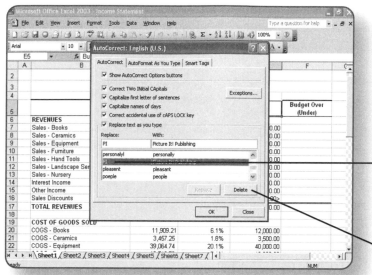

1. **Click** on an **entry** from the AutoCorrect list. The entry will appear in the Replace and With text boxes.

2. **Click** on **Delete**. The entry will be deleted.

Using the Excel Research Tools

A new feature and a powerful gem included with Excel is the Research Library, which is a built-in research tool that allows you to search various information sources. Some of these research sources are built into Office and others are external services and require an Internet connection to use them. The following list describes just a few of the tools the research pane can provide:

• Reference tools and sites such as translation tools and a thesaurus

• Web research sites such as Encarta Encyclopedia, Factiva, and eLibrary

• Business and financial sites such as MSN Money and Gale

> **NOTE**
>
> Factiva provides news content from such sources as Dow Jones, Reuters Newswires, and The Wall Street Journal, and eLibrary is an archive for maps, photos, major newspapers, and magazines. Gale is an information provider used by many libraries, schools, and businesses.

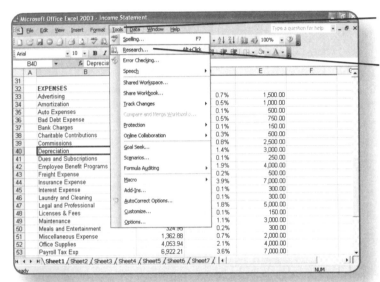

1. Click on **Tools**. The Tools menu will appear.

2. Click on **Research**. Excel will display the research library as a task pane.

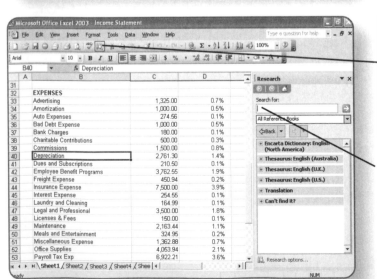

> **TIP**
>
> Optionally, click on the Research button to open or close the Research task pane.

3. Click in the **Search for text box**. A blinking insertion point will appear.

TIP

Hold down the Alt key and click on text in your worksheet to automatically open the Research pane. Excel will automatically place the text into the Search for text box.

4. Type in the **text** you want to search in the Search for text box. The text could be a word or phrase.

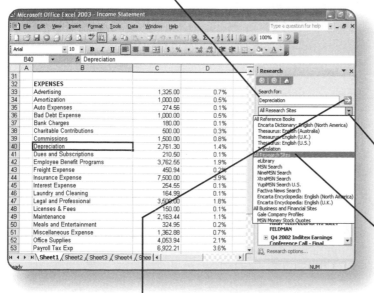

Resources are grouped into several classifications including reference books such as a dictionary or a thesaurus, Web research sites such as eLibrary and Factiva, and Web financial sites such as MSN Money or Gale.

5. Click on the **down arrow** next to the resource list. A list of available research services will appear.

6. Select the **research source** type you would like to use. The name will appear in the resource list.

7. Click on the **Go arrow**. Excel will access the selected research source.

Navigating the Research Pane

The Research task pane offers a Back and Forward button similar to a Web browser for reviewing previous searches. The Research task pane displays the results of the search.

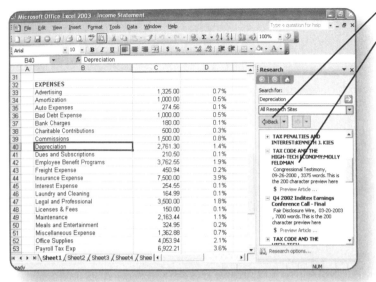

The Back button

Several articles regarding depreciation from different news sources through eLibrary

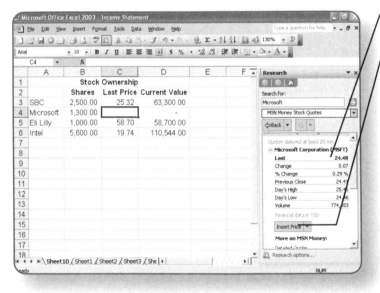

A stock price quote through MSN Money

Click on Insert price to insert the stock information into the current file.

Translating Words

The Research pane can help you translate a word, phrase, or your entire worksheet into various languages.

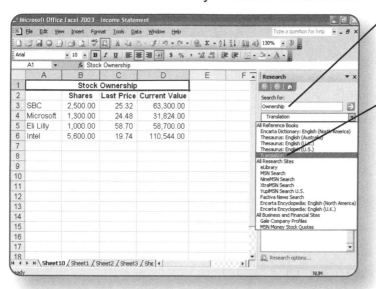

1. **Type** the **word or phrase** you want translated in the Search for box. The text will appear in the Search for text box.

2. **Select Translation** from the research service list. Translation options will appear.

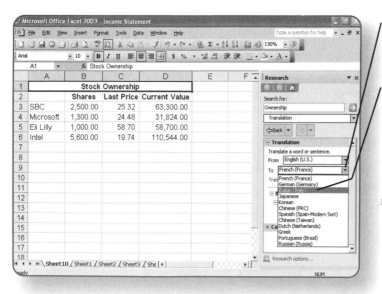

3. **Click** the **To language arrow**. A list of available languages will appear.

4. **Select** the **language** you want to translate to.

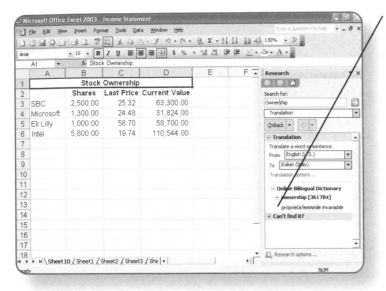

Excel will display the translated word or phrase along with any other available options.

Checking for Errors

Since the Excel worksheet displays the results of a formula calculation, it's sometimes difficult to tell if there is an error in your formula which could be giving you erroneous values. Excel includes an Error Checking feature which reviews the worksheet formulas for potential errors then describes and offers to help correct the problem. Here are a few of the formula errors Excel tries to note with the Error Checking feature:

- Formulas that result in an error message such as the divide by zero error.

- References used in a formula that are not consistent with those in the adjacent formulas

- Formulas that omit cells in an area

- Unlocked cells containing formulas in a protected worksheet

- Formulas referencing empty cells

1. Click on **Tools**. The Tools menu will appear.

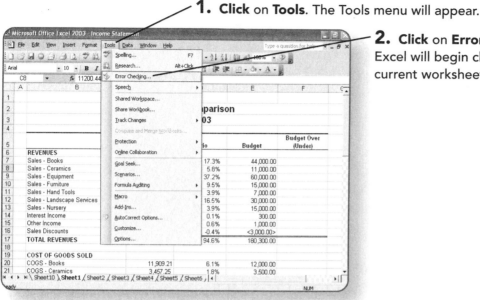

2. Click on **Error Checking**. Excel will begin checking the current worksheet for errors.

If Excel locates a potential error, it will highlight the cell and display the Error Checking dialog box.

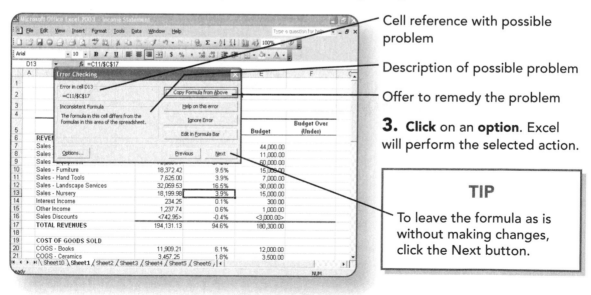

Cell reference with possible problem

Description of possible problem

Offer to remedy the problem

3. Click on an **option**. Excel will perform the selected action.

TIP

To leave the formula as is without making changes, click the Next button.

If no more errors are found, Excel will display a message box stating the error check is complete.

4. Click on **OK**. The message box will close.

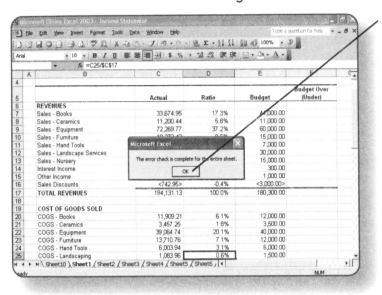

Understanding Smart Tags

Excel recognizes certain types of data that it labels with a very powerful, time-saving feature called smart tags. There are several types of smart tags, some of which look at your data entry and recognize it as a particular type of data or as a formula with a potential problem. The smart tag indicators appear in the cell on your worksheet as you type. The types of actions you can take depend on the data that Excel recognizes and labels with a smart tag.

By default, smart tags are turned off, so you need to activate the feature to take advantage of its help.

1. Click on **Tools**. The Tools menu will appear.

2. Click on **AutoCorrect Options**. The AutoCorrect Options dialog box will open.

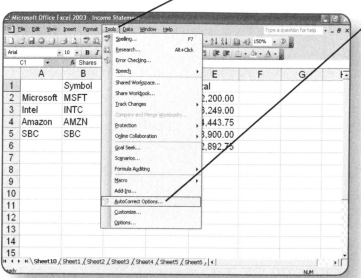

3. Click on the **Smart Tags tab**. The smart tags tab will come to the front.

4. Click on **Label data with smart tags**. The feature will be activated.

5. Click on **OK**. The AutoCorrect Options dialog box will close.

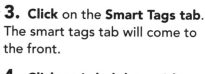

Some categories of smart tags include the following:

- Error Checking smart tags look for potential errors in the same manner as the Error Checking feature.

- Paste smart tags appear over cells that have been pasted and offer options about pasting the data, such as whether to include formatting, values, or both.

- Financial smart tags appear over a cell with a US stock symbol and offers options to check stock prices and other financial information.

- Outlook Name smart tags look for names in the worksheet that cross reference to entries in your Microsoft Outlook contact list.

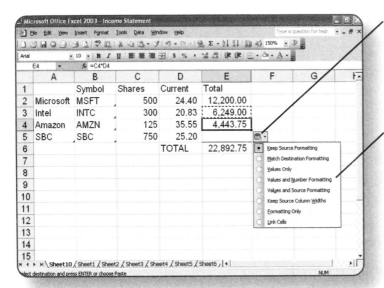

6. Click on a SmartTag **icon**. A list of options will appear.

7. Optionally, **click** on a smart tag **option**. The selected action will occur.

Paste smart tag options include options to paste with or without formatting.

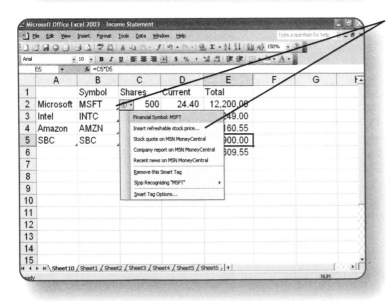

Financial smart tags are indicated by a purple triangle in the lower-right corner of a worksheet cell.

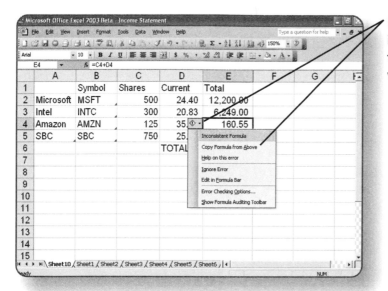

Error Checking smart tags are indicated by a small green triangle in the upper left of a worksheet cell.

15

Customizing Excel

Excel includes a series of preset behavior patterns—patterns which determine where and how your files are saved, where Excel should move the insertion point, how items on the screen are displayed, and many other options. You can control Excel's behavior patterns by modifying preferences.

Excel begins with a blank worksheet; however, sometimes you have a worksheet where you use the same layout over and over again. Instead of retyping and reformating the headings, categories, and other information that you entered in a previous worksheet, you can use an Excel template to store the static information and produce your professional looking worksheet by entering just the new data.

In this chapter, you'll learn how to:

- Modify Excel preferences
- Open an Excel template
- Save a template
- Modify a template

Setting Preferences

Some Excel preferences modify the way Excel displays on your screen while others enable timesaving or safety features. There are so many ways to customize Excel, the Options dialog box is broken into 13 different tabs.

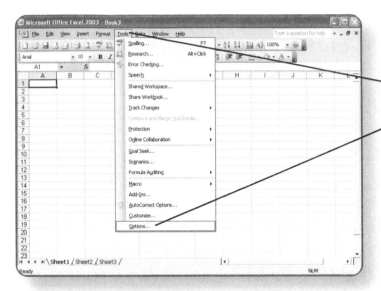

1. **Click** on **Tools**. The Tools menu will appear.

2. **Click** on **Options**. The Options dialog box will appear.

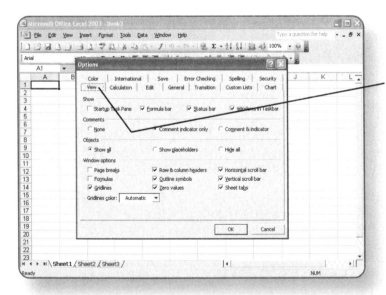

Each of the 13 tabs contains a number of settings pertaining to the tab topic:

- **View**. The View tab controls what and how Excel displays items on the screen such as the status bar or formulas.

- **Calculation**. The Calculation tab controls the calculation procedures Excel should follow when working with formulas.

- **Edit**. The Edit tab controls the direction Excel should move after you press the Enter key as well as other options pertaining to editing data in a worksheet cell.

- **General**. The General tab controls the default font in a blank worksheet, the default file location, the default number of worksheets in a workbook, and other general options.

- **Transition**. The Transition tab provides options to help former Lotus 1-2-3 users make an easier transition to Excel.

- **Custom Lists**. The Custom Lists tab allows you to create your own customized lists that you use with the Excel Fill feature. You used the Fill feature in Chapter 3, "Editing a Worksheet."

- **Chart**. The Chart tab contains a few default options for working with charts. You discovered working with charts in Chapter 11, "Creating Charts from Excel Data."

- **Color**. The Color tab is where you can set your default color selection for new Excel worksheets.

- **International**. The International tab allows you to set different Excel international preferences than those used by your Windows operating system.

- **Save**. The Save tab stores the setting for Excel's AutoRecover feature. You learned about AutoRecover in Chapter 2, "Creating a Simple Worksheet."

- **Error Checking**. The Error Checking tab maintains options for Excel's automatic error checking. Error checking was discussed in Chapter 14, "Discovering Tools for Speed and Quality."

- **Spelling**. The Spelling tab tells Excel where to locate the dictionary used to check spelling. You learned about spelling in Chapter 14.

- **Security**. The Security tab holds passwords to access or edit the current workbook. You will learn more about security features including passwords in Chapter 18, "Collaborating with Others."

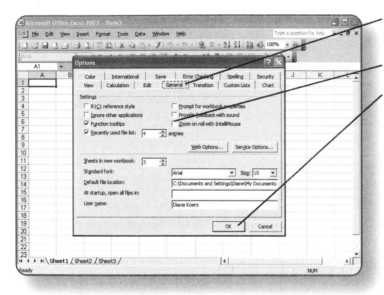

3. Click on a **tab**. A list of options will appear.

4. Select any desired **options**.

5. Click on **OK**. The Options dialog box will close and the new options will take effect.

NOTE

With the exception of the Security tab options, most options affect all, not just the current, Excel workbooks.

Working with Templates

Excel includes several common templates including a Balance Sheet, Expense Statement, Loan Amortization, and Timecard. Each template provides formatting, sample text, and formulas suited to the particular task. Many more templates are also available online from the Microsoft.com website.

Using a Predefined Template

You access templates from the Excel task pane. Excel calls their templates "Spreadsheet Solutions."

1. **Click** on **File**. The File menu will appear.

2. **Click** on **New**. The task pane will reopen if not already on the screen.

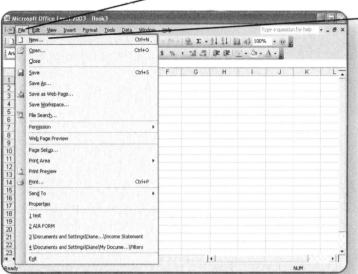

3. **Click** on **On my computer**. The Templates dialog box will open.

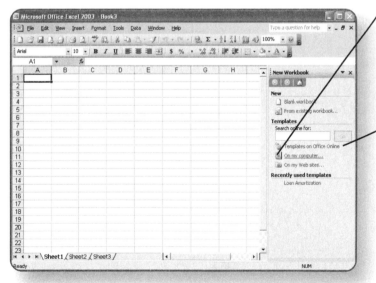

TIP

Click on Templates on Office Online to see a plethora of other Excel templates—some created by Excel, others created by Excel users who want to share their template with others.

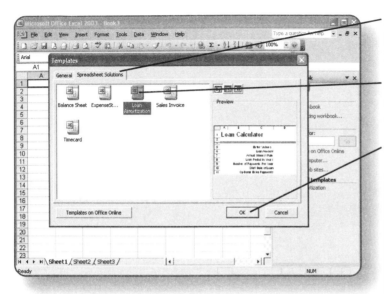

4. **Click** on the **Spreadsheet Solutions tab**. A selection of templates will appear.

5. **Click** on the **template** you want to use. The template name will be highlighted.

6. **Click** on **OK**.

NOTE

The first time you use these templates, Excel may prompt you for your Office CD.

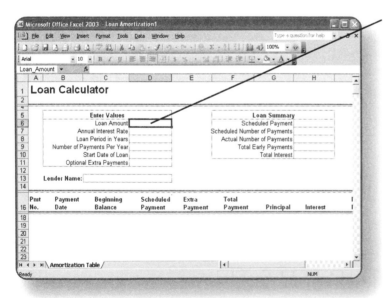

An unnamed, unsaved copy of the predefined template will appear on your screen, including formatting and formulas, ready for you to enter your own data.

Saving a Template

If you have a worksheet you use regularly, but create a new version of the worksheet each time, save it first as a template. Then when you need a new sheet, the preliminary work will be complete and ready for you.

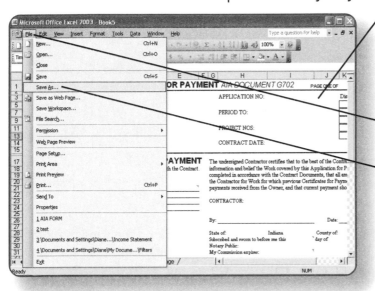

1. Create the **worksheet** including formulas and formatting, but omit any actual variable data. The worksheet will appear on your screen.

2. Click on **File**. The File menu will appear.

3. Click on **Save As**. The Save As dialog box will open.

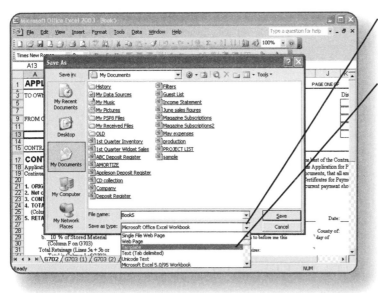

4. Click on the **Save as type down arrow**. A list of options will appear.

5. Click on **Template**.

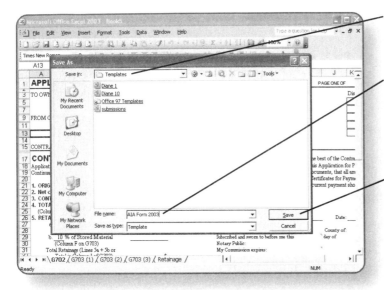

Excel will automatically change the Save in folder to the Templates folder.

6. Type a **descriptive name** for the template such as ABC Invoice or Monthly Sales Report. The name you type will appear in the Name box.

7. Click on **Save**. Excel will save the template.

8. Click on the **Close box** to close the existing file template. You are ready to use the newly saved template whenever you need it.

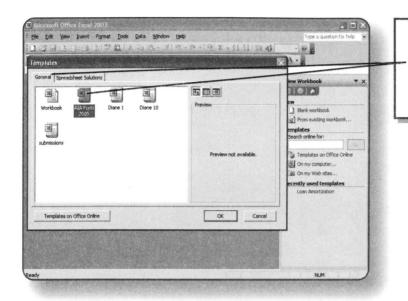

Editing a Template

If you find an error on the template or need to change the master copy, you can easily edit any template you create. Template changes affect only new worksheets based on the template. It does not change any existing saved worksheets based on the template.

1. Click on **File**. The File menu will appear.

2. Click on **Open**. The Open dialog box will open.

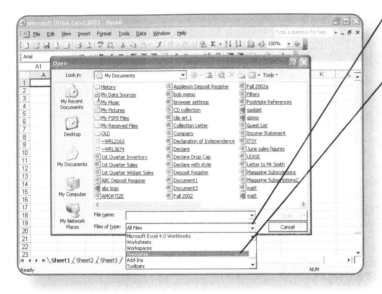

3. Click on the **Files of type down arrow**. A list of file types will appear.

4. Scroll down and click on **Templates**. The Look in folder will change to the Templates folder.

NOTE

Typically, Excel will store Office templates in the C:\Documents and Settings\ your name\Application Data\Microsoft\Templates folder.

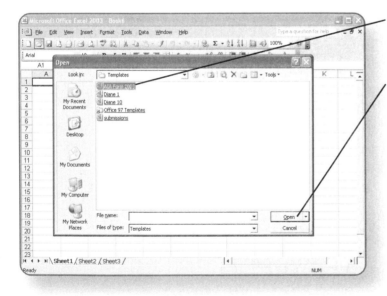

5. Click on the **template** you want to modify. The template name will be highlighted.

6. Click on **Open**. Excel will display the actual template on the screen.

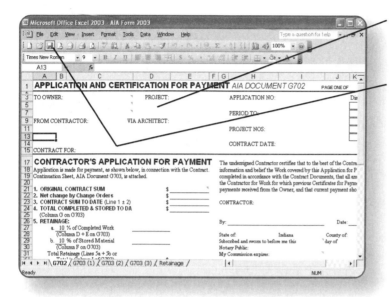

7. Make any desired **modifications**. The changes will appear on your screen.

8. Click on the **Save button**. The template file will be updated.

Deleting a Template

If you no longer want a template, you can easily delete it. You delete the file through the Open dialog box.

1. Click on **File**. The File menu will appear.

2. Click on **Open**. The Open dialog box will open.

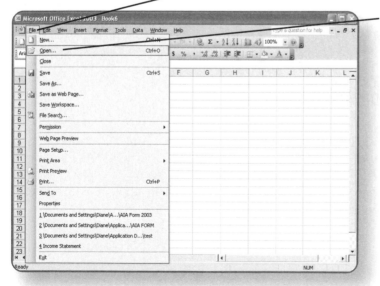

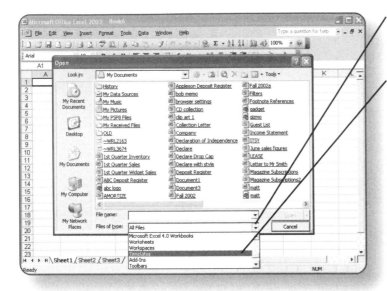

3. Click on the **Files of type down arrow**. A list of file types will appear.

4. Scroll down and click on **Templates**. The Look in folder will change to the Templates folder.

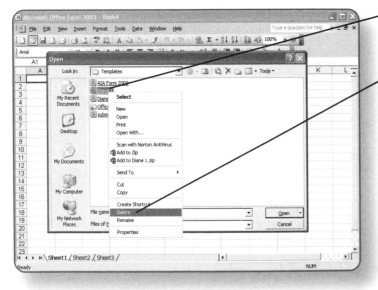

5. Right-click on the **template** you want to delete. A shortcut menu will appear.

6. Click on **Delete**. A confirmation dialog box will open.

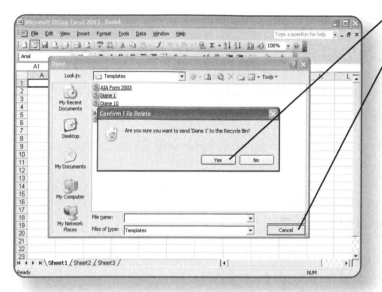

7. Click on **Yes**. Excel will delete the template.

8. Click on **Cancel**. The Open dialog box will close.

Part IV Review Questions

1. When working with an Excel database, where do you find records? *See 'Working with Data' in Chapter 13*

2. By default, if you sort a column of months, how will Excel display them? *See 'Sorting by Dates' in Chapter 13*

3. What character represents a single character in a filter search? *See 'Creating Custom Filters' in Chapter 13*

4. Before creating data subtotals, how must you sort an Excel worksheet? *See 'Subtotaling Data' in Chapter 13*

5. What does AutoCorrect do? *See 'Working with AutoCorrect' in Chapter 14*

6. What is the name of Excel's built-in research tool that allows you to search various information sources? *See 'Using the Excel Research Tools' in Chapter 14*

7. What feature does Excel provide that can spot potential formula errors? *See 'Checking for Errors' in Chapter 14*

8. Name three of the Smart Tags you might see on an Excel worksheet? *See 'Understanding Smart Tags' in Chapter 14*

9. Does changing options affect only the current workbook? *See 'Setting Preferences' in Chapter 15*

10. What types of items are provided in an Excel template? *See 'Working with Templates' in Chapter 15*

PART V

Integrating Excel Technology

16

Integrating Excel with Word

Microsoft Word is the word processing application portion of Microsoft Office. You use Word to create documents such as letters, memos, or proposals. Excel and Word work nicely together so you can combine an Excel worksheet with a Word document. For example, you can create a memo in Word that contains financial data you created in Excel.

In this chapter, you'll learn how to:

- Create an Excel worksheet from within Word
- Insert an existing Excel worksheet into a Word document
- Import Word data into Excel

TIP

If you are not familiar with using Microsoft Word, you should consider purchasing *Microsoft Office Word 2003 Fast and Easy*, ISBN 1-59200-080-0.

Using Excel Worksheets in Word

While you are in Microsoft Word, you can create an Excel worksheet in the document. The worksheet is part of and saved as part of the Word file. The process of saving a document created by an outside application inside of another application is called *embedding.*

Creating an Excel Worksheet from Within Word

The fastest method to insert an Excel worksheet is to use the Toolbar button available in Word.

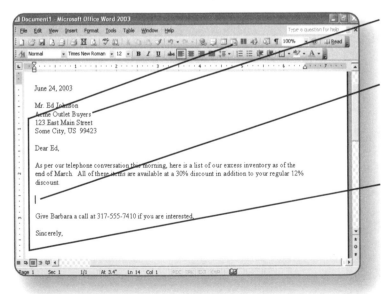

1. Type some **text** in a Word document. The text will appear on the screen.

2. Click in the Word **document** at the location you want your Excel worksheet to appear. A blinking insertion point will appear at that location.

3. Click on the **Insert Microsoft Excel Worksheet button**. A grid will appear under the button.

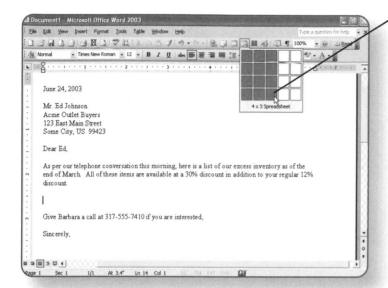

4. Click and drag over the **grid** until you highlight the number of rows and columns you want in your worksheet. The number of rows and columns will appear at the bottom of the grid.

NOTE

Don't worry too much about the worksheet size. The size you specify is an estimate and Excel will provide access to the same number of cells as in a normal Excel worksheet; 256 columns and 65,536 rows.

5. Release the **mouse button** to accept the number of highlighted rows and columns. Word will display an Excel worksheet in the document.

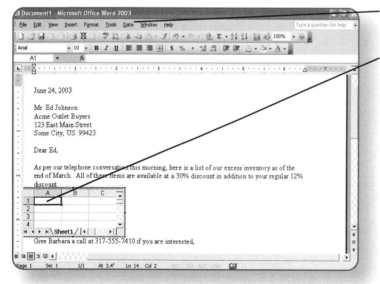

The toolbar and menu bar will display Excel options.

6. Click in the **cell** where you want to enter data. The cell will be selected.

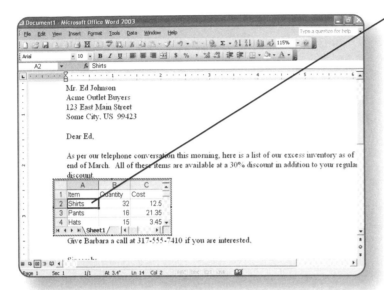

7. **Type** the **data** you want in the cell.

8. **Press** the **Enter key**. The data will be accepted and the next cell down will be highlighted.

9. **Continue entering** data as needed into your worksheet.

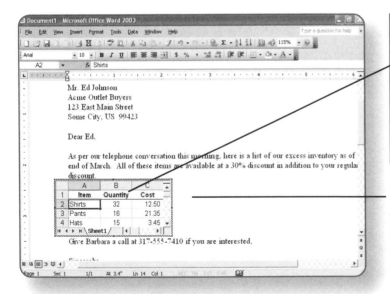

NOTE

You can insert rows or columns, create formulas, format cells, or otherwise move around the worksheet as you would any other Excel worksheet.

10. **Click** anywhere **outside** of the worksheet. The embedded worksheet will be deselected and the Word menu and toolbar will reappear.

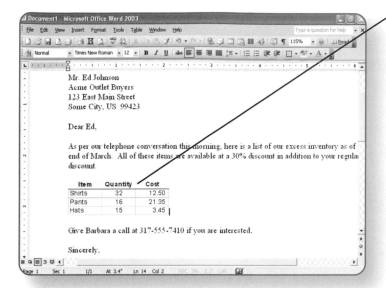

When the worksheet is deselected, the Excel column and row headings disappear. Word displays the worksheet as an Excel table.

TIP

Double-click anywhere inside the worksheet to reselect it and continue working.

Resizing the Excel Worksheet in Word

Even though when you first inserted the worksheet, you specified the number of rows and columns, Excel still provides access to the full worksheet size. You can continue entering data in additional rows and columns, although the entire worksheet may not be visible in the Word document. You can resize the worksheet to view more cells.

NOTE

When you deselect the worksheet, the table will display only the current cells. If all the data cells are not visible, they will not be displayed in the Word table either.

---

1. **Double-click** on the **worksheet**. The worksheet will be activated.

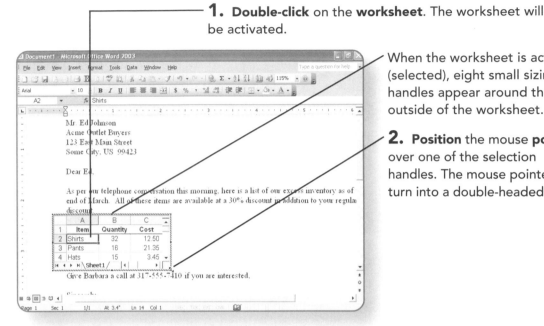

When the worksheet is activated (selected), eight small sizing handles appear around the outside of the worksheet.

2. **Position** the mouse **pointer** over one of the selection handles. The mouse pointer will turn into a double-headed arrow.

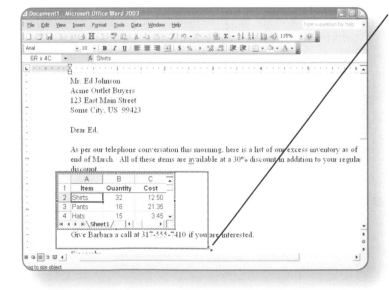

3. **Click and drag** the **handle** until the worksheet is the desired size. If you enlarge the worksheet, more rows and/or columns will display.

- Dragging a corner handle will enlarge or shrink the worksheet in both height and width in proportion to its original size.

- Dragging a side handle will modify the worksheet width only.

- Dragging a top or bottom handle will modify the worksheet height only.

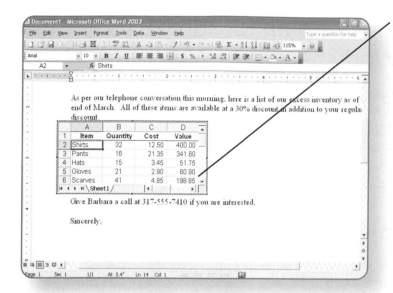

4. Release the **mouse button**. The worksheet will remain at the new size.

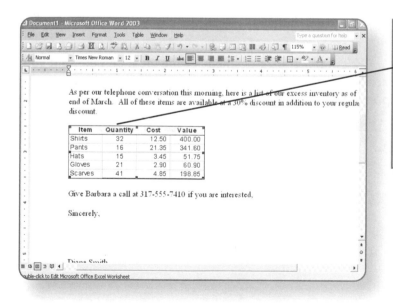

TIP

Click once anywhere on the Excel table to select the table but not activate the Excel worksheet. Press the Delete key to delete the Excel table.

Inserting an Existing Excel Worksheet into Word

If you already have a worksheet created in Excel, you can insert it directly into the Word document without having to retype the data. You can insert the worksheet in its original state which doesn't change, or you can insert the worksheet as a link that will update the Word document if the Excel worksheet changes.

Inserting an Entire Workbook

You can insert an entire previously created Excel workbook into a Word document, including multiple sheets. However, if a workbook has multiple sheets, only the currently displayed sheet will print in the document.

1. **Type** some **text** in a Word document. The text will appear on the screen.

2. **Click** in the Word **document** at the location you want your Excel worksheet to appear. A blinking insertion point will appear at that location.

3. **Click** on **Insert**. The Insert menu will appear.

4. **Click** on **Object**. The Insert Object dialog box will open.

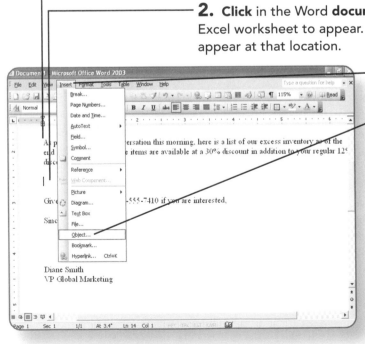

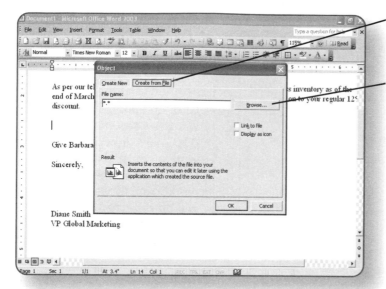

5. Click on **Create from File**. The Create from File tab will come to the front.

6. Click on **Browse**. The Browse dialog box will open.

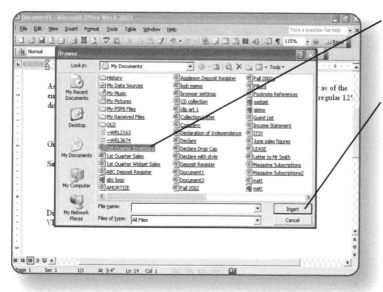

7. Click on the Excel **worksheet** you want to insert. The file name will be highlighted.

8. Click on **Insert**. The Browse dialog box will close.

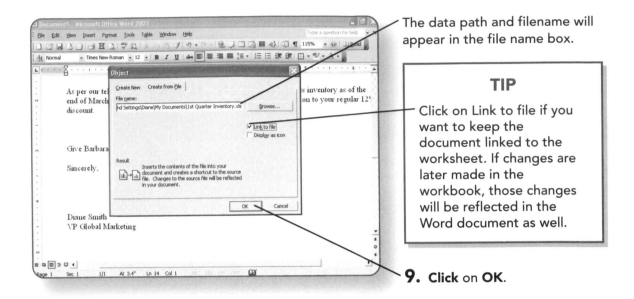

The data path and filename will appear in the file name box.

TIP

Click on Link to file if you want to keep the document linked to the worksheet. If changes are later made in the workbook, those changes will be reflected in the Word document as well.

9. Click on **OK.**

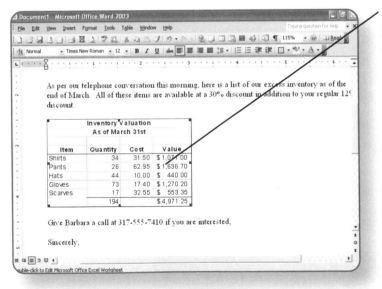

The entire workbook will be inserted into the Word document.

Copying a Workbook Portion

If you only want to place a portion of the Excel workbook into the Word document, you can use the copy and paste options to transfer the information.

1. In Excel, **select** the **cells** you want to copy. The cells will be highlighted.

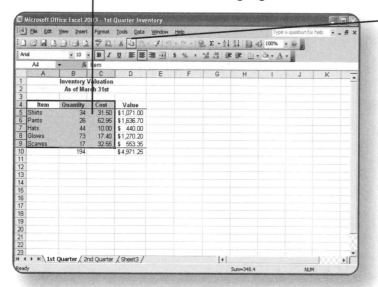

2. Click on the **Copy button**. The cells will be copied to the Windows clipboard.

TIP

Optionally, click on the Edit menu and select Copy.

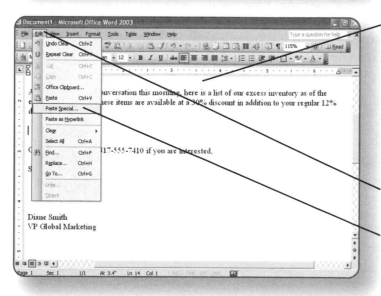

3. Open or create the Word **document** in which you want to place the Excel data. The Word document will appear on the screen.

4. Click in the **location** you want the Excel data. The blinking insertion point will appear.

5. Click on **Edit**. The Edit menu will appear.

6. Click on **Paste Special**. The Paste Special dialog box will open.

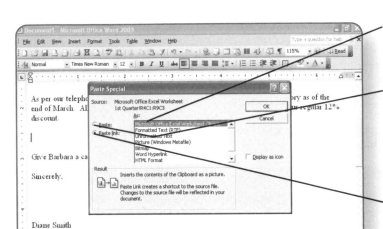

7. **Click** on **Microsoft Office Excel Worksheet Object**. The option will be selected.

8a. **Click** on **Paste** to create a one-time copy of the originally selected cells. The option will be selected.

OR

8b. **Click** on **Paste link** to create a link to the original workbook. The option will be selected.

9. **Click** on **OK**. The cells will be pasted into the Word document.

Inserting Word Data into Excel

If you created information in Word, or even data in a Word table that you later think would be better if it were in an Excel spreadsheet, you can easily convert the Word document to Excel. You use the Windows clipboard to copy the text from one program to another.

Inserting Paragraphs

If you copy regular Word paragraph text into an Excel worksheet, Excel will place each paragraph in a single cell.

1. **Select** the Word **paragraphs** you want to copy. The paragraphs will be highlighted.

2. **Click** on the **Copy button**. The text will be copied to the Windows clipboard.

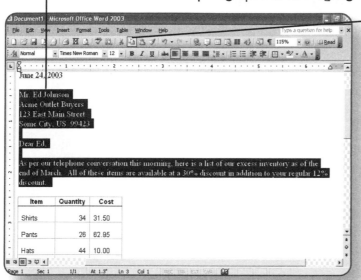

3. **Click** the **cell** in the Excel workbook where you want the text. The cell will be selected.

4. **Click** on the **Paste button**.

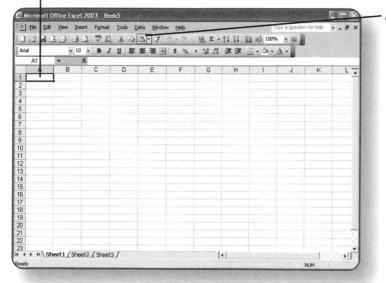

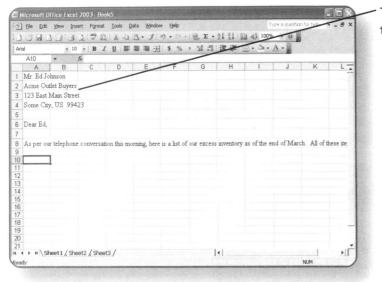

The copied text will appear in the Excel workbook.

Inserting Word Tables

If you copy a Word table, when you paste it into the Excel workbook, Excel will treat each cell of the Word table as a cell in the Excel worksheet.

1. Select the Word **table** you want to copy. The table will be highlighted.

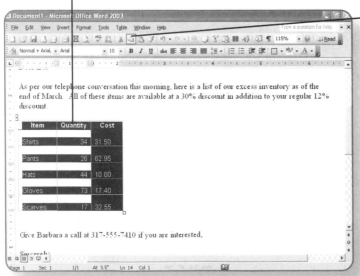

2. Click on the **Copy button**. The table will be copied to the Windows clipboard

3. Click the **beginning cell** in the Excel workbook where you want the table. The cell will be selected.

4. Click on the **Paste button**.

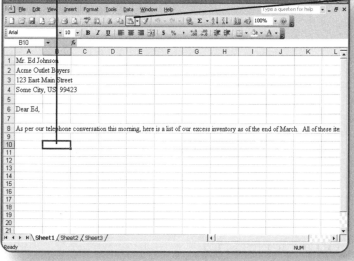

The copied table will appear in the Excel workbook.

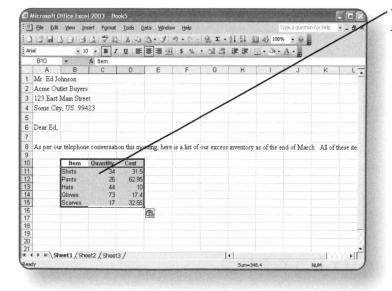

17

Using Excel with Access

Just as easily as Excel and Word interact, so do Excel and Access. Both Excel and Access work with data in rows and columns which makes it seamless to transfer data between the two applications.

In this chapter, you'll learn how to:

- Export Access data into Excel
- Import Excel data into Access
- Create a link from an Excel worksheet to Access

Exporting an Access Table or Query to Excel

If you have already used Access to create data that you now want to manipulate in an Excel spreadsheet, you can export the information directly from Access into Excel. You can export either an Access table or a query.

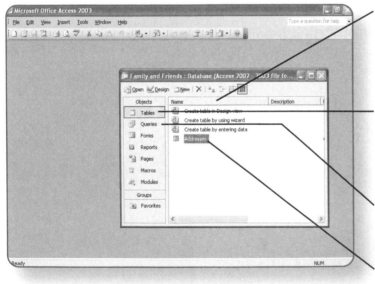

1. Open the Access **database** that contains the table or query you want to export. The database window will appear on your screen.

2a. Click on **Tables** if you want to export a table. A list of available tables will appear.

OR

2b. Click on **Queries** if you want to export a query. A list of available queries will appear.

3. Double-click the **table or query** you want to export. The table or query will open in Access Datasheet view.

4. Click on **Tools**. The Tools menu will appear.

5. Click on **Office Links**. A submenu will appear.

6. Click on **Analyze It with Microsoft Office Excel**.

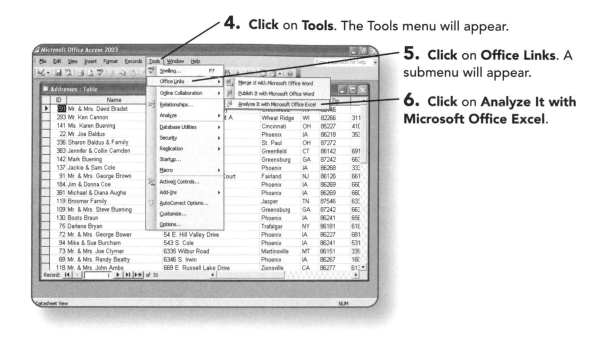

Excel will open and the selected table or query data will display in an Excel worksheet.

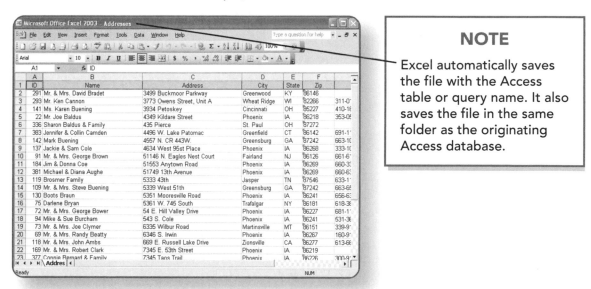

NOTE

Excel automatically saves the file with the Access table or query name. It also saves the file in the same folder as the originating Access database.

Importing Excel Data into Access

You can import data from Excel into Access by placing the new data in a new Access table or by appending it to an existing Access table.

Beginning a Data Import from Excel to Access

Whether you want to place the new data in a new table or append it to an existing table, the procedure begins the same.

1. **Open** the Access **database** in Access. The Access main menu will appear on your screen.

2. **Click** on **File**. The File menu will appear.

3. **Click** on **Get External Data**. A submenu will appear.

4. **Click** on **Import**. The Import dialog box will open.

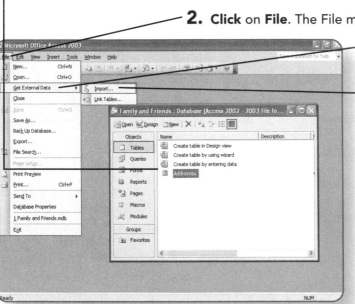

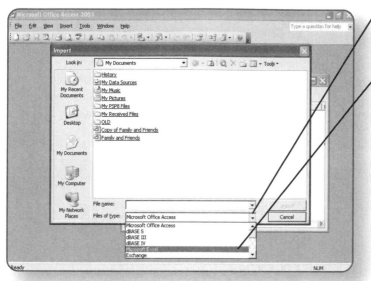

5. Click on the **Files of type down arrow**. A list of options will appear.

6. Click on **Microsoft Excel**. The option will be selected and a list of Excel file names will display.

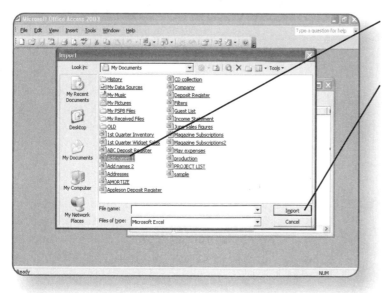

7. Click on the Excel **workbook** you want to import. The file name will be highlighted.

8. Click on **Import**. The Import Spreadsheet Wizard will open.

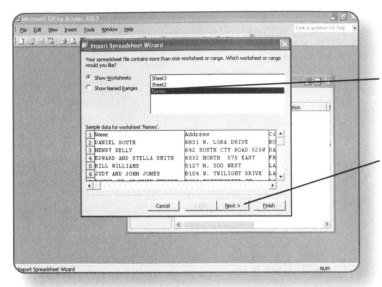

If your Excel worksheet has multiple worksheets, you can only import one sheet at a time.

9. **Click** on the **worksheet** you want to import. A preview of the worksheet data will appear in the sample area.

10. **Click** on **Next**. The next screen of the wizard will appear.

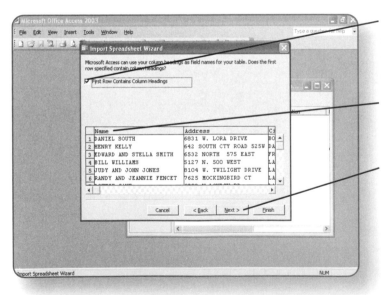

11. **Click** on **First Row Contains Column Headings** if the first row of the worksheet contains field names.

The first row of the preview will become headings in the Import Spreadsheet Wizard.

12. **Click** on **Next**. The next screen of the wizard will appear.

If you want to import the data into a new Access table, see the following section, "Importing Excel Data as a New Table."

If you want to append the data into an existing Access table, see "Appending Excel Data to an Existing Table," later in this chapter.

Importing Excel Data as a New Table

If you want to import the Excel data into a new Access table, Access will automatically create a field for each column of worksheet data.

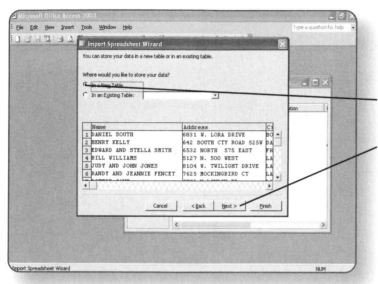

1. Follow steps 1-12 in the previous section, "Beginning a Data Import from Excel to Access."

2. Click on **In a New Table**. The option will be selected.

3. Click on **Next**. The next screen of the wizard will appear.

The Import Spreadsheet Wizard will now attempt to identify the data you want to import. The first column of data will be highlighted. Access will create fields based on each column.

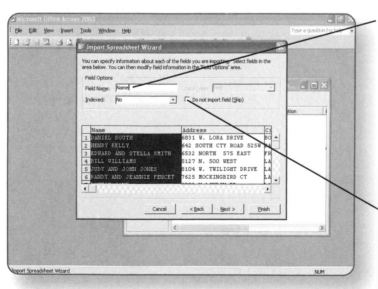

4. Type, edit, or accept the **field name** in the Field Name text box. This is usually the name of the column heading, but if your spreadsheet does not have column headings, you will need to enter something to identify this field of information.

TIP

Click on Do not import field (Skip) if you do not want to import the currently highlighted field.

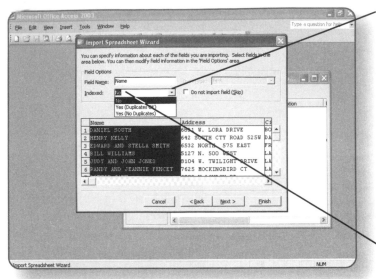

5. Click on the **Indexed down arrow**. A list of indexing options will appear.

Unless your data contains a large number of records, 1000 or more, you do not need to index the field. If your data does contain a lot of records, you may want to index the records for faster data access. You can index them so that each item in the field is unique or not.

6. Click on an index **option**. The option will be selected.

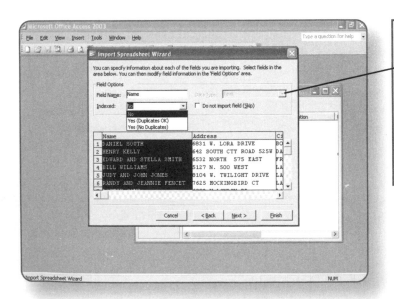

TIP

If available, click the Data Type down arrow and select a data type. The Data Type option may be unavailable based on the values in the currently selected field.

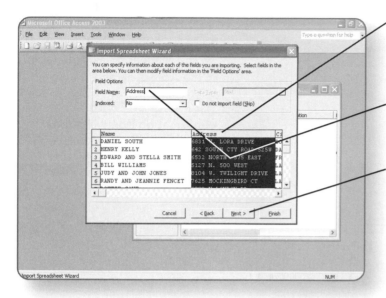

7. Click on the **next column of data** you want to import. The column of data will be highlighted.

8. Repeat steps 4-8 for each column of data you want to import.

9. Click on **Next**. The next screen of the Import Spreadsheet Wizard will appear.

Now you must determine which field you want as the primary key field. The *primary key* field is a unique field in a table that differentiates one record from another.

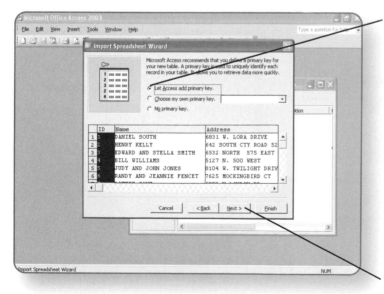

10. Make a primary key **selection**:

- **Let Access add primary key**. This allows Access to create a field for the primary key.

- **Choose my own primary key**. This allows you to select which field is unique and can be used as the primary key.

- **No primary key**. A primary key is not required, but highly recommended.

11. Click on **Next**. The next screen of the wizard will appear.

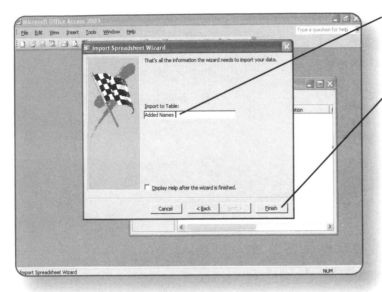

12. **Type** a **name** for the new table. The new table name cannot be the same as an existing table in the Access database.

13. **Click** on **Finish**. A confirmation box will appear.

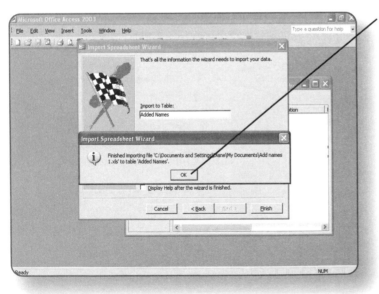

14. **Click** on **OK**. The Excel data will be imported into the new Access table.

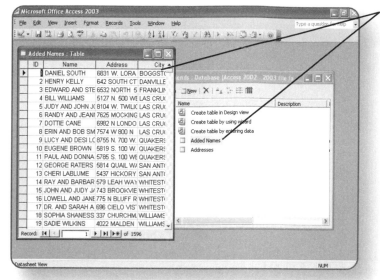

The new table will appear on the Tables list. Double-click on the table to view the data.

Appending Excel Data to an Existing Table

If your Excel data fields match up exactly with the fields in an existing Access table, you can add (append) the Excel rows into the Access table as new records. The important thing to remember is that the field names and their order must match *exactly*.

1. Follow steps 1-12 in the earlier section, "Beginning a Data Import from Excel to Access."

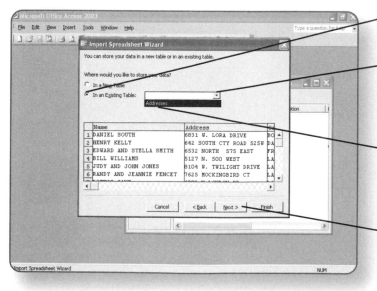

2. Click on **In an Existing Table**. The option will be selected.

3. Click the **In an Existing Table down arrow**. A list of tables in the Access database will appear.

4. Click on the **table name** in which you want to append the new data. The table name will be selected.

5. Click on **Next**. The next screen of the wizard will appear.

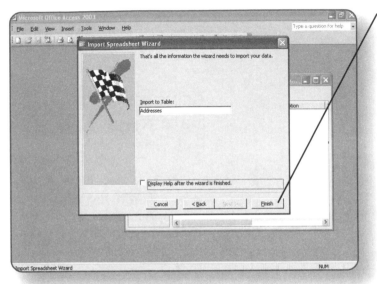

6. Click on **Finish**. A confirmation box will appear.

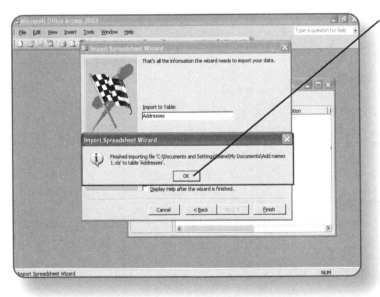

7. Click on **OK**. Access will import the Excel records in to the specified Access table.

Linking an Excel Worksheet to Access

Another way to connect an Excel worksheet to an Access database is by creating a link. When you create a link, you can update the data in Excel as needed, and the changes will be reflected in the Access database as well. There is no need to re-import the data each time you change it in Excel.

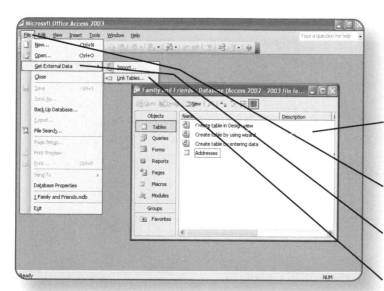

1. **Open** the Access **database** in Access. The Access main menu will appear on your screen.

2. **Click** on **File**. The File menu will appear.

3. **Click** on **Get External Data**. A submenu will appear.

4. **Click** on **Link Tables**. The Link dialog box will open.

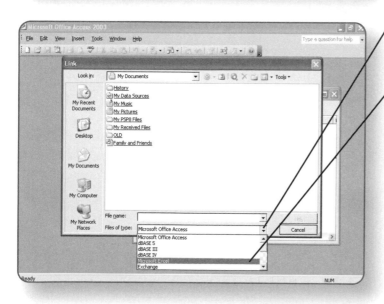

5. **Click** on the **Files of type down arrow**. A list of options will appear.

6. **Click** on **Microsoft Excel**. The option will be selected and a list of Excel files will display.

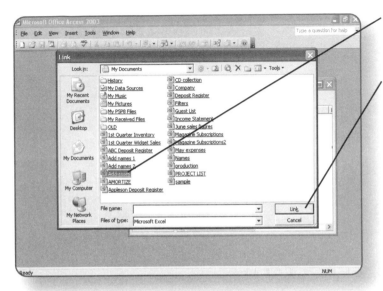

7. Click on the Excel **workbook** you want to link. The file name will be highlighted.

8. Click on **Link**. The Link Spreadsheet Wizard will open.

If your Excel worksheet has multiple worksheets, you can only link one sheet at a time.

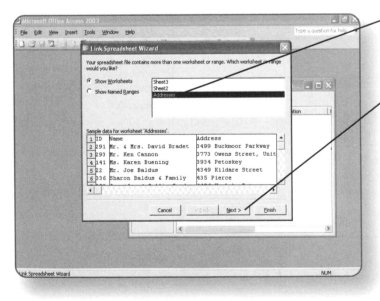

9. Click on the **worksheet** you want to link. A preview of the worksheet data will appear in the sample area.

10. Click on **Next**. The next screen of the wizard will appear.

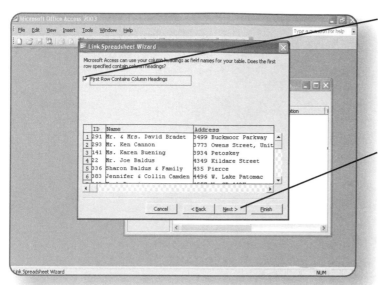

11. Click on **First Row Contains Column Headings** if the first row of the worksheet contains field names. The first row of the preview will become headings in the Link Spreadsheet Wizard.

12. Click on **Next**. The next screen of the wizard will appear.

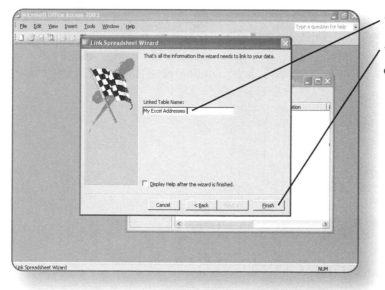

13. Type a **name** for the link.

14. Click on **Finish**. A confirmation box will appear.

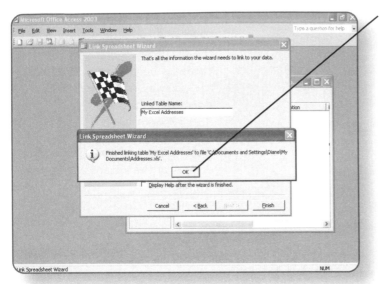

15. Click on **OK**. A link between the Excel worksheet and the Access database will be created.

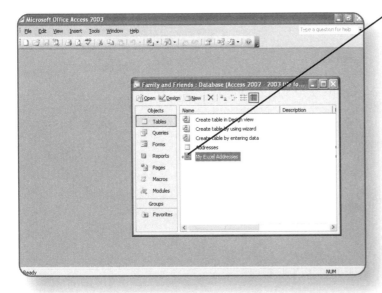

The linked worksheet will appear on the Access tables list; however, an icon appears next to the table name, which indicates it is a linked table.

18

Collaborating with Others

Chances are, you have an Excel workbook that others need to access. You might copy the workbook to another disk and hand it to them, have others access it directly from your computer, or you may even e-mail or post the file on the Internet. Any way you want to do it, Excel provides several features aimed at helping people work together as a group on a workbook. Each user can add their own comments, track revisions as multiple people edit the workbook, and protect the workbook from others making changes to it.

In this chapter, you'll learn how to:

- Work with Excel comments
- Use revision marks to track changes
- Work with workbook security features

Working with Comments

Comments are notes that you attach to a cell, separate from other cell content. Using comments allows you or others reviewing a workbook the opportunity to provide instructions such as noting how a complex formula works, or entering thoughts, questions, and even instructions as to the type of information you want the end user to enter into the cells. Adding a comment does not change the overall appearance of the worksheet. You can think of comments as Post-It notes for individual worksheets cells.

When a cell has an attached comment, a triangle appears in its upper-right corner. You can point at the triangle to display the actual comment text.

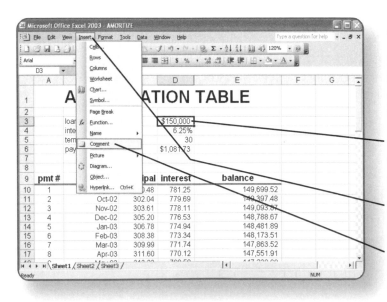

Adding a Comment

Each cell can have a comment, but only one comment per cell is permitted. Comments can be up to 32,767 characters in length.

1. Click on a **cell** to which you want to attach a comment. The cell will be selected.

2. Click on **Insert**. The Insert menu will appear.

3. Click on **Comment**. A small comment frame will appear next to the cell.

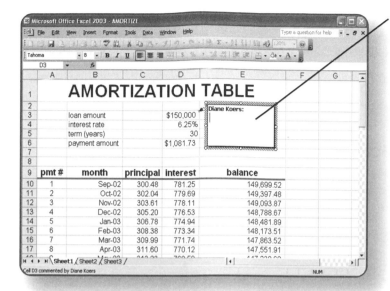

Excel automatically adds your name to the comment which it picked up from the Options dialog box. If there is no name in the Excel Options box, it will use the default name entered when setting up your computer.

TIP

To remove your name from a comment, select your name and then press the Delete key.

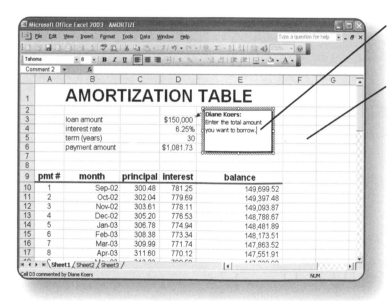

4. Type your comment **text**. A comment can be larger than the comment box.

5. Click on a **cell** different than the commented cell. Excel will accept the comment and display a triangle in the upper-right corner of the commented cell.

Editing a Comment

Similar to editing cell contents, you can easily edit a comment at any time. You can edit the contents or resize or move the comment box. You can also format the comment text.

Editing Comment Contents

You edit the comments content as you would any text paragraph.

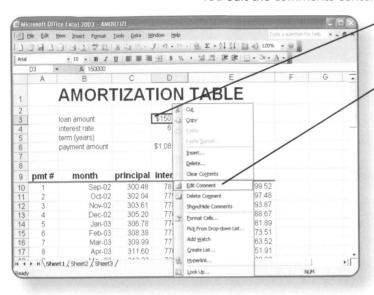

1. Right-click on the **cell** with the comment you want to edit. A shortcut menu will appear.

2. Click on **Edit Comment**. The comment box will open for editing.

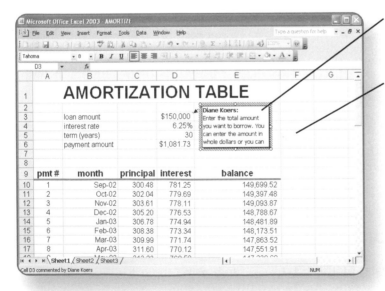

3. Edit the **comment** as needed. The comment will reflect the changes.

4. Click on a **cell** different than the commented cell. Excel will accept the comment changes.

Displaying a Comment Box

If you pause your mouse over a comment marker, you can read the comment. Sometimes, however, you want to keep the comment displayed on the screen as you edit other cells.

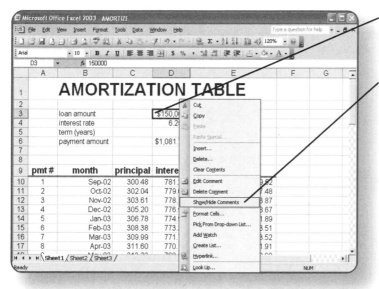

1. Right-click the **cell** with the comment you want to change. A shortcut menu will appear.

2. Click on **Show/Hide Comments**. The comment box will remain open on the screen.

The comment will remain visible until you tell Excel to hide it.

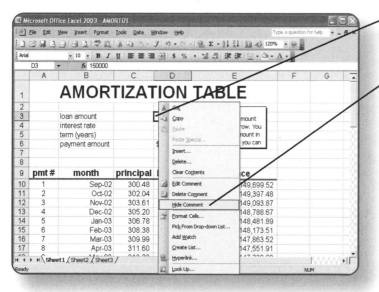

3. Right-click the **cell** with the comment. A shortcut menu will appear.

4. Click on **Hide Comment**. The comment box will hide.

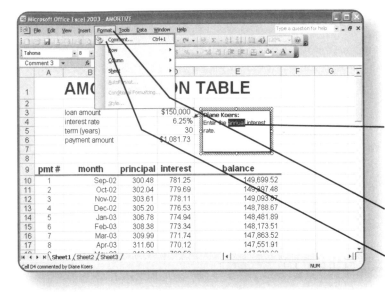

Formatting a Comment Box

Just as you can format Excel cells, you can also format comment text.

1. Click and drag over the **comment text** you want to format. The text will be highlighted.

2. Click on **Format**. The Format menu will appear.

3. Click on **Comment**. The Format Comment dialog box will appear.

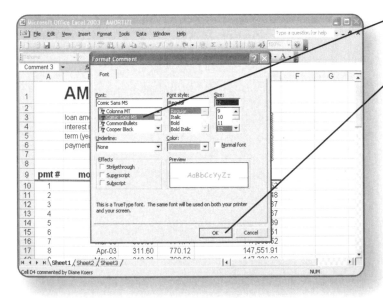

4. Select the formatting **options** you want. A sample will appear in the Preview box.

5. Click on **OK**. The Format Comment dialog box will close.

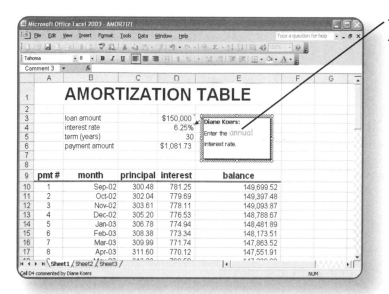

The formatting will be applied to the selected comment text.

Resizing a Comment Box

If the comment box is not large enough to display your entire comment, you can resize it.

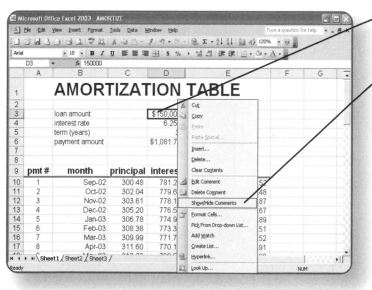

1. Right-click the **cell** with the comment you want to change. A shortcut menu will appear.

2. Click on **Show/Hide Comments**. The comment box will remain open on the screen.

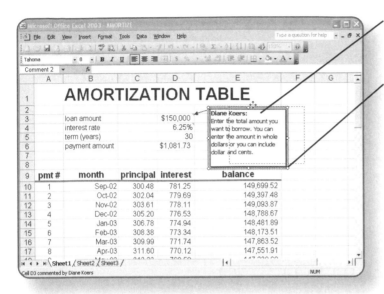

3. Click on the **Comment**. A series of handles will appear around the comment.

4. Position the **mouse pointer** over any of the handles. The mouse pointer will turn into a double-headed arrow.

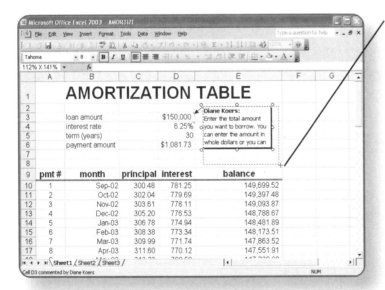

5. Click and drag any of the **handles**. The comment box will resize.

6. Release the **mouse button**. The comment box will remain at the new size.

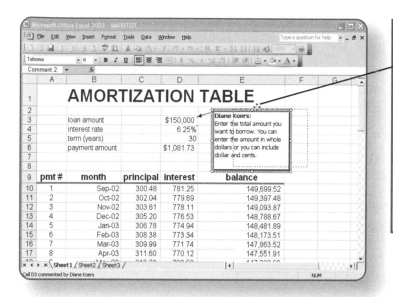

TIP

Optionally, you can move the comment box by dragging the border of the comment box to a new position. An arrow will point from the comment box to the commented cell. If you hide and redisplay the comment, it will return to its default position.

Printing Comments

By default, comments do not print with the worksheet. You can, however, instruct Excel to print comments either at the end of the worksheet or at their cell location on the worksheet.

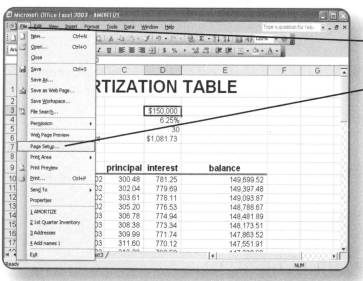

1. Click on **File**. The File menu will appear.

2. Click on **Page Setup**. The Page Setup dialog box will open.

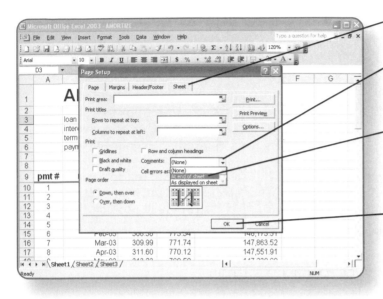

3. Click on the **Sheet tab**. The Sheet tab will come to the front.

4. Click on the **Comments down arrow**. A selection of choices will appear.

5. Click on a comment printing **option**. The option you select will appear in the Page Setup dialog box.

6. Click on **OK**. The Page Setup dialog box will close.

Deleting a Comment

If you no longer need or want the comment in the cell, you can delete it.

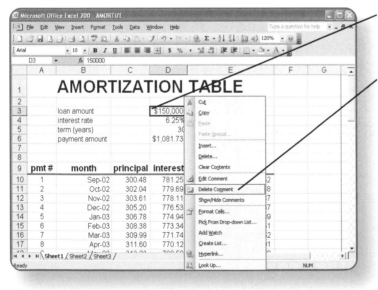

1. Right-click on the **cell** with the comment. A shortcut menu will appear.

2. Click on **Delete Comment**. Excel will delete the comment.

Working with Revisions

When multiple people edit a workbook it can be difficult to determine which person made which changes to the workbook. Excel includes a feature which helps you determine who made changes. Excel calls these Revision marks.

Tracking Revisions

Similar to the Comments feature, Excel tracks the users by the name assigned in the Options dialog box.

1. Click on **Tools**. The Tools menu will appear.

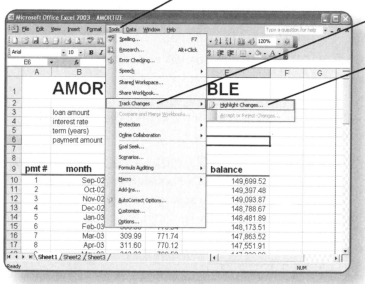

2. Click on **Track Changes**. A submenu will appear.

3. Click on **Highlight Changes**. The Highlight Changes dialog box will open.

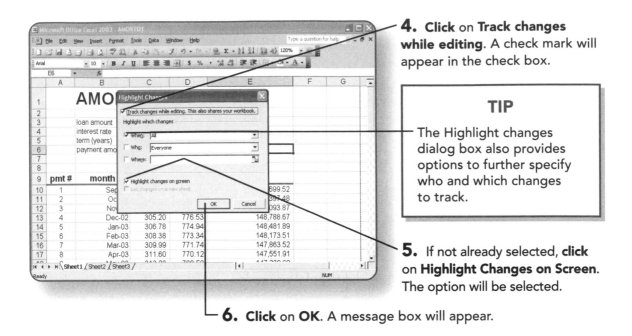

4. **Click** on **Track changes while editing**. A check mark will appear in the check box.

TIP

The Highlight changes dialog box also provides options to further specify who and which changes to track.

5. If not already selected, **click** on **Highlight Changes on Screen**. The option will be selected.

6. **Click** on **OK**. A message box will appear.

Before Excel can activate revision tracking, the workbook must be saved.

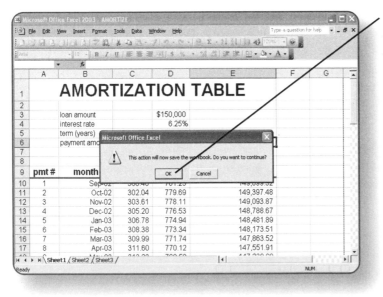

7. **Click** on **OK**. The workbook will be saved and the revision tracking feature activated.

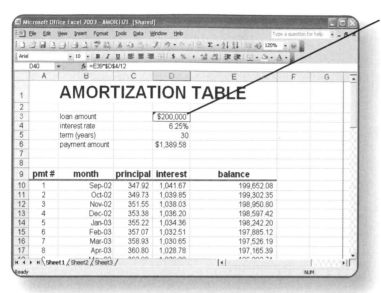

8. **Make** a **change** in the workbook. The modified cell will display a small triangle in the top left cell corner and a colored border appears around the cell.

Examining Revisions

Besides displaying the user's name, Excel also shows each user's changes with a different color.

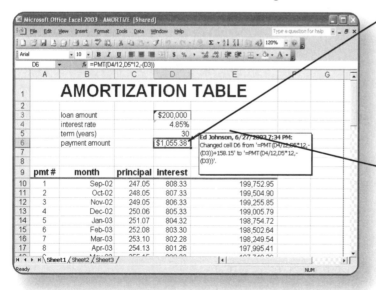

1. **Pause** the **mouse** over the changed cell. A revision box will appear displaying the change and the name of the person who made the change.

The text box also displays when the change was made.

2. **Move** the **mouse pointer** away from the changed cell. The revision box will disappear.

Accepting or Rejecting Revisions

Excel provides the option of reviewing all the tracked revisions and accepting or rejecting the changes as a group or individually.

1. Click on **Tools**. The Tools menu will appear.

2. Click on **Track Changes**. A submenu will appear.

3. Click on **Accept or Reject Changes**. Excel may prompt you to save the workbook.

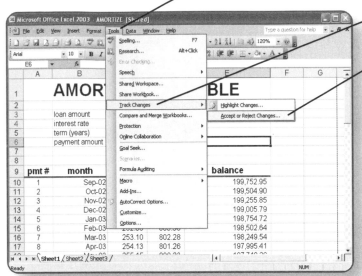

4. Click on **OK**. Excel will resave the workbook and the Select Changes to Accept or Reject dialog box will open.

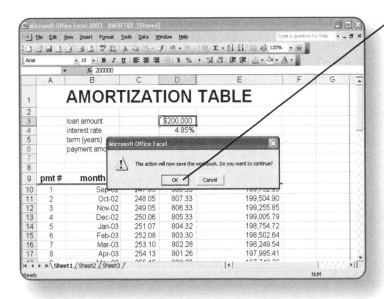

You can select which changes to review or review changes made by a specific person, or even changes made since a specified date.

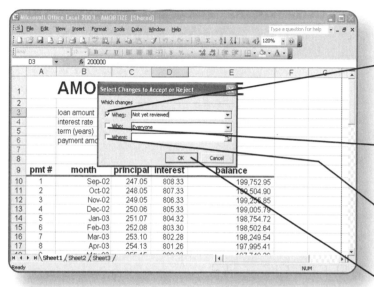

5. Select from the following **options**:

- **When**: Allows you to select all changes not yet reviewed or only changes made since a specified date.

- **Who**: Allows you to choose which users changes you want to check.

- **Where**: Allows you to highlight the specific cells you want to review.

6. Click on **OK**. A dialog box will appear showing the first change in your workbook.

You must accept or reject a change before you can advance to the next change.

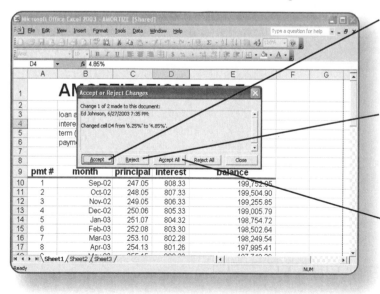

7a. Click on **Accept** to accept the change and move to the next change.

OR

7b. Click on **Reject** to return the cell to its previous state and move to the next change.

TIP

You can accept or reject all remaining changes at once by clicking Accept All or Reject All.

When all changes have been reviewed, the Accept or Reject Changes dialog box will close.

You can easily turn off the display of revision marks.

8. Click on **Tools**. The Tools menu will appear.

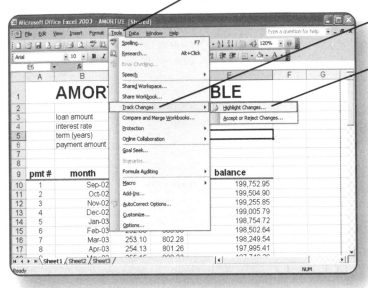

9. Click on **Track Changes**. A submenu will appear.

10. Click on **Highlight Changes**. The Highlight Changes dialog box will open.

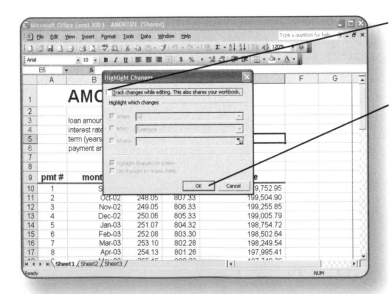

11. Remove the **check mark** from Track changes while editing. The check mark will be removed.

12. Click on **OK**. The Highlight Changes dialog box will close.

Sharing a Workbook

If you want to allow multiuser editing of your workbook, you must first share the workbook. *Multiuser* editing allows several people to edit the workbook simultaneously. Some Excel features, such as revision tracking, require sharing be activated.

If the feature you are using does not automatically activate sharing, you can activate it through the Tools menu.

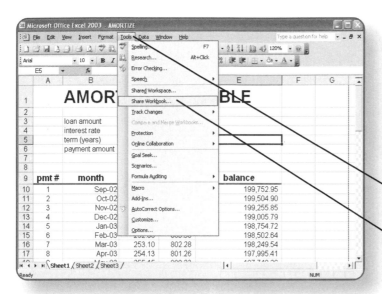

1. **Click** on **Tools**. The Tools menu will appear.

2. **Click** on **Share Workbook**. The Share Workbook dialog box will open.

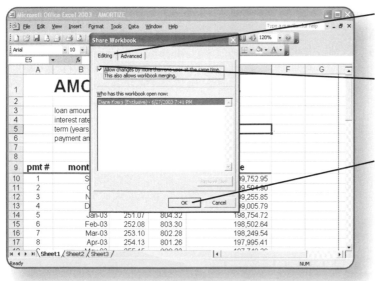

3. **Click** on the **Editing tab**. The Editing tab will come to the front.

4. **Click** on **Allow changes by more than one user at the same time**. The option will be checked.

5. **Click** on **OK**. The Share Workbook dialog box will close.

If any changes have been made to the workbook, Excel will prompt you to save the file.

6. Click on **OK**. Excel will resave the workbook.

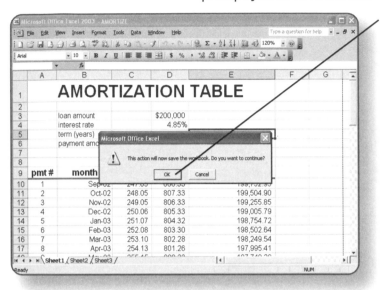

Excel denotes a shared workbook with the word [Shared] in the title bar.

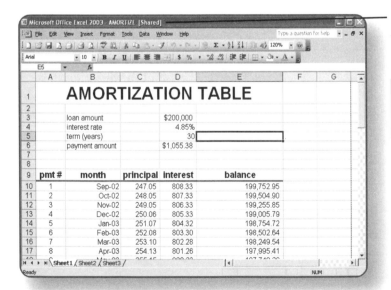

TIP

Repeat the above steps and remove the check mark to unshare a workbook. Excel will display a confirmation box.

Securing a Workbook

You will probably want to be sure that no one can either by accident or intentionally make unauthorized changes to your data. Excel provides protection at several different levels including protecting the worksheet, specific cells of the worksheet, or the entire workbook.

Protecting a Worksheet

You can protect your work at the worksheet level by allowing others to view but not edit the worksheet without a password. Protecting a worksheet prevents others from changing data or changing formatting.

1. From the worksheet you want to protect, **click** on **Tools**. The Tools menu will appear.

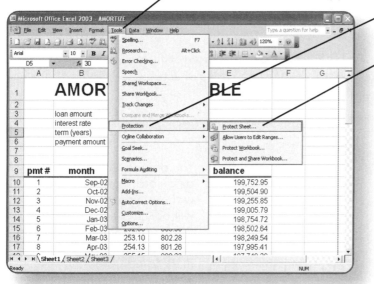

2. **Click** on **Protection**. A submenu will appear.

3. **Click** on **Protect Sheet**. The Protect Sheet dialog box will open.

4. If not already checked, **click** on **Protect worksheet and contents of locked cells**. A check mark will appear in the check box.

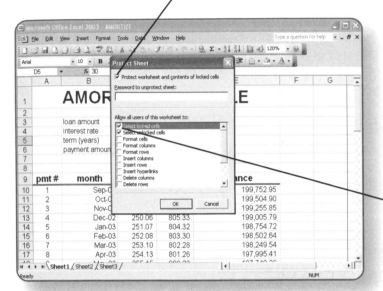

NOTE

When protecting a worksheet, Excel assumes all cells are to be locked. You'll learn later in this chapter how to unlock specific cells.

5. Click on any **options** you want to enable for users of the worksheet. Adding a check mark to an option gives the user permission to change the selected settings.

6. Type a **password** in the Password box. The password you type will display as a series of asterisks. Passwords are case sensitive.

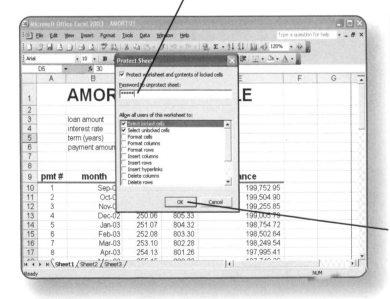

TIP

You do not have to assign a password; however, without a password, users will only have to return to the Protect Sheet dialog box and remove the check mark to edit the worksheet.

7. Click on **OK**. The Confirm Password dialog box will open.

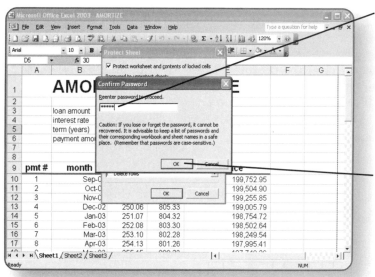

8. Retype the **password**. Again, only a series of asterisks will appear.

9. Click on **OK**. The Confirm Password dialog box will close.

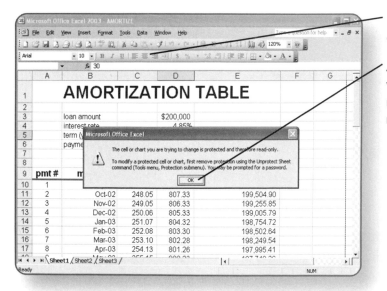

Most toolbar options are grayed out and unavailable.

Anyone can open and view the worksheet, but if an attempt is made to edit any data, a message box will appear.

Removing Worksheet Protection

If you no longer want to protect your worksheet, you can easily remove the protection. You cannot remove password protection without the password.

1. **Click** on **Tools**. The Tools menu will appear.

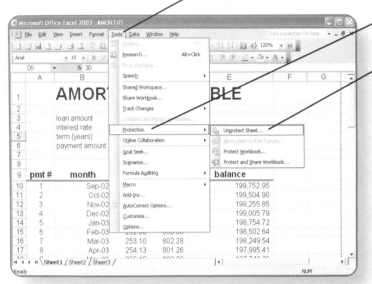

2. **Click** on **Protection**. A submenu will appear.

3. **Click** on **Unprotect Sheet**. The Unprotect Sheet dialog box will appear.

NOTE

If you did not assign a password, the Unprotect Sheet dialog box will not appear. The sheet will simply become unprotected.

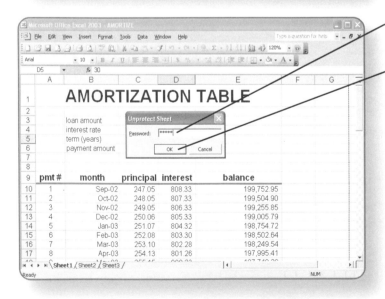

4. **Type** the **password**. A series of asterisks will appear.

5. **Click** on **OK**. The worksheet will be unprotected.

Unprotecting Specific Worksheet Cells

You may have a worksheet where you only want yourself or others to enter data in specific cells and to not have access to formulas or other definite data. You can designate the cells you want editable and leave the remainder of the worksheet protected.

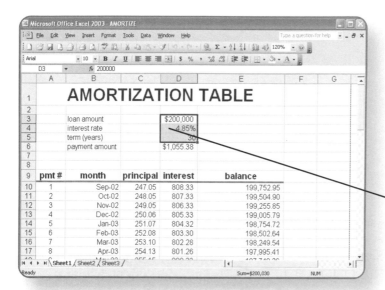

TIP

Make sure the worksheet is not protected before you proceed with these steps.

1. Select the **cells** you do *not* want protected. The cells will be highlighted.

2. Click on **Tools**. The Tools menu will appear.

3. Click on **Protection**. The Protection submenu will appear.

4. Click on **Allow Users to Edit Ranges**. The Allow Users to Edit Ranges dialog box will open.

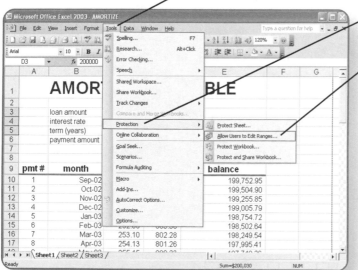

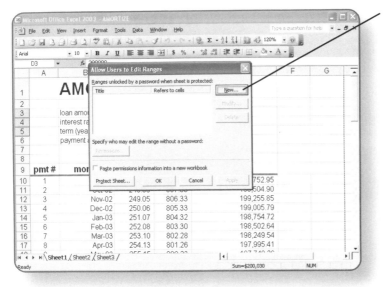

5. **Click** on **New**. The New Range dialog box will open.

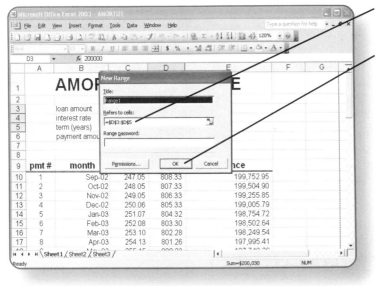

The New Range dialog box references the highlighted cells.

6. **Click** on **OK**. The Allow Users to Edit Ranges dialog box will reopen.

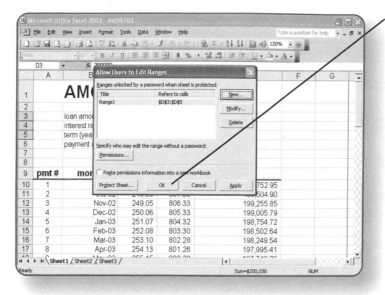

7. Click on **OK**. The Allow Users to Edit Ranges dialog box will close.

You must now protect the worksheet as you learned in an earlier section, "Protecting a Worksheet."

The cells you flagged are the only cells a user can edit without removing worksheet protection.

Preventing Others from Opening a Workbook

Another method to protect your workbook is a password to keep others from even opening the workbook. You can also apply a password to allow them to view it but not make any changes, anywhere in the entire workbook. This type of password protection, called *file level* protection, is accomplished through the Save As dialog box.

1. **Click** on **File**. The File menu will appear.

2. **Click** on **Save As**. The Save As dialog box will appear.

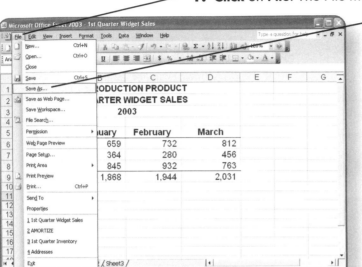

3. **Click** on **Tools**. The Tools menu will appear.

4. **Click** on **General Options**. The Save Options dialog box will open.

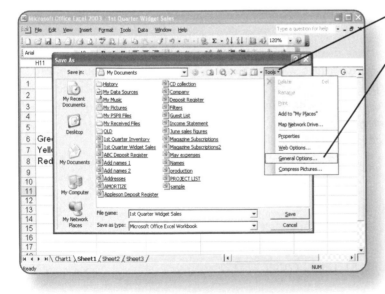

Excel provides two levels of password protection. You can use either or both password options.

The Password to open box prevents unauthorized users from opening the workbook.

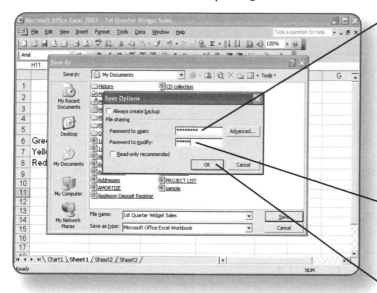

5. Type a **password** in the Password to open box. The password will appear as a series of asterisks. Again, passwords are case sensitive.

The Password to modify box prevents users, once the workbook is open, from making any changes.

6. Type a **password** in the Password to modify box. The password will appear as a series of asterisks.

7. Click on **OK**. The Confirm Password dialog box will open.

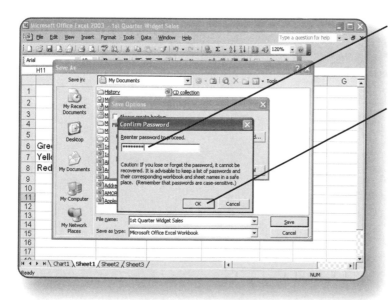

8. Type the Password to open **password** again. This is to confirm you didn't type it incorrectly the first time.

9. Click on **OK**. If you assigned a Password to modify, another Confirm Password dialog box will open.

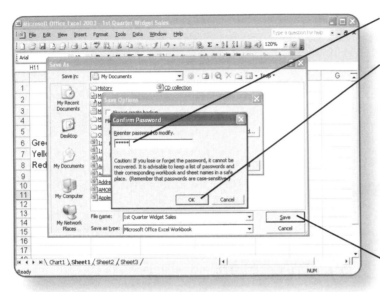

10. **Type** the Password to modify **password** again.

11. **Click** on **OK**. The Save As dialog box will return.

TIP

To remove file passwords, repeat the above steps, but leave the password boxes empty.

12. **Click** on **Save**. A dialog box will open.

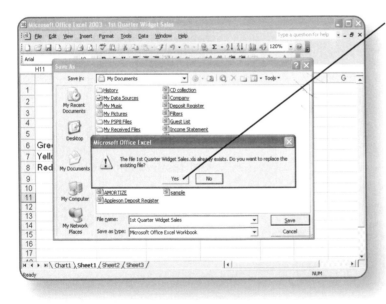

13. **Click** on **Yes**. Excel will save the workbook with the passwords.

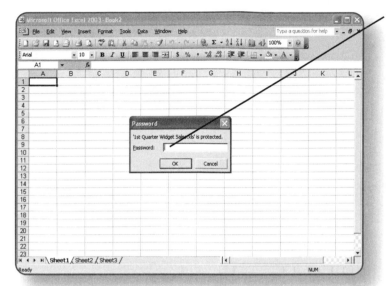

A password must be entered to open the file.

Part V Review Questions

1. What is the name of the process of saving a document created by an outside application inside of another application? *See 'Using Excel Worksheets in Word' in Chapter 16*

2. If you copy a Word table and paste it into an Excel workbook, how will Excel treat each cell of the Word table? *See 'Inserting Word Tables' in Chapter 16*

3. What file name does Excel automatically assign when saving a file from an Access table or query name? *See 'Exporting an Access Table or Query to Excel' in Chapter 17*

4. Why might you want to index your records? *See 'Importing Excel Data as a New Table' in Chapter 17*

5. What happens to an Access database when you change data in a linked Excel worksheet? *See 'Linking an Excel Worksheet to Access' in Chapter 17*

6. In an Access tables list, how does Access indicate the table is linked to an Excel worksheet? *See 'Linking an Excel Worksheet to Access' in Chapter 17*

7. What are cell comments? *See 'Working with Comments' in Chapter 18*

8. How many comments can each cell have? *See 'Adding a Comment' in Chapter 18*

9. Which Excel feature helps you determine who made changes to a worksheet? *See 'Working with Revisions' in Chapter 18*

10. What is multiuser editing? *See 'Sharing a Workbook' in Chapter 18*

A
Excel Shortcut Keys

Keyboard shortcuts are keys or key combinations you can press as alternatives to selecting menu commands. You may have noticed the keyboard shortcuts listed on the right side of several of the menus. You can use these shortcuts to execute commands without using the mouse to activate menus. You may want to memorize these keyboard shortcuts. Not only will they speed your productivity, but they will also help decrease wrist strain caused by excessive mouse usage.

When several keys are listed together, you hold down the first key while tapping the second key. For example, if you see Ctrl+N, you first press and hold down the Ctrl key, tap the N, then release the Ctrl key.

In this appendix, you'll learn how to:

- Get up to speed with frequently used keyboard shortcuts
- Use keyboard combinations to edit text
- Use the speech shortcut keys

Learning the Basic Shortcuts

Trying to memorize all these keyboard shortcuts isn't as hard as you may think. Windows applications all share the same keyboard combinations to execute common commands. Once you get accustomed to using some of these keyboard shortcuts in Excel, try them out on some of the other Office programs.

Working with Menus

You can make selections from the Excel menu without using the mouse. Perhaps you noticed the underlined letters on menus and commands. Those are *selection letters* and they allow you to work with menus and commands by using the following shortcuts.

To execute this command	Do this
Open a menu	Press Alt then the menu's selection letter
Select a menu command	Press the menu item's selection letter.
Close a menu or dialog box	Press Esc
Show a shortcut menu	Press Shift+F10

Getting Help

You don't need to wade through menus to get some help using the program. Try these useful keyboard shortcuts.

To execute this command	Do this
Use Help	Press the F1 key
Use the What's This? Button	Press Shift+F1

Working with Workbook Files

The following table shows you a few of the more common keyboard shortcuts that you may want to use when working with any type of Office file.

To execute this command	Do this
Create a new workbook	Press Ctrl+N
Open a different workbook	Press Ctrl+O
Switch between open workbooks	Press Ctrl+F6
Save a workbook	Press Ctrl+S
Use the Save As command	Press F12
Print a file	Press Ctrl+P
Close a file	Press Ctrl+W
Exit Excel	Press Alt+F4

Working inside Workbooks

While working with a workbook, Excel provides a plethora of shortcut key strokes to speed up your data entry or worksheet movement.

Moving around a Workbook

To quickly move around in a workbook, use these shortcut keys:

To move	Do this
One cell in any direction	Press an arrow key
To the next cell on the right	Press Tab
To the next cell on the left	Press Shift+Tab
One screen page in any direction	Press Alt+ an arrow key
One screen up or down	Page Up or Page Down
One screen left or one screen right	Alt+Page Up or Page Down
To the beginning of the current row	Press Home
To cell A1	Press Ctrl+Home
To the last used cell in the worksheet	Press Ctrl+End
To the next worksheet	Press Ctrl+Page Down
To the previous worksheet	Press Ctrl+Page Up
To specfiy an exact cell	Press F5

Typing and Editing Cell Data

When you are typing data, you can save time with these shortcut keys:

To execute this command	Do this
Edit the current cell	Press F2
Start a new formula	Press = (equal sign)
Start an AutoSum formula	Press Alt+=(equal sign)
Start a new line in the same cell	Press Alt+Enter
Insert today's date	Press Ctrl+' (apostrophe)
Insert the current time	Press Ctrl+Shift+: (colon)
Cancel typing entry	Press Esc
Undo the last action	Press Ctrl+Z
Repeat last action	Press Ctrl+Y
Cut	Press Ctrl+X
Copy	Press Ctrl+C
Paste	Press Ctrl+V
Clear cell contents	Press Delete
Delete the selected cells	Press Ctrl+- (hyphen)
Insert blank cells.	Press Ctrl+Shift++ (plus sign)
Insert a hyperlink	Press Ctrl+K
Fill down	Press Ctrl+D
Fill right	Press Ctrl+R
Insert a new worksheet	Press Shift+F11

Selecting Ranges of Cells

You can use your mouse to select a range of cells for editing, or you can use these keyboard shortcuts.

To select this	Do this
The entire worksheet	Press Ctrl+A
The current selection by one cell	Press Shift+arrow key
The current selection to the end of a row	Press Ctrl+Shift+right arrow
The current selection to the end of a column	Press Ctrl+Shift+down arrow
The current selection to the last used worksheet cell	Press Ctrl+Shift+End
The current selection to cell A1	Press Ctrl+Shift+Home
An entire column	Press Ctrl+Spacebar
An entire row	Press Shift+Spacebar
The current selection to the beginning of a row	Press Shift+Home

Formatting Data

Many formatting commands have a toolbar button, but you can also access the commands with keyboard shortcuts. Both common character formatting and number formatting commands have shortcuts.

To apply this format	Do this
Bold	Press Ctrl+B
Italics	Press Ctrl+I
Underline	Press Ctrl+U
Open the Format dialog box	Press Ctrl+1
Number	Press Ctrl+Shift+! (exclamation point)
Date	Press Ctrl+Shift+# (number sign)
Currency	Press Ctrl+Shift+$ (dollar sign)
Percentage	Press Ctrl+Shift+% (percent symbol)
Time	Press Ctrl+Shift+@ (at symbol)
General	Press Ctrl+Shift+~ (tilde)
Apply the outline border	Press Ctrl+Shift+& (ampersand)
Remove the outline border	Press Ctrl+Shift+_ (underscore)

Miscellaneous Commands

These keyboard shortcut commands don't seem to fit in any of the standard categories, but are very useful when working with Excel.

To do this	Do this
Create a chart	Press F11
Hide the selected rows	Press Ctrl+9
Unhide any hidden rows within the selection	Press Ctrl+Shift+((opening parenthesis)
Hide the selected columns	Press Ctrl+0 (zero)
Unhide any hidden columns within the selection	Press Ctrl+Shift+) (closing parenthesis)
Check Spelling	Press F7

Glossary

+ Addition operator

- Subtraction operator

= Initiates all Excel formulas

* Multiplication operator

/ Division operator

> Greater than operator

< Less than operator

=AVERAGE. An Excel function that calculates the average of a list of values. SYNTAX: =AVERAGE(*list*)

=COUNT. An Excel function that counts the nonblank cells in a list of ranges. SYNTAX: =COUNT(*list*)

=IF. An Excel function that evaluates a condition and returns one of two values, depending on the result of the evaluation. If condition is true, =IF returns x; if condition is false, =IF returns y. SYNTAX: =IF(*condition;x;y*).

=MAX. An Excel function that finds the largest value in a list. SYNTAX: =MAX(*list*)

=MIN. An Excel function that finds the smallest value in list. SYNTAX: =MIN(*list*)

=SUM. An Excel function that adds a range of cells. See also *AutoSum*. SYNTAX: =SUM(*list*)

A

Absolute reference. In a formula, a reference to a cell that does not change when you copy the formula. An absolute reference always refers to the same cell or range. It is designated in a formula by the dollar sign ($).

Active cell. The selected cell in a worksheet. Designated with a border surrounding the cell.

Address. The intersection of a column and row.

Alignment. The position of data in a cell, range, or text block; for example, centered, right-aligned, or left-aligned. Also called *justification*.

Array. A contiguous set of cells in a worksheet.

Attributes. Items that determine the appearance of text, such as bolding, underlining, italics, or point size.

AutoFormat. Pre-defined sets of styles that allow you to quickly apply formatting (color, font, and so on) to your Excel worksheet.

AutoSum. A function that adds a row or column of figures by clicking on the AutoSum button on the toolbar. Same as *=SUM.*

Axes. Lines that form a frame of reference for the chart data. Most charts have an x-axis and a y-axis.

B

Bar chart. A type of chart that uses bars to represent values. Normally used to compare items.

Bold. A font attribute that makes text thicker and brighter.

Border. A line surrounding on any of the four sides of cells or groups of cells in a worksheet.

C

Cell. The area where a row and column intersect in a worksheet.

Cell reference. The column and row indication of a specified cell. For example, E27.

Chart. A graphic representation of data. Also called *graph.*

Choose. See *Click on.*

Circular reference. A cell that has a formula that contains a reference to itself.

Click on. To use the mouse or keyboard to pick a menu item or option in a dialog box.

Clip art. Ready-made drawings that can be inserted into an Excel worksheet.

Clipboard. An area of computer memory where text or graphics can be temporarily stored.

Close button. Used to shut down or exit a dialog box, window, or application.

Column. A set of cells that appear vertically on a worksheet. A single Excel worksheet has 256 columns.

Comment. Used to add annotations to a worksheet cell. Comments do not print with the worksheet.

Copy. To take a selection from the worksheet and duplicate it on the Clipboard.

Cut. To take a selection from the worksheet and move it to the Clipboard.

D

Data. The information to be entered into a worksheet.

Default. A setting or action predetermined by the program unless changed by the user.

Desktop. The screen background and main area of Windows where you can open and manage files and programs.

Dialog box. A box that appears and lets you select options, or displays warnings and messages.

Drag and drop. To move text or an object by positioning the mouse pointer on the item you want to move, pressing and holding the mouse button, moving the mouse, then releasing the mouse button to drop it into its new location.

F

File. Information stored on a disk under a single name.

File format. The arrangement and organization of information in a file. File format is determined by the application that created the file.

Fill. The changing of interior colors and patterns in cells, ranges, sheets, and many graphic objects.

Fill handle. A block at the lower-right corner of each cell that allows Excel to automatically complete a series of numbers or words based on an established pattern.

Filter. To hide data that does not meet specified criteria.

Flip. To turn an object 180 degrees.

Font. A group of letters, numbers, and symbols with a common typeface.

Footer. Text repeated at the bottom of each page of a worksheet.

Format. To change the appearance of text or objects with features such as the font, style, color, borders, and size.

Formula. A formula is an entry in a worksheet that performs a calculation on numbers, text, or other formulas.

Formula bar. The location where all data and formulas are entered for a selected cell.

Freezing. The preventing of sections of a worksheet from scrolling off-screen when you move down the page.

Function. Built-in formulas that perform specialized calculations automatically.

G

Go To. A feature that enables you to jump to a specific cell or worksheet location quickly.

Graphs. See *Charts*.

Greater than. A mathematical operator that limits the results of a formula to be higher than a named number or cell.

Gridlines. The lines dividing rows and columns in a worksheet.

H

Handles. Small black squares that appear when you select an object that will enable you to resize the object.

Header. Text repeated at the top of each page of a worksheet.

Hide. To temporarily turn off the display of certain cells, rows, or columns.

Hypertext link. Used to provide a connection from the current document to another document or to a document on the World Wide Web.

I

Icon. A small graphic image that represents an application, command, or a tool. An action is performed when an icon is clicked or double-clicked.

J

Justification. See *Alignment*.

L

Label. Any cell entry you begin with a letter or label-prefix character.

Landscape. Orientation of a page in which the long edge of the paper runs horizontally.

Legend. A box containing symbols and text, explaining what each data series represents. Each symbol is a color pattern or marker that corresponds to one data series in the chart.

Less than. A mathematical operator that limits the results of a formula to be lower than a named number or cell.

M

Maps. Representing data in charts with geographical maps rather than traditional chart elements such as bars and lines.

Margin. The width of blank space from the edge of the page to the edge of the text. All four sides of a page have a margin.

Mouse pointer. A symbol that indicates a position on screen as you move the mouse around on your Desktop.

N

Named ranges. The Excel feature that provides an alternative "English" name for a cell or group of cells.

O

Object. A picture, map, or other graphic element that you can place in an Excel worksheet.

Open. To start an application, to insert a worksheet into a new worksheet window, or to access a dialog box.

Operator. The element of a formula that suggests an action to be performed, such as addition (+), subtraction (-), division (/), multiplication (*), greater than (>) or less than (<).

Orientation. A setting that designates whether a worksheet will print with text running along the long or short side of a piece of paper.

P

Page break. A command that tells Excel where to begin a new page.

Passwords. A secret code that restricts access to a file. Without the password, the file cannot be opened.

Paste. The process of retrieving the information stored on the clipboard and inserting a copy of it into An Excel worksheet.

Patterns. Pre-defined shading and line arrangements used to format cells in a worksheet.

Pie chart. A round chart type in which each pie wedge represents values.

Point. To move the mouse until the tip of the mouse pointer rests on an item.

Point size. A unit of measurement used to indicate font size. One point is 1/72 inch in height.

Portrait. The orientation of the page in which the long edge of the page runs vertically.

Print area. The portion of a worksheet you designate to print.

Print Preview. Will enable you to see a preview of how your printed worksheet will look on-screen before you print it.

Protection. To make settings to a worksheet so that only authorized users can modify the worksheet.

R

Range. A collection of cells, ranging from the first named cell to the last.

Range name. A "English" name that identifies a range and that can be used in commands and formulas instead of the range address.

Redo. An Excel feature that allows you to repeat an action you reversed using the Undo feature.

Reference. In a formula, a name or range that refers the formula to a cell or set of cells.

Relative. In a formula, a reference to a cell or a range that changes when you copy the formula. A relative reference refers to the location of the data in relation to the formula. A relative reference can be an address or range name.

Right align. Text that is lined up with the right side of a tab setting or worksheet margin, as with a row of numbers in a column.

Row. Cells running from left to right across a worksheet. Excel has 65,536 rows in each worksheet.

S

Save. The process of taking a worksheet residing in the memory of the computer and creating a file to be stored on a disk.

Save as. To save a previously saved worksheet with a new name or properties.

Script. A series of commands and keystrokes stored in a file that can be replayed by a few keystrokes or a mouse click. Sometimes called a *macro*.

Scroll bar. The bars on the right side and bottom of a window that let you move vertically and horizontally through a worksheet.

Shape. Drawing items, such as arrows, circles, rectangles, lines, polygons, and polylines in your worksheet.

Sort. To arrange data in alphabetical order.

Spreadsheet. A software program such as Excel that can perform calculations on data.

Sheet. See *Worksheet*.

Spelling. A feature of Excel that checks the spelling of words in your worksheet against a dictionary and flags possible errors for correction.

Status bar. The line at the bottom of an Excel window that shows information, such as the current formatting of a cell.

Style. A way to format similar types of text, such as headings and lists.

Syntax. The exact structure of functions and formulas.

T

Target cell. The cell where the results of a formula should be placed.

Task pane. A window that appears to the right of the worksheet, providing shortcuts to commonly used commands.

Template. A worksheet file with customized formatting, content, and features. Frequently used to create invoices and other forms.

Text box. A graphic object, shaped as a rectangle or square, that contains text. Can be used in a worksheet or chart.

Titles. Descriptive pieces of text. Used in charts and worksheets.

Toolbars. Appears at the top of the application window and is used to access many of the commonly used features of Excel.

U

Undo. An Excel feature which reverses the last editing action.

Unhide. To display cells, rows or columns previously hidden in a worksheet.

V

Value. An entry that is a number, a formula, or a function.

Variable. Cells that are changed to see what results from that change.

Views

Views. Ways of displaying worksheets to see different perspectives of the information in that worksheet.

W

Wizard. An Excel feature that walks you through a procedure step-by-step.

Workbook. A single Excel file containing a collection of Excel worksheets.

Worksheet. One of several pages in an Excel workbook.

Wrapping. A function that causes text to automatically wrap to the next line when it reaches the right edge of a cell.

X

X-axis. In a chart, a reference line marked in regular intervals to display the categories with descriptive labels.

Y

Y-axis. In a chart, a reference line marked in regular intervals to display the values of a chart.

Z

Zoom. Used to enlarge or reduce the way the text is displayed on the screen. It does not affect how the worksheet will print.

Index